GROUPON'S
BIGGEST DEAL EVER

GROUPON'S
BIGGEST DEAL EVER

THE INSIDE STORY OF HOW
ONE INSANE GAMBLE, TONS OF
UNBELIEVABLE HYPE, AND MILLIONS
OF WILD DEALS MADE BILLIONS
FOR ONE BALLSY JOKER

FRANK SENNETT

ST. MARTIN'S PRESS 🙢 NEW YORK

GROUPON'S BIGGEST DEAL EVER. Copyright © 2012 by Frank Sennett. All rights reserved. Printed in the United States of America. For information, address St. Martin's Press, 175 Fifth Avenue, New York, N.Y. 10010.

www.stmartins.com

Library of Congress Cataloging-in-Publication Data

Sennett, Frank.
     Groupon's biggest deal ever : the inside story of how one insane gamble, tons of unbelievable hype, and millions of wild deals made billions for one ballsy joker / Frank Sennett.—1st ed.
          p. cm.
     ISBN 978-1-250-00084-2 (hardcover)
     ISBN 978-1-250-01741-3 (first international trade paperback edition)
     ISBN 978-1-250-01494-8 (e-book)
     1. Mason, Andrew, 1981–   2. Groupon (Firm).   3. Coupons (Retail trade).
4. Internet marketing.   5. Internet advertising.   I. Title.
HF6127.S46 2012
381'.14206573—dc23

                                                                          2012009440

First Edition: June 2012

10   9   8   7   6   5   4   3   2   1

For Emma Grace, who was born on the same day
as Groupon Now! And for Nick,
who was along for the whole ride.

You can't connect the dots looking forward; you can only connect them looking backwards. So you have to trust that the dots will somehow connect in your future. You have to trust in something: your gut, destiny, life, karma, whatever. Because believing that the dots will connect down the road will give you the confidence to follow your heart, even when it leads you off the well-worn path. And that will make all the difference.

—Apple founder Steve Jobs, in his 2005
Stanford University commencement address

I think that's one thing characteristic of Andrew: He's always had confidence in spades. He has always been confident, even when he didn't have reason to be.

—Bob Mason, Andrew Mason's father,
in a November 2010 interview

Life is too short to be a boring company. Our path will include some moments of brilliance and others of sheer stupidity. Knowing that this will at times be a bumpy ride, we thank you for considering joining us.

—Andrew Mason, in a letter to potential investors
included in Groupon's IPO prospectus

GROUPON'S
BIGGEST DEAL EVER

AUGUST 2010

Andrew Mason crossed the lobby of the landmark Montgomery Ward headquarters building a mile northwest of downtown Chicago, boarded an elevator, and punched 6. Reaching his floor, he strode down the carpeted hallway to Groupon's reception area, pulled open the glass door, and stepped inside. Ignoring the large video screen displaying his company's cheerful green-and-black logo, he turned to face the exposed red brick on his left.

The art project was complete.

Nine magazine covers were suspended in midair, three across and three down, on pop-out ladder frames anchored to the wall by silver wire. In the center of the square, twenty-nine-year-old Andrew Mason grinned and squinted out at himself from under the *Forbes* logo, hands shoved awkwardly into the pockets of his jeans, brown hair tousled like he'd just rolled out of bed in his untucked casual dress shirt, sleeves rolled to the elbows, his gangly, six-foot-four frame slouching slightly to the right.

"The Next Web Phenom," the headline read.

When the issue had come out earlier in the month, Groupon's marketing chief had suggested creating a brag wall to highlight positive press coverage of the daily-deals powerhouse. Mason hated the idea so much that he gave it a perverse twist: All of the covers surrounding his *Forbes* debut would depict hugely hyped tech companies that had crashed and burned.

"Don't mess with MySpace," warned *Fast Company*. Equally laughable were *BusinessWeek*'s cover on "The MySpace Generation" and *Fortune*'s feature on the "MySpace Cowboys." Not to be outdone, *Time* asked: "What's next for Napster?" (Answer: Getting its ass sued out of existence.) The horror show continued. Friendster, essayed by *Inc.*, had to move to Asia to find any friends before pulling the plug on its social network and relaunching as a games site in 2011. Netscape, lauded on the covers of *Time* and *BusinessWeek*, owned 90 percent of the Web browser market in 1996; a decade later, its share had fallen to under 1 percent as a forgotten property of America Online. Speaking of which, that faded giant had its own *Time* cover on the wall of shame touting its "big coup"—buying CompuServe.

This was no time to pop the champagne, Mason thought as he took in this collection of dashed dreams. The wall would serve as a reminder to employees—and to himself—that everything Groupon had accomplished was built on sand. He might even soon be forced by his investors to sell off the company well before realizing his vision for it. If the fastest-growing company of all time was to be more than a footnote in the Web's bubble-filled history, the young CEO had to keep everyone moving forward before the ground could shift beneath them.

Of course, that didn't mean they couldn't have a little fun along the way.

ONE

If you believe the rumored numbers, it would have been the biggest acquisition in Internet history—and you definitely should believe the numbers. In the fall of 2010, online search giant Google offered nearly $6 billion to purchase Groupon, the up-start daily-deals site dubbed by *Forbes* as the fastest-growing company ever after it had become the quickest firm to rack up $1 billion in sales and the second-quickest, behind video behemoth YouTube, to hit a billion-dollar valuation.

From early October of 2010, when Yahoo! began targeting Groupon for purchase (more on that—a lot fucking more, as then-Yahoo! CEO Carol Bartz might put it—later), through sale negotiations with Google that lasted into December, the tension on the board ratcheted up to Cuban Missile Crisis levels. Online acquisitions didn't get any bigger than this.

Andrew Mason, the inexperienced CEO hiding a brilliant analytical mind behind a goofball demeanor, turned thirty on October 22 in the midst of dismissing Yahoo!'s interest. A few weeks later, Google came calling, contacting Groupon via Allen & Company, one of the investment banks Groupon was working with.

Mason was invited to Google's large Chicago sales office, along with Groupon chairman and co-founder Eric Lefkofsky, and then-president and -COO Rob Solomon. There they met with Stephanie Tilenius, Google's head of commerce, and Margo Georgiadis, VP of global sales. Everyone left the session feeling good about a potential team-up.

Negotiations proceeded at a rapid clip after the initial conversation. Mason visited Google founders Larry Page and Sergey Brin at the legendary Googleplex in Mountain View, California. Lefkofsky started working on deal points with Google chief business officer Nikesh Arora. You know that button on Google's main page that says: "I'm feeling lucky"? Arora was ready to push it. Except that Groupon was starting to enter a period of hyper-growth, increasing pressure on Google to raise its bid, which at that point had reached $3 billion.

By mid-November, negotiations had stalled over the final number, but the prospect of a sale was tantalizing to both Groupon's leadership and its venture-capital investors. On November 22, Lefkofsky told Solomon to grab some clean underwear: They were going to California to salvage the deal. They left with Mason, product VP David Jesse, senior VP of global operations Nick Cioffi, and Lefkofsky's investment partner (and fellow Groupon co-founder) Brad Keywell that afternoon in a chartered jet from Chicago's Midway Airport to San Jose. Even gaining two hours heading west, they didn't arrive at the Googleplex until after 5:00 P.M.

Mason, Lefkofsky, and Solomon were quickly shown to Arora's office, where they were joined by Web godfather Eric Schmidt, Google's CEO at the time and now the company's executive chairman, along with Page (who took back the CEO reins from Schmidt two months later), and deal architect David Drummond, Google's senior VP of corporate development. It was a high-wattage meeting by any measure.

Mason at that point was seven years out of Northwestern University, where he had majored in music. At six-foot-four, he struck some in Silicon Valley as a taller, more cherubic version of the comedian Dane Cook. When Mason wasn't intensely focused on solving a business problem, he could disarm even the harshest critic with a warmhearted grin that crinkled his eyelids. He was highly guarded about his personal life and emotions, which sometimes made him come across as cold to those who reported to him. But Mason was always willing to make himself physically vulnerable for the sake of a comedy bit—such as cultivating bizarre sideburns and performing a boot-scooting boogie as the cowboy-hatted pitchman for a monkey-rental service Groupon rolled out one April Fool's Day. Rumpled clothing and unkempt hair gave him a perennial Sunday-morning-in-the-dorm vibe—in fact, he briefly experimented with sleeping in his clothes so he could wake up a bit later in the morning—and he was so committed to defying the business world's superficial rules of behavior and appearance that he once showed up to lunch with a billionaire decked out in a bright-green tracksuit. But he did own business suits as well, and he cleaned up nicely when he wore them—not that he cared if anyone thought so.

Lefkofsky had already successfully taken other Web companies public, most notably InnerWorkings and Echo Global Logistics, both of which helped other businesses find efficiencies in their supply chains. Half a head shorter than Mason, Lefkofsky had something of a bantamweight boxer's aspect, the physical impression of coiled energy underscored by the fact that he was not afraid of conflict. He was a trim, youthful forty-two, and with his dark bushy eyebrows, ever-present glasses, and gray-blue eyes that conveyed both wry wit and sharp intelligence, he looked a bit like Groucho Marx without the greasepaint. Add in facial hair that just barely exceeded the definition of stubble and a wardrobe that consisted mostly of jeans, casual button-up shirts, and muted sweaters and you had the very portrait of an online mogul who seemed increasingly comfortable with himself.

Solomon also had been around the block a few times: Now in his early forties, he had enjoyed a six-year run growing revenues as the head of Yahoo! Shopping and became a corporate officer at Yahoo! An easygoing, well-liked, shaggy-haired former Berkeley water polo player who knows his way around a surfboard, he moved to travel start-up SideStep as president and CEO in 2006, overseeing its sale the next year to rival Kayak for $200 million, and then served a stint at VC firm Technology Crossover Ventures.

Still, this was a plunge into the deep end of the pool for all of them.

The meeting consisted largely of both sides telling each other how great this partnership would be. After observing the niceties, Lefkofsky, Mason, and Solomon were invited into a conference room with a whiteboard, where they negotiated for more than two hours with Arora and Drummond until they reached a number—the magic $5.75 billion—that they felt comfortable taking back to Groupon's board.

Around 9:00 P.M., Mason, Lefkofsky, and Solomon returned to the Rosewood Sand Hill, a luxury hotel in Menlo Park on Sand Hill Road, the fabled street of dreams for seekers of venture capital in Silicon Valley. The trio retired to Madera, the Rosewood restaurant where many a high-tech deal is sealed and celebrated. It was just before closing time, and they had the place all to themselves.

Lefkofsky marked the occasion with the premium tequila he's fond of, Solomon toasted him with a few fingers of Scotch, and Mason had red wine. It was a giddy, potentially historic moment: They were heading back to the Midwest in the morning on a glide path to being Google's biggest-ever acquisition. It was an astonishing outcome for a team of Chicago upstarts who'd started fleshing out the idea for a group-buying site just a few years earlier. The trio finished their drinks and, warmed by the glow of the restaurant's large fireplace, contemplated futures growing brighter by the moment.

Only one significant hurdle remained: Google couldn't guarantee the deal would close. The company did offer a sky-high $800 million breakup fee, but if antitrust concerns held up the sale for a year to eighteen months—and perhaps ultimately led the Justice Department to quash the deal—that would be cold comfort for Groupon. In the worst case, the Chicago company could be crippled. Stuck in limbo, it wouldn't be able to make key hires and strategic acquisitions to supercharge growth, and it couldn't go after new customers as aggressively as needed. Lefkofsky devoted two full weeks to building a workable contract from the term sheet, but without that guaranteed close, no one was comfortable with the deal. Meanwhile, the prospects for Groupon successfully staying independent were looking increasingly rosy.

After the last California trip, Mason and Lefkofsky initiated several tension-packed board calls from Groupon headquarters. The conversations, some of which took place on weekends as the sense of urgency grew, centered around a simple yet exceedingly difficult-to-answer question: Would it be absolutely nuts to turn down this deal? One thing's certain: The negotiations forced Groupon's leaders to explore the depths of the gold mine they were sitting on.

Those kinds of figures tend to focus the mind.

Groupon had cracked a code the Silicon Valley giants had failed repeatedly to solve: It had hooked local merchants up to a giant e-commerce machine and then delivered the resulting bargains directly to millions of consumers worldwide. Executed properly, this could be one of those once-every-decade business breakthroughs, perhaps on a par with Amazon's creation of an online-only retail superstore in the nineties. But if Groupon was a special company, Google's offer was pretty damn special, too.

As the biggest technology firm in the world, Google could provide Groupon with key advantages. Integrating daily deals into the dominant online search product could rapidly increase the reach of those offers. And Google's respectful post-acquisition management of YouTube suggested Groupon's team would be able to operate as a truly autonomous business unit, an impression Google did everything it could to reinforce.

So the model worked, in theory. But some of Groupon's key players, Mason chief among them, had the nagging sense that YouTube had sold itself too early. And even though the offer now on the table was nearly four times as large as the one that landed YouTube, the Chicago crew couldn't shake the feeling that they still might be cashing out too soon. But every argument against consummating the deal kept butting up against one number: 6 billion.

As the negotiations dragged on, most of the board came around to supporting the sale. Among the leadership team, Lefkofsky also leaned toward selling, Solomon was ready to accept either outcome, and Mason expressed both a desire to keep running the company and a willingness to go with Google if it could speed Groupon toward its goal of creating a new ecosystem for local commerce. If the majority shareholders wanted to sell, Mason could get excited about the ways in which the search leader might help his company grow, even though he was nervous about the fact that such acquisitions often fail.

But there were a few key voices—such as board member Kevin Efrusy, the man who'd led Accel Partners to invest in a nascent Facebook—pushing Groupon to see how far it could go on its own. Efrusy was joined in the pro-independence camp by board observer Roger Lee, general partner of VC firm Battery Ventures, another Groupon investor.

German entrepreneur Oliver Samwer, a big Groupon equity holder thanks to the sale of his European CityDeal clone to the company earlier that year, swung back and forth on the question like a weather vane in a tornado. Some days he'd insist on selling to Google at once; on others he'd argue that Groupon must remain independent because it soon could be churning $200 million a month in gross sales, way up from the $50 million it was doing at the time. The projected sales number seemed crazy, and by most standards it was. But by the second half of 2011, less than a year later, Groupon's gross billings actually topped $400 million a month.

By early December, it was time to make a decision. Solomon was fond of telling colleagues that if they turned down the largest deal ever offered to an Internet start-up, they'd ultimately look like either the biggest idiots in the world or the guys with the biggest balls. Toward the end of the process, Mason brought in Nitin Sharma, a data scientist who worked for Groupon, to make a presentation to Lefkofsky, Keywell, and Solomon. Sharma had crunched the numbers and, based on his jaw-dropping projections—Groupon could end up more than ten times larger if it fully optimized its data processes—he strongly recommended that the company remain independent.

That's when everyone started climbing down off the fence. Lefkofsky was neurotic enough that he might not sleep for the next eighteen months if antitrust concerns held up the Google deal, and now these new projections supported the Groupon founders' gut feeling that they had a lot of running room left with this still largely unexploited commerce model.

In the six weeks during which the Yahoo! and Google negotiations played out, the company's sales had exploded to some $50 million a month—twice what they had been just three months earlier. The leadership team started wondering if gross revenues in 2011 might top a billion dollars—or even $2 billion.

It was hard to project how steep the curve might be. The most successful Groupon to date, a November 24, 2010, Nordstrom Rack deal that sold $50 gift cards for $25 and grossed more than $15.6 million (representing about 2.5 percent of Groupon's cumulative total sales up to that time), pointed toward strong continued growth on the national retail front. Add in the fact that international sales were exploding and now accounted for more than half of the company's revenue and staying independent started to seem almost irresistible.

Mason and Lefkofsky holed up in a Groupon conference room and talked the proposed deal through one last time. They now believed their company was worth well more than $6 billion, but it was difficult to say precisely how much more—unless they chose to believe leaks from New York investment bankers who pegged Groupon's valuation at anywhere from $20 to $30 billion. That overheated speculation emerged as competition between Morgan Stanley and Goldman Sachs for lead underwriter status became so intense that Goldman CEO Lloyd Blankfein scheduled a visit to Groupon headquarters for two weeks into the new year so that Blankfein, one of banking's true masters of the universe, could pitch Mason and Lefkofsky in person.

Ultimately, they concluded the company had so much growth

potential, and they were so passionate about the business model, that the only move left was to call Google on December 3 and kill the deal—a deal that likely would have been done if only the search giant had been able to guarantee a close. After Lefkofsky confirmed Keywell and Solomon's support for the plan, he pulled the plug.

"Emerging from that process, it felt like a butterfly emerging from the cocoon," Mason said. "We went through a period of introspection and self-doubt, and then ultimately emerged in a state of supreme confidence. Like, okay, we're the best company in the world."

That's not how it looked from the outside, though. Groupon's rejection of Google sent heads spinning in Silicon Valley and shocked the rest of the world, even as it whetted the appetites of the banks for a Groupon IPO that might eclipse Google's own.

Was it hubris that led Groupon to remain independent? Seemingly millions of people drew that conclusion. And it's true that $5.75 billion would have represented an eye-popping payday for a two-year-old start-up. After all, Google had landed YouTube for the bargain price of $1.65 billion in 2006 and then picked up online advertising powerhouse DoubleClick for $3.1 billion a year later. Auction site eBay had earlier set the online-acquisition bar by paying $2.5 billion for videophone service Skype in 2005. Even accounting for inflation, Groupon would have set the all-time private cash-out mark for a Web start-up if it had only said yes to Google.

But with the steep revenue trajectory management saw in late 2010, they knew there was a significant possibility that if and when Google finally delivered the big check, Groupon's founders could be selling at a discount much steeper than the half-off sushi, mani-pedi, and boat-tour deals the company was known for.

Even so, no one would have criticized Groupon for taking the money.

As the year drew to a close and serious competition began to emerge in the daily-deals space, only one question remained: Would Groupon's $6 billion gamble pay off?

TWO

Andrew Mason tried so hard to make his friends laugh in high school that he drove his exasperated freshman math teacher to tears on more than one occasion. One pal in particular, Rob Garrity, now CEO of a New York–based renewable energy company, would crack up at Mason's bits until the class was thoroughly disrupted. "It was great stuff," Garrity said. "Although I feel bad a little in retrospect."

Absolute commitment to a bit regardless of audience response remains a hallmark of Mason's humor. But long before he became the Andy Kaufman of CEOs, his friends saw him as the go-to guy for outrageous stunts. They recall the times, for instance, that he pledged to eat nothing but pizza for a month and tried to go a full week without wearing shoes—even going so far as to cut the soles out of an old pair of sneakers so that he could attend classes while technically keeping his promise. When his decoy shoes were discovered, though, he was forced to go back to regular footwear to avoid a suspension. Even the best gags have to end sometime.

Actually, there's one that never should have begun in the first place, but it illustrates a core aspect of Mason's personality.

Once when he went along on a trip to visit Garrity's grand-parents in suburban Philadelphia, the two teens took Garrity's husky for a long walk and happened upon a Blockbuster Video store. They didn't dare leave the rambunctious dog outside, but they wanted to choose a movie together. Garrity suggested that Mason pretend to be blind and have the husky lead him around the store like a service dog.

It was a typical politically incorrect high school prank of the kind most people end up reliving over a few beers at their class reunions. With the husky pulling one way and Mason another, a customer walked up to him and said, "My, that's a beautiful dog." Mason stared blankly into space, head turned away from the speaker, and deadpanned, "Thank you, but I wouldn't know." He then began feeling the fronts of video cases as if their titles might be printed in Braille.

It was a groan-worthy performance, to be sure.

But although the dog wasn't his, he took the leash because Andrew Mason was always *that guy*. He didn't just turn his life into a humor routine at school or when he was out with friends. Even as a teenager, Mason took his act into the workplace. When he worked as a host and server at a Chi-Chi's Mexican restaurant for eight months starting in 1998, he turned the gig into performance art.

While seating customers, Mason would grab menus from the host stand, take off at a quick pace, and then abruptly stop so the diners would run into him. When he started walking again, he would make indeterminate gestures toward various tables. People would start to sit down, only to see Mason walk off to a different table.

"Because I never went out and ate at restaurants, I thought the role of the waiter was to entertain the customers," Mason said. "So I'd wear a sombrero and I'd bring an accordion and play songs. And now, as someone who goes to restaurants, if I ever had to deal with that person, I'd get them fired."

But how far had he really come from those nights working at Chi-Chi's? And given the controversy Mason has often generated with his Groupon hijinks, could it be that he might someday look back on his early CEO days and conclude that his performative behavior had caused him and his company more trouble than it was worth?

"No," Mason said toward the end of 2011, "because you only live once, and all I'm doing is being myself. I think a normal CEO is trying to appear in some way that's not actually them. That's probably not what they're like. They have an idea of what it means to be professional and appear smart, and I just don't want to compete" on those terms.

That attitude has enabled a cartoon version of Mason to take hold in the popular mind, meaning he seldom gets credit for how seriously he takes the business offstage, nor for the strategic acumen he's demonstrated in building Groupon into a powerhouse. Even internally, his wacky public persona led some employees to mistakenly believe the company was happy to coddle mediocre performers. When they began to see the fun corporate culture as an end in itself instead of a reward for hard work, Mason bluntly disabused them of the notion during a series of town-hall-style meetings. The CEO had made a mistake common among start-up leaders watching their companies scale: He'd assumed newer employees shared the core team's all-out commitment to Groupon's success when in reality many of them saw it simply as a job instead of a mission.

"I'm confident that it will work out in the long term," Mason said of the image disconnect and its unintended consequences. "But you have to be able to live with yourself. And it just wouldn't feel right to try and do this and not be myself. I have to do it on my own terms, in the way that I enjoy. When I look at the ways that typical companies conduct themselves, it's really not something that I want to be a part of. When I look back at the mistakes I've made, that's not one of them."

Rob Solomon, Groupon's first president and COO, thinks otherwise. "Andrew at thirty-five and forty is going to hate Andrew at twenty-nine and thirty; I guarantee it," he said. Undeniably, our adult lives have stages. Behaviors we see as essential to our nature in our twenties we end up outgrowing as easily as we outgrew the Steve Miller Band greatest-hits CD we loved in high school.

Even if Mason doesn't end up loathing his younger self, Solomon said, "He won't like him as much as the guy he evolves into." That's true for many of us, but outside of athletic phenoms, child stars, and start-up CEOs, most people don't spend their formative years under such a glaring spotlight.

Mason matured early in ways that count. He created businesses between comedy bits in high school, too, including a scheme to resell candy purchased in bulk at Costco at a nice profit to classmates in the cafeteria. Mason and his friend Garrity also launched a Geek Squad–style computer repair service in the late nineties, relying on the fact that they knew a lot about PCs just from tinkering with them.

To impress clueless middle-aged clients, they removed the top of every computer they worked on, so that it looked like they were in the midst of complex diagnostics even if they were just reconnecting a printer cable. The pair finally got in over their heads when they were asked to troubleshoot why a mouse wasn't working properly and found themselves stumped.

"What are we doing?" Garrity asked after the home owner left them to the task. "We've got to get out of here," which they did, leaving the money on the client's kitchen counter and hightailing it out of the house without another word. So ended Mason's first tech start-up.

"It was absolutely ridiculous," Garrity said. "It was just so unprofessional."

The duo also drew up plans to start a bagel home delivery service. Even though that enterprise never really took off, Garrity believed Mason was a creative genius long before he founded Groupon. "He's so smart; he was always doing his own thing. And he was very, very principled."

Still, Mason's senior yearbook records that he was voted his high school's most unique and hilarious student. With Andrew Mason, it seems, it's impossible to separate the sizzle from the Chi-Chi's steak fajita.

OCTOBER 21, 2010

Andrew Mason was running late for lunch at Buddy Guy's Legends, an iconic blues club in Chicago's South Loop neighborhood. It was a couple of months after the *Forbes* cover, just before the Yahoo! and Google negotiations heated up, and one day before his thirtieth birthday. The roller coaster was clicking its way to the top of the big hill, but no one knew yet how wild the ride was going to get.

Guitar picker Fruteland Jackson was playing an acoustic set to a room that was alarmingly empty for a Thursday when Mason walked in trailing a camera crew. He'd been roped into filming a weird interview segment with a woman from a button company, and he was clearly annoyed as he apologized for the delay while going through the awkward removal-of-the-mike-transmitter-from-his-pants routine.

He was dressed in dark jeans and a button-down shirt, tails out, sleeves rolled up to his elbows. Slender, with a mop of brown hair, Mason had a thoughtful, engaging demeanor some might call boyish.

The CEO had been commuting to work by Vespa since that past April. "It's changed my life," he said. His scooter, a 275cc model, just happened to be green. "I haven't had anything close to a near-death experience" on Chicago roads, he noted, adding, "I'm trying to go all-winter scooter." He would soon splurge on a new Mercedes, though, which was a good thing because the winter of 2010–11 in Chicago included a blizzard that shut down the city's famed Lake Shore Drive for the first time ever. Scooter weather it wasn't.

After lunch (purchased with a Groupon), he geeked out on his new American Express Centurion Card, the black one made of anodized titanium. The one you have to be personally invited to carry. He was amazed that it gave him a free companion seat every time he flew to Europe. He clearly was still coming to terms with being a budding mogul.

His down-to-earth nature kept winning out during what turned out to be the first of our many meetings. Mason was delighted to see the vegetarian menu options, for instance. "It's rare that you'll see a meatless steak at a blues club," he said. "It's pretty startling." He readily drank a beer; he didn't get all weird about alcohol at a business lunch like so many people do these days. He talked about his then-fiancée, Jenny Gillespie, who had recently left a job at a children's magazine to pursue a music career.

The next day, colleagues would fly Mason's parents in from Pittsburgh and proceed to roast him for his birthday in what he later termed "the most embarrassing ninety minutes of my life."

October was turning out to be a big month for Mason. It was the month he was born, the month Groupon debuted, and the month he planned to get married. If all went well, it might also be the month the huge new category of online commerce he created would transform him into one of the world's youngest billionaires.

THREE

One of the standard shorthand references reporters employ to illustrate Andrew Mason's improbable rise to CEO of one of the planet's hottest online companies is to note that he graduated from Northwestern University in 2003 as a music major and went on to work with indie-rock producing icon Steve Albini at his Electrical Audio recording studios in Chicago. That's all true. And Mason has good piano-playing chops—during his rare off-hours, he works his way through Bach's Goldberg Variations on the Steinway Model B grand piano he bought as "my one splurge when I finally got some money from Groupon." (He was on variation three of thirty-two.)

But don't pigeonhole Mason as a musician who got lucky. He coded Web sites as a teenager, and he enrolled at Northwestern in engineering before changing his major. Prior to creating Groupon precursor The Point, he attended grad school in public policy at the University of Chicago because he wanted to get funding for a Web site called Policy Tree.

He knew nothing about the world of venture capital, but he had studied FactCheck.org, a site funded by the Wharton School at the University of Pennsylvania. Why couldn't Policy Tree be the FactCheck of the University of Chicago? he wondered.

Think about that for a moment: Mason was so determined to pursue his vision that he enrolled in graduate school because it was the only way he could think of to secure backing for his brainchild. It was a fairly creative move, albeit one made by a guy who'd managed to make it to the age of twenty-six without a rudimentary knowledge of how tech start-ups normally get bankrolled.

The idea behind Policy Tree was to give people on opposite sides of a given public-policy issue an online tool they could use to find common ground and ultimately act together for the good of society. Before Mason enrolled at the U of C's Harris School of Public Policy to refine the site concept, he got a job in January 2006 as a FileMaker developer for one of Lefkofsky's companies, Echo Global Logistics, which uses online tracking and analytics technology to help businesses move cargo more efficiently.

For the first several months on the job, Mason was a nonentity to Lefkofsky, who was overseeing both Echo Global and another start-up, InnerWorkings, which leverages technology to lower printing and marketing costs for clients. But Lefkofsky quickly made an impression—a bad one—on Mason.

In those early days, Mason had the unfortunate luck to be sitting in a cubicle outside the office of an Echo Global employee who frequently incurred Lefkofsky's wrath. After hearing him, an admitted loud talker, repeatedly dressing down the staff member, Mason came up with a nickname for Lefkofsky: Punchable.

"He just seemed like a guy I wanted to punch," Mason said. "Because he's just completely insensitive to creating any kind of decorum or comfort for anybody."

"That's so true," Lefkofsky said. "I'm not warm and fuzzy."

Mason had an epiphany a couple of years later when they had lunch together at Chipotle and Lefkofsky behaved as much like an alpha dog there as he did at the office, barking orders at fast-food workers like he owned the place.

"I have one setting from morning until I go home at night," Lefkofsky said.

"Including with his kids," Mason said. "It's freaky. You should watch him interact with his kids at some point."

Mason and Lefkofsky harass each other freely, but with affection. In fact, the Groupon chairman is fiercely protective of Mason, publicly backing without hesitation some of the young CEO's more questionable moves. Lefkofsky's got Mason's back in private, too, such as the time he shouted down a Groupon investor who demanded a larger share of the equity than Mason held. The theatrics worked. The meeting ended with the investor accepting that the size of his stake would not eclipse the CEO's.

Within a few months of starting with Echo Global, Mason had shifted to InnerWorkings, also housed in the same building on Chicago's near north side that would eventually serve as Groupon headquarters, when Lefkofsky's other company needed some extra tech help. Having distinguished himself with both hard work and creative thinking, Mason was now the lead developer tasked with redesigning the print technology interface for InnerWorkings.

That was when Mason's impatient drive to improve every piece of technology he touches led to his big break. One of the company's back-end systems was not scaling properly to meet the needs of a growing client base. That frustrated Mason, who devised a solution he knew would work. The project didn't fit into his job description, but when he heard that InnerWorkings had tried and failed to fix the problem three times he shared his plan with the development team.

"There's a guy back in Technology who wants to rebuild our entire system on his own and he says he can do it in six weeks," Mason's supervisor told Lefkofsky. It was a ridiculous statement; the company had wasted years trying to fix the problem, and now this kid was going to make everything right on his own in under two months? Lefkofsky and InnerWorkings management decided to roll the dice, thinking the worst that could happen was the brief loss of one employee's productivity.

This was the first time Lefkofsky became aware of Mason. He was soon impressed by the younger man's drive and self-confidence. Mason had had to sleep at the office to meet his self-imposed deadline, and every time Lefkofsky saw him he was coding.

"It was just clear work that had to be done," Mason said. "Coding is fun. That's all it was."

When Mason actually delivered on his promise, fixing the system where others had failed, Lefkofsky was bowled over.

Yet the thrill of meeting that challenge quickly wore off for Mason. After all, he had never dreamed of a career in business-to-business print technology. That fall he decided to enroll at the U of C. Lefkofsky had other plans and was determined to keep his new star around.

If it was money Mason wanted, no problem. InnerWorkings was prepared to raise his salary from the low five figures to $200,000. Amazingly, Mason was unmoved by the offer.

"Nah," he said. "I'm just going to go to school."

Mason did indeed start grad school, but he agreed to come back to InnerWorkings one day a week to help hand off his projects. The rest of the time, he was at the U of C cooking up Policy Tree, living the life of a brilliant idealist uncorrupted by get-rich-quick dreams and untempted by a high-paying job that didn't speak to his soul. A rewarding career in the world of academia and non-profits undoubtedly awaited him in a world where people still saved money by clipping coupons out of the newspaper.

FOUR

Policy Tree wasn't the only idea for a site vying for Mason's attention. He also wanted to launch one that would improve the world by harnessing the power of collective action. At one point, he told Lefkofsky that he wanted to run the concept by him, but he never actually spit it out. Mason did outline the proposal to Eric Belcher, the president and CEO of InnerWorkings. Luckily, Belcher mentioned it to Lefkofsky, who called Mason one day between classes and asked him to lay out his idea.

For a guy who had enrolled in grad school because it was the only way he could imagine getting a Web project funded, this represented a surprising opportunity to meet with an angel investor—albeit one who also happened to be his boss—and present his concept for the collective-action site that would come to be known as The Point and eventually spin off Groupon.

Put on the spot by the call, an unprepared Mason rushed through the pitch session, failing to explain many of the concept's finer points. Lefkofsky was intrigued nonetheless.

The core idea was for users to post campaigns for collective action on the site—whether it was to start a boycott to force a cell-phone company to change onerous contract provisions (Mason got the idea for the site after suffering through a terrible customer-service experience with his wireless provider) or even to finance a climate-controlling glass dome that would turn the city of Chicago into a temperate paradise, as Mason famously lobbied for soon after The Point launched.

Each campaign would only be triggered after it reached a pre-set tipping point of resources committed, from volunteer labor to cash donations. If the minimum resources weren't in place by a set date, the proposed campaign would simply expire and everyone who had pledged to pitch in would be let off the hook.

Mason's idea was as simple as it was powerful: The site would foster efficient social change by enabling people to commit time and money to a cause only when they could be sure it would make a difference. If you wouldn't write a $25 check to someone who came to the door raising money for a neighborhood park that might never be built, you'd be much more likely to consider donating if you knew the check would only be cashed when construction began.

"That sounds pretty cool," Lefkofsky told Mason when he concluded his impromptu phone pitch. "Why don't you put together a five-page outline and bring it in, and we'll see if this is something we can fund and work on together."

Lefkofsky was inclined to look past Mason's rough pitching skills in part because he was so impressed with the person behind the proposal. In addition to Mason's coding talents, Lefkofsky appreciated the young man's remarkably blunt approach to assessing any given situation. At a time when Mason was a junior staffer among a couple of thousand employees at the two companies, he was fearless in critiquing organizational shortcomings.

"This guy sucks, he's an idiot, and you've got to get rid of him," Mason told Lefkofsky of one employee. Mason felt it was his duty to let the boss know, in case he was too occupied with strategic issues to pay close attention to day-to-day operations. That had to be it, Mason thought. Lefkofsky was a smart, take-no-prisoners guy, so why would he put up with incompetence?

"You think I don't know that?" Lefkofsky responded when informed that one of his managers was a fuckup. "Of course I know that. But there's a reason that it's okay."

Mason was shocked. But it was his first lesson in corporate management—that a big-picture perspective sometimes requires living with a less-than-ideal employee until the time is right to replace him. It was one of many such instructions Mason soon would put into practice on a scale that would have been impossible for him to dream of at the time.

So Mason was smart, he was effective, and he spoke in the same blunt terms as his boss. But Mason also had something important that Lefkofsky badly needed: a window into a younger generation, one that had been raised on the Web and could sense where it might be headed.

The emergence of YouTube as an essential online platform with a multi-billion-dollar valuation had taken Lefkofsky by surprise. He understood the business-to-business sector, but he needed more insights into the consumer-focused Web if he was going to be a player there.

Lefkofsky liked the Web site idea, but he was perhaps even more interested in the fact that Mason was spending ten hours a day online. The notion that a young guy who thought a lot like Lefkofsky could serve as his guide to this new world was an intoxicating one, and it could be worth serious money.

NOVEMBER 2006

Mason's five-page outline for his site was much better than the verbal pitch, so much so that Lefkofsky was ready to invest as soon as he read it.

"What do you want for this?" Lefkofsky asked.

"I can sell you the idea," Mason said. "Why don't you just buy it for, like, fifteen grand?"

"I don't want to buy the idea," Lefkofsky replied. "What am I going to do with it? I have no one to run the site. You've got to run it."

How would that work? Mason wondered. After all, he was in grad school and finals week was coming up.

That's when Lefkofsky uttered the magic words: "Let's put a million dollars into this thing and turn it into a company."

There was only one catch: If Mason wanted the money from Lefkofsky to develop the site, he would have to quit the University of Chicago at the end of the current term.

He asked for a few days to consider his options. After all, this could be a life-defining decision.

FIVE

Accepting the investment would be a huge leap, one complicated by Mason's belief that Policy Tree had a clearer path to success than The Point, which was a much more expansive, difficult-to-execute idea. But the grad student didn't have the resources to ramp up Policy Tree on his own, and Lefkofsky's seven-figure offer was tough to dismiss. The University of Chicago was about to start finals week leading into holiday break; 2007 was around the corner. The time might be right for a fresh start.

Mason visited with his professors, who gave their blessing. At that point Mason knew he would drop out. He started working in earnest on a business plan for the collective action site, but he kept studying for his finals as well. He would finish the quarter and try to get decent grades, in case he needed to go back someday. It would be foolish to count on this start-up venture making him rich. (When he got his first big check, he deposited it at one of his bank's supermarket counters only to be told by the surprised clerk that he should open multiple savings accounts and divvy the money up to ensure the entire sum got FDIC coverage, which maxes out at $250,000 per account.)

Mason started setting up the project out of Lefkofsky and Keywell's offices in January of 2007. By the end of the month, Mason had posted a message on the embryonic front page of PolicyTree.org: "Hello! Policy Tree is indefinitely on hold—I'm busy working on The Point. Want to take over?"

The Point's working title had been "Big Vox." No one liked it, but after a few weeks spent throwing out every potential alternative they could come up with—hundreds of names—a better candidate proved elusive.

The naming difficulties underscored a key problem with the site, Mason ultimately concluded: The underlying concept was so abstract and amorphous that it was impossible to come up with a Web address that adequately conveyed its purpose.

They finally hit on "The Point" in late January. They liked the name because it reinforced the concept of tipping points, which was core to the site's functionality. A campaign could only be launched after it "tipped," after all.

Tipping points were already being used by some more narrowly targeted collective action sites, notably the non-profit DonorsChoose, which educator Charles Best launched from Brooklyn in 2000 to help fund classroom projects posted by teachers from around the country. In fact, one could easily make the case that The Point was essentially DonorsChoose without a specific hook. And The Point wasn't the last such site to launch: Kickstarter, which debuted in 2009 just as Groupon was picking up steam, has also successfully harnessed the power of the tipping point to spur collective action, in its case to fund creative projects from theater and dance productions to films and video games.

Ironically, the Point's Groupon spin-off grew so big so fast that the tipping point quickly faded in importance—most deals now tip immediately, and few hit their expiration date without doing so. But in the early days, the tipping point was a critical part of the package.

When Lefkofsky set up The Point in early 2007, he took the lion's share of the stock and gave Andrew 15 percent, which underscores the leverage deep-pocketed angel investors bring to the table. But Mason showed once again that money wasn't his primary motivation.

"Just do whatever you think is fair," he told Lefkofsky. "I'm not going to negotiate it in any way. Because if I do, I'll feel like I always could have gotten more and then I'll feel bad, so let's just do whatever."

The investment left Mason feeling wildly optimistic. After the money came through, he walked around downtown Chicago with a few friends and told them, "It's in the bag—I'm basically going to have, like, thirty million dollars in a couple years. I can't see a way that doesn't end up happening."

Lefkofsky took a more realistic view. He figured the lopsided equity split was warranted because he was throwing a million bucks at a decidedly iffy idea. "The equity typically is a mess in these early-stage start-ups," Lefkofsky added. "The first time an entrepreneur does a business, it's rare that they end up making a killing. Unless it's an experience like Microsoft where the founders have incredible early success and don't need tons of capital to operate their business. Even at Facebook, Mark Zuckerberg is down to like 28 percent, and that's after an unbelievably meteoric rise."

Even before they got rich off the business, Mason and Lefkofsky didn't dwell on the ownership disparity. But there was something else about the structure that bothered both men.

"There are people that own a lot of this company that don't do much," Lefkofsky said. "That's far more frustrating. If someone owns a ton and they're killing themselves, like Brad and I do, you never feel nearly as angry as when people have a ton and they don't do anything. And we have people who have a ton of stock and they're gone; they're not even around."

There was a final wrinkle in the way the business was set up, one that could have a profound impact on the ultimate financial rewards for the founders. Since Lefkofsky was going to invest a million dollars of his personal funds into The Point, he had to decide how much equity, if any, to give his business partner Brad Keywell, who hadn't put in a dime.

Under their standard arrangement, both men received a set share of the equity in start-ups they either invested in or founded, with Keywell down for a somewhat smaller chunk than Lefkofsky. But The Point was an unusual hybrid that made the distribution decision tricky: The duo would serve as co-founders, while Lefkofsky put up almost all of the money as well. In the end, Lefkofsky awarded Keywell his usual stake, which was slightly less than the 15 percent Mason ended up with. Cutting Keywell out would have increased Lefkofsky's stake by some 50 percent.

The bald, bright-eyed Keywell called Lefkofsky's decision a testament to their twenty-year partnership and a friendship that blossomed at the University of Michigan after they'd known each other since attending the same temple as children. In law school in their early twenties, they found themselves assigned to the same section, which meant they would take every first-year class together. Within a few days after the term started, the pair became inseparable. They realized they had no interest in ever working for anyone and they both wanted to build businesses. They ended up collaborating on several business plans while still in law school, and continued down the entrepreneurial path together upon graduating.

"It was a non-issue," Keywell said of the equity question. "Most partnerships don't work, for a long list of reasons. The ones that do work generally work for a short list of reasons: There's trust, complementary skills, respect, and true friendship. If those four things exist, you've got a great partnership." Keywell and Lefkofsky had them all.

These days, Keywell is most active as co–managing director of Lightbank, with Lefkofsky. "There is no one like him," Lefkofsky said of his partner. "He's raw energy and intellect. One of the best early-stage entrepreneurs I've ever seen."

Once the equity split was decided, Lefkofsky quickly got the company off the ground. When The Point was incorporated in 2007, the founders capitalized it with nominal sums in exchange for equity stakes. Lefkofsky ponied up $8,275 on top of his million bucks, and Keywell put in $7,150. Andrew Mason contributed all of $375, earning the rest of his stake through his work. Now it was time to staff up. Mason actually already had an employee before The Point started. With the $35 an hour he'd been making as a developer at InnerWorkings, Mason had been paying a guy his age named Joe Harrow $10 an hour off the books to come to his apartment and help develop the Policy Tree project.

Harrow, who went on to join The Point and eventually took on Groupon's customer-service function, got the gig by responding to a Craigslist posting. But before Mason officially shifted Harrow over to The Point, he needed to finish writing the business plan and hire a senior developer, Brendan Baldwin. Baldwin ended up sticking around for seventeen months and building The Point's interface on the Ruby on Rails platform with Mason and five other coders.

When Mason turned in the business plan, which mentioned group buying in several places by, for instance, promising to integrate consumer requests for deals with specific merchants into the site's search architecture and by contemplating that users might "bargain with a local farmer to deliver fresh produce to a neighborhood at a discount rate" or otherwise "buy something . . . that requires a large body of people," Lefkofsky sensed he had bet on the right guy. Every other business plan that had been submitted to him he'd hated. Beyond being poorly written, they were often incoherent. He or Keywell ended up rewriting all of them. Until this one. Lefkofsky reviewed every section after Mason wrote it and simply told him to keep going. After very little editing, Lefkofsky said, "It really served as the business plan of The Point for eighteen months."

Lefkofsky might be the dyed-in-the-wool capitalist to Mason's geeked-out coder, but they have a similarly difficult time finding collaborators they click with. Mason is notorious for rejecting and rewriting Groupon's customer-service letters and other external communications. But when he reads over finance presentations prepared by Lefkofsky, he typically signs off on them without a second thought.

These two control freaks were indeed fortunate to find each other, because neither of them would have been able to tolerate a situation where they didn't agree on details as granular as the slides in a PowerPoint presentation. "We work great together or this would be a disaster," Lefkofsky said. "We pretty much see the world the same way."

They also share an unsentimental management style that can be off-putting, even though they often leaven it with humor. One day, for instance, Lefkofsky walked up to Nick Cioffi, Groupon's global operations SVP, to have a word with him. When a colleague mentioned it was Cioffi's birthday, Lefkofsky replied, "I don't give a shit. Right now, we're at work. And at work, we make money." Then he softened, adding, "When I leave work tonight, and I'm at home playing with my kids, I'll wish you happy birthday."

Another time, an employee called Mason out for ignoring someone who was speaking directly to him. He quickly apologized, but the question arose: "Was that CEO assholeness or standard assholeness?" Joe Harrow recounted. "I don't know that becoming CEO has changed Andrew that much. He's a weird dude and he doesn't apologize for it. He's got an edge."

If you're in tune with Mason and Lefkofsky—and they value you—they're great to work with. But if you can't keep up with the pace they set or key into their incisive style, it's best for you to move along quickly.

As 2008 dawned without a profitable business model for The Point, Mason and Brad Keywell went prospecting for VC funding up and down Silicon Valley's famed Sand Hill Road for three full days in January. There they were lectured and then turned down by heavy hitters at Sequoia Capital, Benchmark Capital, and Kleiner Perkins.

"There were all these guys telling us what was wrong with this idea," Keywell said. "All of them have since revisited the fact that they remember the meeting, and they remember telling us how so-and-so company's got it right and we're missing it." It was essentially the twenty-first-century VC version of denying the Beatles a recording contract, and Keywell, who's been pitching VCs in Silicon Valley since 1998, relishes the story.

The Point finally hit pay dirt with New Enterprise Associates, which had funded previous Lefkofsky and Keywell ventures. The partners had hoped to diversify their funding base beyond NEA, but it was not yet to be. "What it took was faith in this team," Keywell said. "We went to all the usual suspects on Sand Hill Road, but at the end of the process, the folks who had had experience with me and Eric were the ones that took the leap." On January 29, The Point announced a $4.8 million Series A investment round led by NEA, with managing general partner Peter Barris joining the board.

Though Keywell focused primarily on national deals, recruiting high-level talent, and closing strategic partnerships, he had the least defined role of the three founders, and his involvement would ebb and flow where Mason and Lefkofsky's would remain constant. But Keywell was happy to serve as needed even as he looked at other start-up opportunities.

"To me, this is happiness," said Keywell, who started his first business, a greeting-card company, at age seven. "This is absolute happiness. Starting stuff, growing stuff, and being entrepreneurially creative is the absolute reason I think I exist. Eric's been doing this forever because this is what he does; I've been doing it forever because this is what I do. It makes me happy, so therefore I do more of it. It makes him happy, so therefore he does more of it."

Meanwhile, Lefkofsky and Mason continued to split up most of the day-to-day duties of running The Point, and later Groupon, in a way that played to each man's strengths. As chairman, Lefkofsky handled the financing and investor relations, evaluated potential strategic partnerships, and dealt with regulatory agencies such as the SEC, among other high-level duties. For instance, during one early board meeting, there was a discussion about who should sit on Groupon's audit committee. Mason volunteered to serve, but Lefkofsky advised him not to. "Yeah," Mason said with a chuckle, "I don't even know what that is."

In addition to serving as the goofy public face of both companies, Mason oversees day-to-day operations without interference from Lefkofsky. So much so that when the duo took New York City mayor Michael Bloomberg on a tour of Groupon in 2011, they ended up in a space that housed ninety salespeople. It was the first time Lefkofsky had even been in the room.

And despite Mason's external persona, inside the company, especially among his management team, he is anything but goofy. His team describes him as superfocused, supercompetitive, and superanalytical. Groupon is a data-driven beast, where numbers rule and business issues are analyzed in a detached, rigorous manner. Mason has also recruited a team of online all-stars that he manages closely. No issue is off-limits or too small for him to dig into. Feedback is direct and sharp. If you're doing something right, you know it. If you're doing something wrong, you know it faster. But the lack of politics and emotion, which at times seems a detriment to Mason personally, creates a management culture that is stable, predictable, and highly functional through enormous external chaos and some of the fastest growth on the planet.

When it comes to setting business strategy, dealing with the board, and securing investments, Lefkofsky—who seems to invest in a new start-up every five minutes through his and Keywell's Lightbank fund—plays a critical role.

"Money and deals: That's where it's much more of a partnership," Lefkofsky said. "But how the business runs from Andrew on down is completely him. This unbelievable culture here I have zero responsibility for."

That may be true. But Lefkofsky did almost take the advice of others who wanted to kill the business before it even got off the ground.

SIX

Remember that little problem of The Point having such an all-encompassing concept that it was almost impossible to pin down? And the fact that it was being run by a twenty-six-year-old creative coder who was not motivated by money and who had never run a real business before? Those factors did not add up to a recipe for quick success at The Point, and they very nearly derailed the entire enterprise before it offered its first daily deal.

Tensions developed between Mason and Lefkofsky as a result of those issues. There was no clear business model, and Mason was more focused on realizing his vision for the site than developing one. Meanwhile, Lefkofsky was so busy running his other companies that he met with Mason no more than once a week. The young CEO was able to make formative mistakes during this period that helped prepare him for his larger role with Groupon, but a bit more operational mentoring from Lefkofsky wouldn't have killed him.

When they did meet, sparks often flew. Mason was obsessed with creating a perfect user experience out of the box no matter how long it took, while Lefkofsky wanted him to launch something good enough in six weeks. As the development process dragged on past three months, Lefkofsky couldn't take it anymore.

"What the fuck?" he said to Mason. "Don't focus on every little detail. The site doesn't have to be perfect; just get something out there and learn from it."

"What are you talking about?" Mason replied. "It has to be a great experience."

The team kept adding new features as they went—the site needed a social-networking component, a messaging system, and ways to distinguish between pledges of money and effort. The goal of solving all the logistical problems of collective action had eluded history's greatest social organizers, but Mason thought he could reach it with a sufficiently robust platform.

Even though Mason's team was small and it wasn't burning through the start-up cash at a rapid clip, Lefkofsky and the board grew increasingly nervous as a product failed to materialize. But lacking the ability to program in Ruby on Rails, there was nothing they could do besides push Mason to launch faster. "He was totally on an island," Lefkofsky said.

The core team developing The Point was putting in crazy hours in a small suite at the back of the InnerWorkings offices. But even then, Mason refused to take life too seriously.

When Matt Loseke, an HTML and CSS coder who eventually became Groupon employee number six, started in April 2008, his workstation was in a back corner facing a wall. His colleagues all sat behind him, out of sight unless he turned away from his computer screen. Immediately after he started, Loseke was getting shot with rubber bands in the back of his head. He'd whirl around and demand to know who was firing at him, but no one ever fessed up. "All day long, rubber bands bounced off my head," he said.

Then one day, Loseke arrived at work earlier than normal.

Mason and one other employee had gotten there ahead of him. No sooner had Loseke booted up his computer than *thwip*, a rubber band hit him in the head.

Loseke turned to Mason. "Dude, what the fuck?" he said.

"What?" Mason replied with a perfect poker face.

"I don't know you well enough to know if you're fucking with me," Loseke said, turning back to his work.

Everyone was taking turns hitting him, Loseke figured. And besides, it was a convivial, fun office environment. He loved his job, quirks and all—like the prank Aaron With, a former college classmate of Mason's who'd been hired from a non-profit to work on The Point, played on the building's other tenants the month Loseke started.

With had sandy hair, a penchant for sweater-vests, a mustache that looked like two caterpillars had crawled onto his upper lip, and the pale complexion of a man who'd spent his life under the glow of fluorescent lights. But assuming he's an old-before-his-time square would be a mistake.

With hated the smell of popcorn that would waft up from the shared kitchen into The Point's offices, so one day he posted a memo next to the microwave. The edict, purportedly from the building's Atmosphere Control Division, banned the popping of corn throughout the premises. With thought that everyone would understand that it was a joke, but several tenants complained, and he ended up posting an abject apology on April 29 after the company's kitchen privileges were almost suspended. "I promise that I will not engage in any such humor again," With wrote. Of course, as the company began colonizing the entire building, it would become a much more humor-friendly environment.

And then there was the day Mason showed up with his hair shaved all the way down the middle of his head from front to back, leaving only sidewalls and stubble. He was shooting an instructional video for The Point in the guise of an older Andrew Mason come to talk from the future.

But the future was closer than he thought. Nine months after plunging down the rabbit hole, Mason was finally forced to launch The Point. It boasted a huge set of features, but none of them worked particularly well. That's when he realized what Lefkofsky had meant by launching quickly. You could create a solid site in a short time frame if you didn't try to incorporate every bell and whistle.

"I still believe you should launch something that's a great experience," Mason said. "I think you should just launch less." It was a critical lesson to learn, but that education almost cost him the business.

Once the imperfect and overly ambitious site finally went live in September 2007, it did not receive the attention Mason had expected. Then the team began casting about for ways to turn it into a viable business. Lefkofsky brought in outsiders, such as Dan Seals—a business consultant and Democratic politician who ran for and failed to win a congressional seat in the Chicago suburbs three times—to brainstorm models that would take The Point to profitability. But months ticked by, and nothing gelled as the start-up funds continued to evaporate.

During The Point's adolescent stage, every moneymaking scheme the team tried turned out to be a dead end. They offered to create white-label campaigns for non-profits, essentially letting organizations brand The Point's back-end system as their own product. As that initiative fizzled, Mason decided the site needed to be completely redone, a reboot that took nearly five months. Unbelievably, Mason made the site even more complex than it already was. The focus shifted from having the tipping point met simply when a certain number of people joined a campaign to including a secondary action component. "It was like, 'We'll all put up this pool of money, but we'll only release it when someone agrees to run for mayor,'" Mason said. Like a plastic-surgery addict trying to achieve a natural look by going under the knife again and again, he stayed in the operating room all summer.

One day, in a scene that would be repeated more than once, a clearly agitated Lefkofsky entered Mason's office for a closed-door session that was so loud it could easily be heard throughout The Point's small work space.

"You've got to find a revenue model," Lefkofsky insisted, his voice rising. "Your fun little start-up bullshit's over. People, not just me, have invested millions of dollars in your dream, and if you don't turn it into reality FAST, this is all going to come to an abrupt end. I can't hold back the other investors forever. They already want to call it quits. We've wasted enough time and this isn't a not-for-profit. Find a business, or let's move on."

Incredibly, Mason refused to panic. Based on no evidence, he told Lefkofsky, "Relax. When it's time to make money, we'll just make a lot of money." He had an innate confidence that when he was ready he could find a way to use the power of the Internet, and the power of collective action, to generate revenues.

Lefkofsky couldn't believe what he was hearing. Mason thought he could somehow flip a switch and—boom!—instant revenue stream. If that was the case, the time to do it was now.

For the idealistic crew, these heated exchanges between the bosses were a wake-up call. They always knew they'd have to monetize The Point someday, but that day had seemed like a vague, far-off reality. Now, the pressure was all too real.

SEVEN

Lefkofsky was seriously thinking that he was going to have to pull the plug. He accused Mason of rearranging deck chairs on the *Titanic*, but something about the project kept Lefkofsky emotionally invested in it.

He saw sparks of creative brilliance when, for instance, Mason launched his campaign to raise $10 billion for a climate-controlled winter dome over the city of Chicago. "The eradication of winter would allow our city to blossom to its full potential," Mason wrote in his public pitch for the dome, which would have "airplane-shaped holes in the sky" and could be collapsed and stored during the summer. "The ability to use bikes as transportation year round would allow people to sell their cars and reduce traffic. We'd be able to get more done in the winter, no longer trapped indoors. The possibilities are endless."

Alas, the campaign stalled out at $239,000 pledged, or just $9,999,761,000 short of the tipping point. But at least it effectively explained how the site worked. As Mason noted, participants "will not spend a dime unless we raise ten billion dollars, which will be more than enough to get the job done. There is no risk whatsoever in joining. Don't think about whether or not enough money will be raised, just think about what it would be worth to you to never again suffer a Chicago winter."

But nothing could fix the fact that the site lacked focus. The concept was too broad for users to get their minds around. They could use The Point to organize a group of friends to go out for a party, or buy a Ping-Pong table for their dorm room, or organize a boycott against a multinational corporation, or try to overturn a federal law, or raise money for a non-profit . . . or do group buying. Mostly, they did none of those things. By trying to be good for everything, the site essentially became good for nothing.

Meanwhile, an online search marketer named Zac Goldberg was busy trying to drive traffic to The Point on the cheap. He started by buying Google ads based on keywords for activist campaigns that had already been set up. Unfortunately, one of the site's first user-generated campaigns was a bid to make marijuana legal by getting a million people to publicly sign onto the cause, so Goldberg started buying ads for The Point based on keywords such as "legalize marijuana." Those ads would pop up on Google whenever someone used that phrase in a search. Within three days, The Point was overrun by fans of an anarchist band called Insane Clown Posse, who proceeded to create one pot-legalization campaign after another. Goldberg immediately switched the ad campaign to focus on preventing cruelty to pets.

Mason contrasted this frustrating state of affairs with his experiences in writing music. "When you're creating art, you want to express your ideas in their fullness, almost disregarding whether or not people understand," he said. "But the most successful business innovations are the ones that are one baby step removed from something that already exists, and that people already understand. So they can look at it for a second and they've got it. 'Oh, it's like this with a twist.' And that's what we eventually boiled Groupon down to."

As DonorsChoose showed, focusing on a specific niche is as yet the only proven way to make the social-funding model work. It's all about simplicity. And under that logic, as Mason is fond of noting, The Point could give birth to other targeted plays in the Groupon mold.

So the next time you get upset seeing the Andrew Masons of the world get rich off of concepts that are just one click over from something that already exists—like, say, store coupons—console yourself with the fact that the very recognizability of such concepts can be the secret to their success. Don't waste your time carping about the kid who liked having his mom trim the crusts off his PB&J sandwiches so much that he grew up to "invent" Uncrustables sandwiches; maybe you can make a mint off of fun new uses for the leftover crusts.

Of course, your business will probably crash and burn, just like The Point almost did. After that tough adolescent period when Lefkofsky looked beyond the lack of a business model to find flashes of promise from May through October 2008, he worried that there might never be a sustainable path for The Point.

It was time for a Hail Mary play. Where Lefkofsky and Keywell had been hands-off, they were now aggressively involved in trying to monetize the site. Lefkofsky suggested adding advertising, but Mason resisted. Meanwhile, the board of directors started pressuring Lefkofsky to pull the plug. These were the same directors who sat on the boards of his companies Inner-Workings and MediaBank, an online media-buying company that he and Keywell had founded. Those firms were doing well, which made The Point look like even more of a dog by comparison.

"Just close it down," one director told Lefkofsky as the leaves started to fall. "We still have three million left over. Distribute the money and let's move on."

It seemed that every conversation between Mason and Lefkofsky during that period turned into a conflict. Their disagreements were fundamental and easily could have become insurmountable. Lefkofsky grew so convinced Mason was wired against the concept of making money that he started referring to the young CEO as a socialist. It became the chairman's personal mission to break Mason of his supposed anti-capitalist ways.

From Mason's perspective, his mentor was behaving idiotically. When Lefkofsky pushed harder to sell advertising on the site, Mason finally blew up at him.

"What's wrong with you?" Mason demanded. "We're getting thirty thousand visitors a month and we'll make nine dollars a month in advertising. Why would I do that? Who in their right mind would try to sell advertising when we have no traffic?"

"You just need to see what it feels like to do something that results in making money," Lefkofsky insisted.

Mason finally agreed to create some ad positions on The Point's blog, but neither party left the argument a winner, and by August it was clear that hosting ads wasn't going to generate meaningful revenue. Offering the technology to non-profits for white-label fund-raising campaigns was another dead end. So the team started to focus on answering one key question: How could they monetize group buying?

While those options were dead ends, Lefkofsky's capitalist reeducation camp did ultimately lead Mason and the other young idealists on his team to seek a non-adversarial business model, one in which every party would leave with something of value. To get to that epiphany, the team closely examined how members were using the site. Interestingly, a few of them had attempted to persuade merchants to offer a discount if a certain number of users agreed to, say, eat dinner at their restaurant.

"There were campaigns people started from early 2008 that are basically Groupon campaigns that existed on The Point," Mason explained. But back then, the company only provided a virtual room for the negotiation to take place and it took no cut for bringing the parties together.

Group buying had been tried on the Internet many times before. So what was ThePoint.com going to do that was different? Mason approached the issue from the perspective of the consumer: If he could get a daily e-mail that highlighted one great business at an even better price, he'd often be moved to buy. But the key insight, which gave rise to Groupon, is actually amazingly simple and, like most great business models, makes you end up asking yourself, "Why didn't I think of that?"

What Mason and his team eventually figured out is this: Every day local merchants have unused inventory. They have food that goes to waste, appointments that don't get filled. They need, like most businesses, more customers. And to get more customers, merchants have to entice them to come in, which often means offering them a discount. But for most merchants, discounts and sales are a catch-22. You only want to lower your price if you know you're going to get new customers. Until Groupon arrived, this was an unsolved equation. Groupon applied the logic of tipping points and said to merchants: "If we can get you one hundred customers, will you give them all 50 percent off?" That created an immediate connection between the incentive offered and the merchant's desired result. Overnight, a new marketplace was formed.

But the logistics needed to be hashed out. In addition to Lefkofsky, Keywell, Mason, Harrow, and Cioffi, who was overseeing day-to-day operations, the job of setting up the site and

developing a sales strategy was also shouldered by Shawn Ber-
cuson, who would become Groupon's first VP of business development, and Mason's college pal Aaron With. By this time,
Mason had moved out of his office and taken a desk between
With and Harrow.

"What do you think we should call the new site?" the CEO
asked them one day. Someone had earlier suggested naming it
Thrill & Chill (offering two deals—one exciting and one
relaxing—each day), but the idea was chilled when it failed to
thrill.

In less than thirty seconds, With responded, "How about
Groupon?" He liked to play around with portmanteaus—
mashing words together to create new ones—and since the concept of The Point's spin-off service was to offer coupons that
people would buy in groups, combining "group" and "coupon"
was a natural.

Mason later jokingly told With, "If you hadn't come up with
that name, at some point I would have myself." As With noted
with a laugh, "It was kind of an asshole thing for him to say,
but it's true."

Regardless, the name Groupon stuck—as did the catchphrase
"get your Groupon."

It was a time of quick decisions. Days after With named the
service, the designers had created screen shots. Soon, the rudimentary programming was complete and Groupon was cleared
for a trial launch. The entire process took no more than six weeks.

That suited Lefkofsky fine. With a rapid rollout, he thought,
the team could fall on its face again without wasting too much
time and then move on to better ideas. He was intrigued by the
group-buying concept, but he didn't think it would be their
killer app.

Mason had applied the lessons he'd learned from The Point's

failures by developing a stripped-down, narrowly focused product on the fly. The first Groupons would be set up on a WordPress blog, with a widget from The Point embedded in each deal post.

"The back end was a piece of shit," Mason said. In fact, when members purchased a Groupon, they would get an e-mail saying: "Thanks for joining this campaign on The Point." User e-mail addresses would then be exported into a FileMaker database. Joe Harrow would run a computer script that opened Apple's e-mail application, created individual messages for every e-mail address associated with a deal purchase, embedded PDF deal coupons into messages, and sent them off one by one. The site was totally hacked together.

With the process ready to test, the crew began trying to sell local merchants on the concept of offering discount deals in exchange for getting a guaranteed number of customers through the door. It could be the win-win everyone was looking for. If it was done right, both customers and merchants would benefit from the group-deal experience and Groupon could take a healthy cut as the market-making middleman that brought them all together.

"The biggest lesson we learned from The Point is, we scoped that thing so big, we couldn't specialize," Harrow said. "Nobody could wrap their head around it; we couldn't even really understand what we were building. When we did Groupon, we said, 'Let's just take a tiny little piece of this and do it great.'"

But if this approach didn't work, there was no certain future for The Point.

OCTOBER 21, 2008

The Point launched its first Groupon deal on a Tuesday. The offer, which you can still see on the site, was dead simple: two pizzas for the price of one at Motel Bar, the joint on the ground floor of Groupon's headquarters building that employees had turned into a pub-grub hangout.

Members of The Point were asked to pay thirteen dollars for twenty-six dollars' worth of pie. Once purchased, the Groupons would expire on October 25, 2009, giving buyers plenty of time to chow down. Motel Bar set a tipping point of twenty-five deals, figuring if it could get at least that many (mostly) new customers through the door, it would be a worthwhile marketing expense to try to build repeat business.

This deal would serve as the template for the Groupon. Going forward, a Groupon would be a deal offering typically 50 percent or more off the price of a merchant's goods or services. Shop owners would usually get half the proceeds from each Groupon purchase, and they would cover the coupon value as well. So if a Groupon offered twenty dollars' worth of a service for ten dollars, Groupon would take five dollars—half of the base purchase price—from every deal sold. The merchant would get the other five dollars but would have to provide twenty dollars' worth of value to each customer.

Factoring in Groupon's cut and the coupon value, then, merchants would be taking a 75 percent hit off the full retail price on every deal sold. It was a margin killer in the short term, but businesses hoped the promotions would pay off by converting deal buyers into long-term customers more effectively than direct mail or old-fashioned newspaper coupons could do. Groupon wouldn't be the best marketing vehicle for every merchant type, but in general the trick was to structure offers so that the expense was justified. Even at such steep discounts, many merchants would profit directly from the deals themselves, thanks in part to upselling customers. If that $20 Groupon was used as part of a $40 purchase, for instance, the margins started looking a lot better.

At 9:18 that evening, with under three hours to go on the offer, the Motel Bar Groupon deal tipped and The Point made its first $325.

That's how once-in-a-decade, market-transforming businesses are born.

EIGHT

There was only one problem: The Point didn't have enough money left to ramp up Groupon without dramatically cutting its fixed costs. Just ten days before the Motel Bar deal went live, Mason slashed The Point's staff from a dozen to six in a last-ditch attempt to buy the Groupon concept more time.

The sales team was begging businesses to give this odd, unproven marketing method a try. But early on, deals often wouldn't tip. And customers and merchants didn't quite know how to handle the deal printouts. The day after the Motel Bar Groupon tipped, Zac Goldberg, who's now Groupon's online marketing VP, and two of his colleagues from The Point went downstairs to redeem one of the deals. But neither they nor the waitress had any idea how the transaction should work. After spending $13 for the $26 Groupon, they ended up giving the server the deal print-out plus an additional $13, thereby paying full price for their pizza.

The second Groupon, for tickets to see *The Dark Knight* at an IMAX theater, didn't look like it was going to tip, even though it only needed to sell ten deals. At the last minute, Goldberg posted flyers about the deal in all of the building's elevators and the Groupon tipped. "It was one of our earliest, and not-very-scalable, marketing tactics," he said.

This was Groupon's chicken-and-egg moment: Without a large customer base, it was difficult to sign up merchants; but without merchants offering cool deals, why would consumers give Groupon a try? Plus, few people outside the building even knew about the service.

To make matters worse, the Motel Bar deal didn't even have a subscription page attached to it. The Point had no method for collecting e-mail addresses to which they could send upcoming offers. Mason quickly coded a landing page that would stop visitors before they got to the deal and ask for their e-mail info. The page included a promise: "The first 500 subscribers will get an amazing gift that you won't believe."

Thanks to some inexpensive search marketing, the offers soon began attracting thousands of new subscribers a day. It was the birth of Groupon's mighty e-mail list. However, Goldberg said, "We may be guilty of still owing those first five hundred subscribers that gift." (Mason thinks they got something, perhaps a credit toward purchasing a Groupon.)

As they were hacking their way forward, there was still so much tension around the office that when Mason and CTO Ken Pelletier called developer Matt Loseke into a meeting one day, he was so sure he was being let go that he didn't take in a word they said.

"Can I use you guys as references?" Loseke finally blurted out.

"What?" Pelletier asked. "No, no, no, no, no. You're not fired. You're okay."

Around that time, Goldberg was called into the office immediately after Mason had fired two of his co-workers. He'd just been hired in September, so he assumed the worst.

"Zac, you're next," the CEO said.

"Okay, what's the bad news?" Goldberg asked as he sat down.

"Oh, I just wanted to let you know you're doing a great job." Mason replied. "You can go now."

Goldberg believed his boss intentionally put a scare into him as a prank. "That's pretty indicative of his humor," the marketer said.

But it was no joke when Aaron With, the man who'd given Groupon its name, got the ax for real. Mason went to With's apartment on October 11 and cut him loose the night before he was to embark on a six-week European tour with his band, Volcano.

Mason was miserable about the turn of events. To With, it felt like a larger defeat than just losing his job. That The Point was likely to fail was a huge disappointment for both of them.

With and Mason had become friends nearly a decade earlier, when they were undergrads at Northwestern. They'd played in an indie-pop band Planet of the Plants, with Mason on keyboard. He and With also played guitar and sang. Through the band, they had formed a bond. Now, Mason told With he could write deal copy on a freelance basis during his tour, but it was hard not to suspect that their professional relationship was coming to an end.

As With embarked on his tour, Mason had no time to reflect on the loss. Despite minimal resources and a hacked-together site—which, ironically, was made possible only by the code written for the The Point reboot that Lefkofsky had criticized—Groupon was actually starting to gain some traction. On November 11, The Point launched Groupon.com, "thus reinventing the coupon," as it said in a press release that day. The company's official communications were often humorous, but they were never modest.

By the time the holiday buying season kicked off, more

merchants were willing to take a chance on the concept and deals started attracting several hundred customers. This was good news, but the manual processes Mason had set up for Groupon began to buckle under the strain. While the e-mails were being generated from a successful deal, Joe Harrow had to walk away from his computer and find something else to do around the office for an hour or more. After coming back to press the send button in window after window, he'd often have to set up a second batch.

That wasn't even the worst of it. If a customer wanted a refund, Harrow would have to log in to Groupon's bank account and issue a credit. He next had to copy the information and send it to Mike Cerna, who was then head of development, and tell him: "Cancel this order. I issued a refund." Only after Cerna manually entered the data into the system was the process complete. And that was for each refund. But even if it wasn't a sustainable system, it would work long enough to prove that Groupon was the business model they were desperate to find after all.

Though restaurant deals proved solid offerings, and remain a staple of the site, Mason soon told his sales crew to start booking deals that would encourage members to enjoy fun new experiences in their city. Inspired by a boat tour of Chicago's architectural highlights he'd taken with his father the previous summer, he wanted Groupon to help people rediscover the joys of urban life.

"Doing one awesome deal a day on these really neat experiences wasn't a no-brainer idea at the time, by any means," Mason said. "It seems so simple now, and people take it for granted. But that's the beauty of the Internet: We're twenty years in, and there are still so many opportunities to come up with really stupid simple ideas that absolutely change the world."

Much of the Groupon formula that seems inevitable in retrospect was actually born of necessity. The deal-a-day concept? It evolved from the fact that Groupon didn't have many customers or merchant clients in the early days, so offers had to be spread out. Single deals were also easy to launch quickly.

Going after local merchants? The company had no access to national merchants. The focus on services and experiences over products? Mason had seen Mercata and other early group-buying sites fizzle after focusing on product sales, which were a low-margin business anyway. Launching during a recession, when workers were easy to find and people were especially hungry for bargains? Pure fate. And where Amazon has fought sales-tax collection battles in many states, Groupon sells gift certificates—bingo, no taxes to collect.

Burned by The Point experience, Mason said, "We always approached Groupon with skepticism: This thing is likely not going to work, so let's really focus on the problems and change direction quickly as soon as we see them, so that there actually is some kind of chance that it is successful. I think our skepticism about the concept in general is what has led to its success, and generally leads to entrepreneurial success." Of course, skepticism is only a useful tool if you're willing to give yourself credit when necessary. Mason admitted, "Sometimes we're too hard on ourselves and it leads us to get very close to making dumb decisions."

Like almost selling to Google too soon.

Still, even after the company's near-death experience, the freshly minted CEO needed to have a little bit of the shine rubbed off him. One of the rare times Lefkofsky hurt his feelings came when Mason bounded into his office to tell him that a Groupon campaign had generated enough gross revenue to pay the salary of his most expensive employee for one day.

"Get out of here, that's nothing," Lefkofsky said. "Come back when you're making ten thousand dollars a day."

Mason realized he'd become a pitchman, constantly telling Lefkofsky, "This thing's going to work." It was time to prove it. *Eric's not buying my bullshit anymore*, he thought.

Even though there were still days when deals didn't tip, the model was showing more and more promise. Less than a month in, Mason was driving through downstate Illinois on his way to meet with someone who might set up a Groupon franchise there, during a brief period when the company was considering building its business on a franchise model. He stopped by the side of a road to check his phone on how that day's deal—for a sushi restaurant—was doing. It had sold five hundred.

"Holy shit!" Mason said to himself out there among the cornfields. He had built it, and they had come.

That's when Groupon was able to rehire Aaron With. Unlike the story of business betrayal told in the Facebook movie, *The Social Network*, Mason and With had a relationship built as much on honesty and integrity as on shared creative vision. Shortly after Volcano returned to Chicago in early December, Mason called his friend and asked him to come back full-time, writing deal copy as the site's editor and selling to merchants on the side.

With seriously considered turning down the offer, but then he thought, *I helped start this thing. If it's going to take off, I want to be there for the ride.* He soon joined Mason as one of Groupon's most essential voices, developing the absurdist copywriting style that helped the daily-deals site attain its loyal following. An example from the company style guide, which recommends goosing deal copy with fake proverbs, illogical comparisons, and ersatz history, says: "If your eyes are the windows to your soul, your hair is the tunnel to your mind. Keep your mind-matter from escaping with today's hair-taming Groupon."

With deserves credit for giving Groupon a distinctive editorial voice that both makes customers feel like they're part of a goofy club and helps spread the company culture to new hires. But With also created an editorial operation with a measure of independence from the sales function. If a merchant looked dodgy, editors could pull the plug on a deal, for instance. Maintaining that integrity helped build trust with customers, even if it was sometimes tough for merchants to swallow that they wouldn't have final sign-off on their deal copy.

Nailing the humor style was critical to making the process work. The first deal write-up With drafted was filled with disgusting, sexual, off-color humor. He and the five writers he hired to staff up the editorial function quickly developed an acceptably offbeat house style, but in the first year some boundary-pushing gags still slipped through. One Groupon sales manager grew so angry at the idea that these sarcastic assholes could alienate his clients that he got into a shouting match with Mason about it.

Typically, Mason was very hard on With in public so as not to be seen as playing favorites. But with the bedrock voice of Groupon under attack, the CEO strongly defended his editor to the sales force, and the complaining manager soon hit the bricks. "That set the tone for us to carve out the editorial independence we needed," With said. "We continued to refine the voice to the point where it was viewed as one of our defining, differentiating assets."

He and Mason later saw *The Social Network* together at the height of the Google and Yahoo! negotiations. Mason liked it as a movie, but he couldn't relate to it as an entrepreneur. "We didn't have a Justin Timberlake at Groupon," he said. "There was no hooking up in the bathroom—as far as I know."

Outside the theater, the editor joked about what a Groupon movie might look like.

"We'd need to create a lot more drama," With told Mason, who hated the idea of a Groupon film. "You'd probably have to fire me again."

But Groupon had more than enough twists and turns in store, even if Aaron With got to keep his job. Meanwhile, it had ended 2008 with gross billings of $94,000, revenues of $5,000, and an operating loss of $1.6 million in its first two official months of operation. Baby steps.

NINE

As Groupon entered its first full calendar year, it was selling two to three hundred deals a day in Chicago, and Lefkofsky brought former AOL executive Ted Leonsis onto the fledgling firm's board of directors. The Point was starting to fade into the rearview mirror, with Mason telling users on January 5, 2009: "In the last few months, most of our time has been spent on Groupon, the collective-buying side of The Point." Soon, Groupon's precursor site would become little more than the answer to a trivia question. Mason's first employee, Joe Harrow, who saw himself as a non-profit guy, felt that The Point was never about making money. But once Groupon started taking off, money seemed to be all anyone talked about there. *I used to be focused on changing the way people make decisions, and now we're selling coupons?* he thought. *What am I doing?*

At a party during that period, Harrow told an acquaintance that he didn't understand why anyone in the world needed to make more than $60,000 a year. Even after a couple of years running Groupon's customer-service department, he said that if his house were to burn down, the only thing worth rescuing would be his laptop—issued to him by the company—which he'd drive off with in his $3,000 car.

"I don't really believe in inheritance," he said. "I think we should try and level things and take care of people who don't have food and water." That was the ethos that informed The Point. Some of that feeling migrated over to the G-Team, Groupon's charitable fund-raising arm, but mostly the transition to a commerce-obsessed company was surreal and even somewhat unsettling for the early guys.

Maybe the direction of the business had been influenced by its surroundings. After all, Groupon was housed, along with Lefkofsky and Keywell's other businesses, in the landmark 1908 Montgomery Ward & Co. Catalog House, a sinuous, terra-cotta-clad gem of early twentieth-century industrial architecture that was set hard against the North Branch of the Chicago River. Didn't it make sense for the new darling of e-commerce to set up shop where the late, great giant of c-commerce once produced its mail-order retail wish books?

Inside, though, it was hard to remember that the building was more than a century old. The million and a half square feet had been transformed into a beehive of modern office suites decked out with glass walls, exposed brick, soft carpets, and brushed-metal accents, all arrayed around a stylish circular atrium that featured a wall of video screens in the lobby waiting area. Groupon started gobbling up space there as fast as it could sublease it, on the way to hitting 340,000 square feet in 2012.

As it colonized new frontiers in fits and starts, desks would sometimes be set up in conference rooms for months to handle the company's relentless workforce growth. But even if it was a briskly efficient, glorified cube farm, Groupon was an often-fun place to work as well.

Visitors know they're in the customer-service section when

they see the wall of head shots next to one group of workstations—many of the reps have improv-comedy backgrounds, which they tap into to keep customers happy with humorously helpful banter (there's also a "wall of shame" where complaints are posted). Doodle-filled whiteboards line other walls. Nearby, one might spy a young woman working with a paper crown on her head because it's her birthday.

The fact that employees sell into cities across North America from this office leads to amusing conversations. On the elevator one day, two women discussed a colleague who laughed every time someone mentioned a particular north-of-the-border market. (In addition to being the capital of Saskatchewan, you see, "Regina" rhymes with "vagina.") That kind of humor plays well in an office with an average age of twenty-five.

From the top down, Grouponistas are expected to adopt the ethic of being transparent, collaborative, and—thanks in large part to the jokey-yet-well-researched deal write-ups Mason calls "the heartbeat of the company"—absurdist humor. Among those employees, always, sits Mason at a workstation just like theirs. In the first few years, he even moved to a different cube every few months. If it was a bit awkward to suddenly have the boss sitting at their elbows, staffers "realized pretty quickly that they don't have to treat me with any respect," he joked. For sensitive meetings, he would hole up in a conference room, but he hadn't had an actual office since the earliest days of The Point.

As the headquarters kept expanding, Mason and Lefkofsky started to realize that Groupon might be not only a new business but an entirely new model for commerce as well. If it scaled, it could bring local merchants online in cities around the world, unlocking a market segment worth trillions of dollars. But that was still a very big if.

After all, though Groupon was on firm footing in Chicago, it was still an entirely local sensation. Even six weeks after Groupon Boston launched on March 16, the expansion looked like a flop.

It had seemed like a natural second market for Groupon. Beyond the "diverse, vibrant local business scene," as the company put it in a blog post that month, Boston could boast "a ton of universities that churn out thousands of web-savvy graduates, some of whom even go so far as to marry their computers."

All the deals in Boston's first week tipped, including the opening offer for forty dollars' worth of Mexican restaurant fare for twenty dollars. But the Boston sales team had very little luck closing deals overall.

That's it, Lefkofsky thought. *It's over. Groupon is a one-town phenomenon. It's not going to work well in other places. We just have an advantage in Chicago because our salesmen know people here.*

In a job posting for a Boston-based editor/community manager, the company had joked: "We don't know anything about Boston. We don't even know how to fake the accent." If understanding the market was a prerequisite for success, Groupon was cooked.

But then, in May, Boston suddenly turned the corner. One day, Lefkofsky walked into a status meeting and asked, "How's Boston doing?" He'd all but given up hope, but still, he had to know.

"Boston's doing unbelievable," came the response.

What? he thought. *Boston's doing unbelievable?*

That was the moment he knew: *This will work everywhere.*

Which meant they were going to change the world after all.

Soon, Groupon had a formula set for rolling out new cities in a couple of weeks: Build a list of prospective merchants, hire two salespeople to call on the market from the Chicago office, add a customer-service staffer and a writer, train them on Groupon protocols, and then pull the trigger.

The mood at Groupon headquarters turned from "Do we have a model?" to "How fast can we get this into every city?"

"Most of us were terrified to go to Boston and thought we weren't ready," editor Aaron With said. "Eric rightly pushed us to move fast. If he hadn't, we'd have lost. The first ten cities were like that. I kept wanting to shore up the operation before we extended it. Eventually, I just submitted to the light-speed reality and soon enough we'd somehow found a way to launch twenty cities a month. We were always being pushed beyond our natural limits and clawing for ways to survive the ridiculously intense scaling."

They were so busy that they barely even noticed the April 27 PR Newswire release headlined: " 'BuyWithMe' & Save at Boston-Area Restaurants, Events, Spas & Retailers."

It read, in part: "BuyWithMe.com, a brand-new daily deal source launching in early May, harnesses Group Buying Power and Social Media to get people their favorite things for less in this tough economy. BuyWithMe brings savings and exclusive offers from Boston's best restaurants, services, events, and retailers to the BuyWithMe community. These deals are often 50% discounts and greater, and are available for purchase during a limited window of time. The concept is the brainchild of a group of young, entrepreneurial Bostonians with strong local ties to their city. BuyWithMe is thrilled to launch this soon-to-be-national concept in their hometown. BuyWithMe is a win-win situation—consumers get great deals and local merchants get tons of new customers."

Coming more than a month after Groupon Boston launched, that "brainchild" must have been an identical twin. This was an audacious lifting of Groupon's concept.

The clone wars had begun.

TEN

Thus opened a chapter in Groupon's history that continues to give the company headaches. The knockoff sites, which have numbered in the hundreds, sometimes simply swiped Groupon's code and marketing copy.

But BuyWithMe, which launched May 18 with a spa deal, caught Groupon completely by surprise. The Chicago-based salespeople would call merchants in Boston only to hear the owners say, "You were already in here, and we got your flyers. We'll call you when we're ready."

What the hell is going on? Mason wondered when he heard about these bizarre calls. *Do we have fans out there that are selling on our behalf?*

It was the opposite. There was another company out to steal Groupon's thunder. In their pre-launch phase, the Boston interlopers were calling themselves Groupies Inc., and they only adopted "BuyWithMe" after Groupon complained about the confusion they were creating in the market.

When Mason finally saw the BuyWithMe site, he couldn't believe how closely the marketing copy mirrored Groupon's. *It's practically verbatim*, he thought. He was furious, but there was little he could do legally to stop even the most blatant copycat sites—such as Groupon.cn, a Chinese operation that ripped off everything, from the company's name and logo to its complete site design. It was surreal.

Other knockoffs soon followed, including LivingSocial, which launched a test run of its daily-deals business around its Washington, D.C., home base with a July 27 restaurant offer, before expanding into New York City at the end of August. LivingSocial's entry into the market was a sobering spectacle, because it had already amassed a base of 80 million users who had signed up to use its Facebook survey apps since 2007. If any of the domestic upstarts could give Groupon a run for its money, this was it.

Occasionally, Groupon took a clone to court, most notably Scoopon, the Australian deals site that had registered the domain Groupon.com.au and forced the real Groupon to enter the market under the name Stardeals while it pursued a domain-squatting lawsuit against its rival. After a months-long legal skirmish, the suit was settled in July 2011, finally clearing the way for Groupon to operate in Australia under its true name.

But mostly, Groupon ignored the clones and simply pressed on, expanding into new markets as rapidly as possible, attempting to reach such a critical mass of cities and customers that no one would be able to beat them at what was, admittedly, an easy game to enter. Mason and Lefkofsky even swallowed their disgust and started acquiring well-run clones in international markets. The strategy would prove a brilliant one.

The eighteen months after the Boston launch were a period of breakneck growth for Groupon. "There was no time to really reflect," Lefkofsky said. "It was moving so fast, it was coming so quick. We'd launch another city, it would go well. We'd launch another city. There was no bad news. There were things that were scary. I remember early on when LivingSocial copied us or when Boston.com did a deal with BuyWithMe. There were a couple moments in the first six months where you thought, 'Is this going to be the end?'"

It got so busy that Mason had to abandon one of his beloved wacky stunts for perhaps the first time ever. In July 2009, Groupon marketing executive Zac Goldberg moved to Providence, Rhode Island, when his wife got a job there, but the company kept him on. That's when the CEO got the idea to build a robot version of Goldberg in the Chicago office that the human version could operate from his computer on the East Coast. Goldberg's face would even appear, via webcam, on a video monitor that would serve as the robot's head as it rolled around the office atop a supply cart.

"Andrew began searching for contractors to build the robot," Goldberg recounted. "He started planning out a wardrobe for it. The only thing that prevented this from coming to fruition was our rapid growth."

The first half of 2009 especially was "just a lot of heads down, crank through, launching city after city after city," Mason said.

That's not to say the CEO didn't find creative ways to make himself useful. One weekend morning during that period, lead designer Steven Walker came into the office and found Mason returning calls to the customer-service line.

"Yeah, hi, this is Andrew," he was saying as Walker passed by his desk. "I'm calling you back about your customer-service issue." And then, after a beat, "Yeah, yeah, this is the CEO. I was just doing customer-service calls today. I wondered what problem you had."

After Boston came Washington, D.C., in May and then New York City and San Francisco in June—the first time the company rolled out two cities in one month. Mason likened the experience to being a baby—every day there was a new formative experience, and the team kept learning more and more about which types of deals worked and which types didn't.

One important early lesson taught Mason the importance of vetting deals in advance for potentially adverse issues—like, say, killing customers. That hit home when the CEO woke up one day that spring at 5:00 A.M. to see how the first skydiving Groupon was selling.

He saw an ominous message on the discussion board along the lines of "A bunch of people have gotten killed here and the owner is in jail. It's weird that you guys are featuring this place." Mason Googled the name of the business and the word "death." Sure enough, the comments were true. Mason was able to pull the deal and replace it with something else before the daily e-mail went out.

Some of the early deals were real duds. Immortalized in a mock school yearbook given to Groupon employees at the end of 2010 under the header "What were we thinking?" are offers for three months of access to a dating site called Omaha Love (two lovelorn souls took the bait), a thirty-minute psychic phone reading (this also sold two, perhaps to the customers wondering why they didn't find their soul mate on Omaha Love), clothing from Ed Hardy Kids (perfect for Junior's first trip to Vegas, three parents must have thought), and this wonderfully confusing offer from Groupon San Antonio: "$20 for a Five-Gallon Water Jug and 14 Refills (20 Refills If You Already Have a Jug) from Krystalina Water (Up to a $41 Value)." That last one sold only three Groupons, not enough to tip the deal, alas.

Around that time, a Chicago pizza parlor went out of business before its Groupon deals expired. A Boston florist then refused to honor its Groupons because the owner's wife had agreed to the deal, only to have him veto it after the offer went out. Adding to the confusion, the shop owner insisted his wife was an intern.

Mason didn't know what to do. Should Groupon issue immediate refunds? Should it take a wait-and-see approach? The company ultimately pulled the deal and returned the cash. *None of these customers will ever buy from us again*, Mason thought.

What happened next is immortalized in the yearbook. There, in the "Early Days" section, is a photo the company sent to customers who purchased the flower deal. All fifteen Groupon employees, with Mason front and center, are standing behind a white poster board sporting a message inked in black marker: "We're sorry!! —your friends [at] Groupon."

"The response we got back was, 'Holy shit, there's actually real people at that company,'" recounted Julie Mossler, Groupon's head of public relations. "And most of them said, 'I'm not going to unsubscribe, I'll stick with you, thanks for refunding my money.'" It was a classic example of how to turn bad PR into a stronger customer connection.

Not that all of Groupon's ideas were that good in the first months—the company's initial logo depicted a naked woman holding a sword and riding on the back of a pterodactyl. Eventually, the company drew a T-shirt on her, a rare example of modesty prevailing.

As to that all-staff apology photo, Mason said, "It's hard to pull those things off when you're bigger because part of being bigger is that you become faceless and you lose that direct connection—people feel less like they're in on something." But the spirit of that day lives on. "We were saying to people no matter what, if they ever feel let down we'll give you your money back," Lefkofsky said. "Those things were in place when we were small, and they're still exactly in place today."

That commitment evolved into the Groupon Promise, a no-questions-asked refund policy. The policy meant a lot to Mason, growing as it did from an epiphany he had in his early twenties after he bought a sweater from the outdoor-clothing company Patagonia. He wore the sweater throughout a summer spent in New Zealand burning brush—along with a few holes in his prized garment.

Hearing about Patagonia's open return policy, Mason decided to swap the singed sweater for a new one. But when he asked to make the exchange, the salesman said, "If you feel this garment didn't live up to your satisfaction, you can absolutely return it." With the responsibility for his actions placed firmly on his shoulders, Mason felt guilty for taking unfair advantage of the company. *They're doing the right thing by me, so I should do the right thing by them*, he concluded. He was impressed that Patagonia had raised the level of its customer-service dialogue.

Years later, Groupon hired a man from Patagonia, and customer-service head Joe Harrow told him Mason's story. The man laughed and said, "That was me! And in fact I told that story to my new hires at Patagonia when I taught them how to explain the return policy to customers."

Mason believes most customers will choose not to abuse return policies if merchants tap into that sense of responsibility and shared social values. As for the unethical few who will inevitably take unfair advantage, "We would much rather suffer that abuse than force the rest of the 98 percent of our customers that are good to endure the bureaucracy of being treated like irresponsible children," Mason said.

It would certainly be lovely if Mason's faith in humanity was always rewarded, but bad-acting customers have become an increasing problem for Groupon, Joe Harrow said in late 2011.

"We used to have almost no fraud, and we had almost no fraud protection; we just trusted our customers," Harrow said. "But now there's more fraud. A customer will use a script to create 150 accounts and use the same promotional code 150 times, because they found a bug, until we fix it."

Perhaps the worst case of customer fraud Groupon has encountered, the one that led the company to call in the FBI, could have cost the company as much as a quarter-million dollars. A scam artist found a vulnerability in the online ordering system and proceeded to exploit it to the hilt.

The glitch allowed customers who used site credits—known as Groupon bucks—to get a double refund if they purchased a deal and then canceled it quickly enough. Earning a few Groupon bucks to get the scam started was easy; Groupon doled them out as customer-referral bonuses, and some of its charitable G-Team offers were sweetened with credit toward the purchase of a future daily deal.

The person who found this bug wrote a computer script that repeated the process over and over. The crime wasn't discovered until the hacker had amassed some $250,000 in credit, which is when Groupon got the feds involved. Because most of the Groupon bucks were still sitting in the scammer's account, the company was able simply to take them back. But it had been a very close call indeed.

When it comes to customers who take advantage of the Groupon Promise to get their money back on deals time and time again—think of them as the ones who would return that beat-up Patagonia jacket even if the burn holes were still smoking—the customer-service team in essence breaks up with them.

Reps tell such frequent fliers, "You can have this refund, but as you keep buying deals from us, we seem to let you down on a disproportionate number of those experiences. So in the interest of not letting you down again, we suggest that we part ways."

Negative feedback from merchants can eventually get a customer fired as well, Harrow said. "If three different merchants say you were a shitty customer, we're going to tell you, 'We value your business, but we also value our merchants'. They are our customers, too, and they hate you. So we can't work with you anymore.'" Actually, Groupon employs more diplomatic language than that, but you get the point.

As many loyal Groupon customers know, merchants who run daily deals can be bad apples, too. Groupon plays the traffic-cop role there as well. "If our customers say, 'This business sucks—they clearly changed their menu prices right before they contacted you, and they're charging $16 for an $8 burrito,' we've got to listen to our customers, too," Harrow said.

In extreme cases, that can mean canceling deals in midstream and immediately refunding all purchases, as in the case of the Boston florist and his intern wife. No vetting system is perfect, so customer calls, e-mails, and comments on deal pages act as a failsafe. Groupon is proud of its track record of putting a stop to merchant scams in real time once the company confirms there's a problem.

"We say, 'This deal does not meet our standards, we've issued you a refund,'" Harrow explained. "Some people get pissed, but mostly they say, 'If it doesn't meet your standards, I don't want it.' Our point is, you can still go shop there, but you can't do it with a piece of paper with our name on it. We have a curator role."

Even while Groupon was establishing the fundamentals of its culture, board member Peter Barris, the venture capitalist from Silicon Valley who'd led The Point's first big funding round, grew impatient at the pace of ramp-up. At a meeting of the directors, he pushed the company to go from launching one city a month to four.

It seemed like a crazy pace, but by the end of 2009 Groupon had launched in thirty U.S. cities and was rolling out ten to fifteen new ones a month. It had grown from a stalwart band of true believers who had fit in CTO Ken Pelletier's kitchen during a party he hosted in January to more than three hundred employees heading into 2010. The company had gross billings of $34.1 million, and revenue of $14.5 million against an operational loss, $1.1 million, that was actually lower than the one Groupon recorded for the two months it was in operation during 2008.

Could total domination be far off?

ELEVEN

That board meeting was a gut-check moment for the fledgling operation, as was the one that came after Groupon raised $30 million from Accel Partners and NEA in October 2009. That's when Accel's Kevin Efrusy, who later became such a steadfast champion of the model's potential, advised against selling to Google and urged the company to take advantage of the global possibilities before Groupon clones pulled off their invasion of the deal snatchers.

With the big cash infusion finally putting Groupon on the map with the Silicon Valley community in a big way, "You have to pay attention to international," Efrusy told Mason and Lefkofsky.

But after the financing round closed and 2010 dawned, more knockoffs popped up as if on cue—many of them overseas, where the daily-deals concept was still new. The company was set to expand into Toronto, but it soon became clear that Groupon needed to partner with one of the clones if it was to quickly advance beyond North America.

Keywell and Lefkofsky began vetting potential European CEOs in January and introducing the ones with at least some promise as acquisitions to Mason, who was not pleased at the prospect of rewarding someone who'd ripped off Groupon's idea.

The Groupon team met with several of their European counterparts. Keywell and Lefkofsky got along with them fine, but Mason disliked most of them instantly and intensely. It was clear to Lefkofsky within five minutes of the first few meetings that his CEO wanted no part of the discussions.

"We all hated the clones," Mason said. "We didn't hate them as businesses, we hated them personally. And I didn't want to meet with any of these people unless it became absolutely necessary for me to get over my hatred because to some degree I felt the hatred was productive."

In his first meeting with an owner of a European knockoff, Mason embarked on a futile search for something he could relate to on a personal level. He asked the man, German serial entrepreneur Oliver Jung, what he did when he wasn't working. It turned out that Jung was a coin collector and had picked up some new ones after arriving in Chicago.

"Oh, that's interesting," Mason said. "What do you like to do with the coins? Are you interested in their history, or do you think about where they came from?"

"No, I just take them out of the safe on Thursdays and look at them and think about how much they're worth," Jung replied.

Mason was incredulous. *What a bizarre thing to say*, he thought. *I'm glad you could take our idea so that you could spend more money on coins.*

"There was a lot of carnage" in those early meetings, Lefkofsky said, and they weren't making much headway with the search.

Speaking of carnage, Groupon was set to take over an adjacent suite of offices on the sixth floor of its headquarters building as it rushed to accommodate hundreds of new employees. Before the build-out began, the company had access to a huge empty room with a linoleum floor. It was too tempting for Mason to leave alone.

One Friday night in March, lead designer Steven Walker, Joe Harrow, and some other colleagues were hanging out in the raw space when Mason said, "This would be a great room for floor hockey."

The next morning, the CEO picked Walker up at his house and they swung by a sporting-goods store, where they bought about five hundred dollars' worth of floor-hockey equipment.

When the crew was assembled, Walker stepped into the goal and the game began. Harrow was shooting the puck at him hard, and there was a lot of horsing around. During the game, Mason mentioned to Walker that his contact at Accel, Andrew Braccia, was trying to hook him up with Rob Solomon as a potential chief operating officer.

Walker was stunned. He wasn't sure what it meant. "Are you getting a boss?" he asked. Mason laughed. He explained the COO role and said Solomon was a long-shot candidate because he was used to running companies as CEO. "You'll never get him," Mason said Braccia told him.

A couple of weeks later, though, Mason told Walker, "We got him. I'm really excited about this."

It's a big-boy company when it gets a COO, Walker thought.

It was pure go-go time when Rob Solomon came aboard as president and COO on March 17. It hadn't been that long ago when his friend Braccia had told him, "You've got to meet Andrew Mason." Braccia knew Mason was looking for an operations-minded number two like Facebook's Mark Zuckerberg had found in Sheryl Sandberg, and he thought Solomon might be a perfect fit culturally.

"There's no chance I'd ever move to Chicago," Solomon told Braccia, "but I'd love to meet this kid." When the two of them did get together, they hit it off. Solomon thought Mason was funny and quirky, a refreshing change from the regular Silicon Valley crew, and Mason saw Solomon as both experienced—thanks to his tours at Yahoo! and SideStep—and different enough from the typical operator that he might shepherd Groupon through its ramp-up period without putting it in a process-oriented straitjacket.

"I'm this weird, long-haired guy who's had a little bit of success in Silicon Valley," Solomon joked, painting himself as a Northern California version of Jeff Bridges' character in *The Big Lebowski*. "And Andrew said, 'Maybe he'd be a good number two.' I didn't think much of it because I wasn't going to move to Chicago."

But Solomon started watching Groupon from his home in Woodside, California, and saw that the company was topping $5 million a month in revenue. *Pretty good for a start-up*, he thought, *but I wouldn't mention it in the same breath as Facebook and Twitter.* Yet the more he thought about it, the more he realized he was bored with his VC gig. At forty-three, he was up for another challenge.

"Maybe we should try this thing out," he told his wife, who happened to have a sister living in the Hyde Park neighborhood that both the University of Chicago and President Obama called home. "Let's just go out there for a weekend. I'll visit the Groupon guys and see if it makes sense for us to move."

Less than two months after his first meeting with Mason, Solomon toured Groupon headquarters. He couldn't believe how much the CEO had accomplished, given that he had virtually no previous experience building a company.

"From that point on I was kind of hooked on moving my three

kids and my three dogs and my wife to Chicago," Solomon said. "Crazy."

If Mason imploded, Solomon knew he could step in and lead the organization. He figured the board saw him as a decent insurance policy and another mentor for the young chief executive. "Andrew was pragmatic enough to say, 'I don't know what the hell I'm doing, I've never done anything like this before, I want somebody to help me,'" Solomon said. "He recognizes that he doesn't know what he doesn't know. But then, he's a very quick study."

Although Solomon figured the job would last two to four years, his wife refused to rent out their house in Woodside that long. She found a family that needed a place while their own home was being built and she told them, "You can rent it for a year and then we'll probably be back."

Solomon was sure his wife was off on the timing. It had to take this thing a few years to scale up and go public, didn't it? Not that he wasn't going to push the envelope as hard as he could. In fact, during his first staff meeting at Groupon he set a truly audacious goal.

"Guys, I'm happy to be here," Solomon said. "This is a great business. We have three million subscribers. One day we're gonna have twenty-five million." Several people in the room thought the suggestion was nuts, but he'd certainly made a memorable first impression.

On March 26, nine days into Solomon's tenure, Groupon enjoyed a purely adolescent outburst. The company turned the occasion of its office expansion into a decidedly non-OSHA-compliant demolition party in which staffers donned helmets and goalie masks, grabbed bottles of beer, drew on the walls leading into the adjoining space—one wrote a haiku: "Breaking walls is fun / at Groupon there are no rules / Momma, please help me!"—and then literally kicked them down. It was a day of joyous destruction. One pair of co-workers used red markers to write the lyrics to "I Wanna Dance with Somebody" on a door that their colleagues soon demolished.

With the board egging them on, Mason, Lefkofsky, Keywell, and now Solomon knew it was time for Groupon to burst through the European wall and find its own dance partner before time ran out. The only problem was, none of the clone operators seemed to be a good fit. If the company didn't find a likely match soon, though, it could end up a regional powerhouse but a global also-ran.

TWELVE

Enter Oliver and Marc Samwer. The duo, along with their youngest brother, Alexander, were legendary for successfully cloning U.S. tech businesses in Europe, notably the eBay knockoff Alando .de that they sold to eBay for $54 million in 1999 when they were in their mid-twenties. The Samwers were poised for even bigger success with CityDeal.de, a daily-deals site that was taking the Continent by storm, launching in eighty cities across sixteen countries with six hundred employees in five months. Groupon, now fifteen months into its existence, had half as many staffers and hadn't even made it into fifty cities by the end of March.

The Samwers' genius has long been to let Silicon Valley do the family's research and development for it. Rather than trying to be the one in a billion people who create the next Google from scratch, the brothers pick the likeliest winners from among hot Web start-ups and then employ extraordinary operational savvy to make their European knockoffs work. The North American market is so large that Silicon Valley entrepreneurs rarely build overseas colonies in time to beat the Samwers to the punch—but they are often willing to acquire well-run clones as a shortcut into global markets. And the brothers don't care if they get credit for originality as long as they end up winning that money game, as they did after cloning eBay and then selling it to the auction company for a huge payday. After their Groupon clone CityDeal, they started Pinspire, a knockoff of photo-sharing site Pinterest, and then hatched a plan to create a billion-dollar e-commerce firm around furniture sales.

Marc Samwer, a sharply intelligent forty-one-year-old with a youthful face, trim physique, and chestnut hair that's slowly retreating from his forehead, became the brothers' Groupon point man in the United States.

"This idea of copying successful businesses came from a certain thought that we learned early on that the absolute biggest risk besides technology risk and execution risk and financing risk and all these risks associated with starting a company, the absolute biggest risk, is the market risk, the customer adoption risk," Samwer explained.

"Is this business idea which sounds theoretically really great and which you may have tested with your friends and your family, is this actually something that people will do and buy and pay money for? You can have analysis over analysis and theory over theory and market research over market research, but the ultimate test is in the real world. So for us it was clear: If we find models which seem to be successful because there's early proof that consumers pay for them, that's the best risk reduction we can do."

On a fact-finding mission to Silicon Valley in 1998, the brothers met with VCs, CEOs, founders, anyone who would talk with them. Many of the Americans treated the Samwers as if they were from a developing country. At first, the siblings proudly pointed out that Germany was actually Europe's largest economy. "But then we said, 'Let's pretend we're coming from a developing country. Let them think that,'" Samwer recalled. "Because U.S. guys love to teach the world how to do everything. I wouldn't describe that as arrogant. But at the same time, we used this attitude, I wouldn't say against you, but at the same time, to our advantage: 'Tell us, tell us, tell us.'"

The Samwers may use U.S. innovation as a shortcut to building successful businesses, but the Germans' operational efficiency ultimately helps the American companies they clone to thrive overseas. "It's a great symbiosis because you guys in the U.S., you have a domestic market, you have this entrepreneurial culture," Samwer said. "Here, people say, 'I'll start a company. If I fail, I'll start another company.' In Germany and the rest of Europe it's considered to be a failure. In Asia it's even worse. But, you guys are not good in internationalization. We are.

"What's better for a company with a billion-dollar idea than to have us copy them and then buy us?" Samwer asked. "Honestly, for Groupon, it was the best deal they ever could have done. Meg Whitman today still says buying Alando for $54 million in 1999 was the best deal eBay ever did next to buying PayPal. Because that $54 million is today $5 billion. Germany for eBay is the most important international market."

Even with eBay as their first big success, though, the brothers didn't get much respect in the United States. "Everyone said, well, it was just a copycat; you're not smart enough to invent something," Samwer recalled.

That stuck in their craw, so the siblings decided to be pioneers their next time out, and they placed a big bet on a mobile-Internet company called Jamba. This was back when smart phones still had black-and-white screens, though, so the Samwers soon found themselves stagnating in a market they'd entered too early.

In casting around for ways to monetize the company sooner, the Samwers hit on ringtones, which immediately exploded in popularity. "What saved us in the end was that we always ask, Where's the business? Where's the money? What are people using and buying and paying for?" Samwer said.

The close call with Jamba helped the brothers finally get comfortable with their place in the online ecosystem. "Being a pioneer can be damn lonely, too early, no money, tough, endless, stupid," Samwer said. "And that healed us. Since then, we basically say, Fuck you. We don't care whether you think we are not smart enough to invent something."

The Samwers' genius lies in innovating within existing models and then operating their knockoffs with ruthless efficiency. They are smart enough *not* to invent something.

The Samwers entered Groupon's orbit when Mason exchanged e-mails about CityDeal with Marc's younger brother Oliver. Oliver Samwer came to Chicago in March for meetings with Keywell and Lefkofsky about selling CityDeal to Groupon and then sticking around to guide the global operation. The Groupon execs were soon convinced Samwer was the right partner. CityDeal was operationally sophisticated and stood out as the fastest moving of all the clones. Their sense of Samwer as a pure capitalist was later confirmed when he famously sent an e-mail to the Groupon leadership team proclaiming: "Hyper growth is better than sex."

The investors had a deal with the Samwers ready to go. There was only one probable obstacle: Mason. Lefkofsky worried that the young CEO wouldn't be able to stand being in the same room with Oli Samwer for two minutes.

But the meeting had to be set up. Because Mason was on the road, he ended up talking to Samwer for forty-five minutes at Chicago's O'Hare Airport. Lefkofsky got a surprising call soon after.

"Yeah, it's great," Mason said. "I like him."

What he liked in particular about Oli Samwer was that he

came across as a no-bullshit guy, as blunt in his assessments as Mason and Lefkofsky were. Right at the outset, Samwer told Mason, "Look, we're not innovators, we're operators, but we're the best at operating."

The Samwers liked what they saw in Mason as well. "Andrew's a great visionary and a great company leader and a great founder," Marc Samwer said. "Oli and I, we respect founders a lot. I think he saw in us immediately great operators and people who can scale and develop further, innovate. We are not only the kings of copycat because we can copy well, but because we can also further develop the models. We improve them. Both sides immediately realized we can be a great team and build a big company together."

"The fact that both Oli and Andrew left that airport meeting saying, 'Holy shit, this could be phenomenal,' is a pivotal moment in the history of Groupon," Keywell said.

The Groupon principals shared several key temperamental traits with the Samwers. Marc Samwer summed his family's values up as "focus, accountability, and no bullshit. There's no time for politics, there's no time for any kind of ego. Oli and I live this every day. We are willing to accept that we did something wrong. Of course, we sometimes say, 'End of the discussion, now we do this this way or that way.'" That fit the Chicago leaders' mind-set to a T.

It also didn't hurt that CityDeal was already in more cities than Groupon. The Samwers were forced to scale more quickly because there was so much competition by the time they entered the space. The end-game strategy was for Groupon to buy the company, but that only happened because the Samwers showed just how well they could exploit the model.

As Groupon worked up the CityDeal purchase agreement, it continued to roll into more markets, finally hitting its fiftieth city, Tucson, Arizona, on April 19—the same day it debuted in Canada, along with Orlando, Florida, and Fort Worth, Texas.

One more thing happened on April 19 as well: Groupon closed an investment round, led by Digital Sky Technologies and Battery Ventures, to the tune of $135 million. Lefkofsky cashed out stock of almost $63 million and Keywell more than $23 million after the round. Mason was now truly wealthy after taking nearly $18 million off the table—and it was hard to argue that he hadn't worked hard enough to earn it. Of course, all of those cash-outs left only $15 million to invest in the business, but operating cash flow was so strong no one seemed particularly concerned at the time.

For DST, the investment was a bet that "social networking and community-based activity will drive, shape, and define the Web's evolution in the years ahead," said CEO Yuri Milner. For Battery, it was a chance to work with a management team that "saw a massive opportunity very early, and have executed flawlessly to define it and take the leadership position," said general partner Roger Lee. "We think there is a lot of runway ahead."

The company that made its mark by offering half-off deals never seemed to do anything halfway. And now they truly were set for takeoff.

THIRTEEN

Rob Solomon likened the process of growing a business so fast to building an airplane in mid-flight. Groupon was full of smart, eager, but inexperienced employees trying to create a new online market category from scratch. The COO immediately gave Lefkofsky a lot of credit for keeping the chaos under control.

"Eric is pretty brilliant and Eric has done this before," Solomon said. "If not for Eric, Groupon really couldn't exist. It wasn't an accident. Eric knows call centers: Echo and InnerWorkings are businesses that have thousands of call-center reps. Nobody in Silicon Valley would have done that. Andrew wouldn't have known how to do that."

That infrastructure—a massive sales force selling to small businesses across the continent from the Chicago office—was a big part of what a Google or Yahoo! might try to buy to get into the space. The Web hadn't been able to tap the local merchant market effectively until Groupon stumbled into it. Silicon Valley had tried to serve it with machines and algorithms, but small businesses needed more hand-holding than a Google Local, Yahoo! Local, or even Yelp could provide. "Local businesses don't care about their branded spotlights or their awareness," Solomon said. "They only care about butts in seats."

Groupon was certainly putting a lot of butts—most of them young urban adventurers with higher-than-average household incomes—in lots of seats. A March 29 Groupon for a Chicago River boat tour sold seventeen thousand offers shortly after Solomon's arrival. *This thing is amazing*, he thought. *We've got to ramp it up to one hundred markets, then two hundred, as fast as possible.*

A critical part of Solomon's job was to make sure Groupon's processes were scalable and its core functions run by experienced people. Lefkofsky had operational expertise, but the company needed many more veteran hands on deck.

Still, Solomon decided to stick with senior sales VP Darren Schwartz, an affable entrepreneur in his early forties with the healthiest head of hair on the management team. Lefkofsky had introduced Schwartz to Groupon's management team the previous fall, following the failure of his communications-training firm, SureSpeak. They had gone to the same high school in Michigan, although they didn't know each other well there.

When Solomon met Schwartz, the sales chief was dealing with the owner of Posies Bakery & Cafe in Portland, Oregon. The woman had run a Groupon on March 9, 2010, that sold nearly one thousand offers to new customers, who then overwhelmed her small shop and made her a cause célèbre among the anti-Groupon crowd after she blogged about the experience.

"She was a small-business owner who didn't understand the power of this tool," Schwartz said. "We weren't wise enough to understand the power of the tool."

Disgruntled merchants who couldn't cope with the flood of customers sent to them by Groupon (often after the owners refused to set a deal cap) were soon giving the company more black eyes than Sylvester Stallone suffered in all six *Rocky* films combined.

Mason responded by ramping up merchant-support options via Groupon Works, an online suite of tips, tricks, and video tutorials from people who'd run successful deals. Sales reps also do a lot of live hand-holding—as some random eavesdropping on sales support calls confirmed. Any Groupon employee who works on a deal can raise questions about the structure and can hold up the offer until those questions are answered. The company also began to insist on capping the number of offers a shop can sell based on how much traffic different types and sizes of businesses can reasonably handle.

"I was told from early on that you need to know how many chairs, how many appointments, how often the tables turn," said saleswoman Sydney Slutzky, who worked the San Francisco market from her Chicago desk. In addition, Groupon deploys on-the-ground sales support in many markets to help businesses that need extra TLC.

"If the reality is some merchants aren't going to educate themselves and need hands held, we're not the kind of business to say that's your fault," Mason said. "As the pioneer of a new business model, it's our responsibility."

And if enough Groupon merchants have bad experiences, of course, competitors will look more appealing to them. It's not altruistic for Groupon to protect its flank. It is a process that needs continual monitoring; more than a year after the Posies fiasco, Groupon suffered a round of negative headlines in the United Kingdom after a bakery there was overwhelmed by orders for 102,000 cupcakes it sold at too low a price. Such highly publicized incidents could prove costly indeed to Groupon's reputation with merchants and customers alike. (In fact, Groupon U.K. settled with a consumer protection agency there in March 2010 after an investigation found that the U.K. operation was not adequately protecting merchants from being swamped and had sold misleading deals to customers.)

In addition to helping create best practices for setting up deals with merchants, Solomon and Schwartz had to overhaul the sales department's management structure. When Solomon arrived, Schwartz was buckling under the burden of carrying some thirty direct reports. When Solomon was at Yahoo!, the sales team was led from on high by regional vice presidents, who had sales directors reporting into them. The directors managed ten or twenty salespeople each. That was the model Solomon directed Schwartz to adopt.

The restructuring freed up Schwartz to move beyond the one-day sales orientation process and adopt a training program that included role-playing exercises, listening in on calls conducted by veteran reps, and weekly sales meetings that focused on everything from selling techniques to improvements in the deal pipeline. Managers were having formal conversations about sales goals, and reporting processes started to improve.

There was only one problem: Groupon was in such constant need of bodies as it added cities that there was never time to cut the deadweight from sales. "As we started to ramp, it was always just, 'Okay, we're going to put two people in a city, two people in a city, two people in a city,'" Schwartz said. Because the money got better and better as Groupon expanded, even marginally talented salespeople stuck around, and only the worst of the worst were fired. As a result, complacency, even a sense of entitlement, began to set in among some poor performers who would have been quickly tossed out of a mature sales organization.

But after putting the training and reporting pieces in place, Schwartz started recruiting divisional sales managers from the ranks, giving some of his most trusted salespeople a career path for the first time. The sales force had yet to be sufficiently weeded out, but this was a start down a better path.

By midyear, Schwartz had added regional vice presidents atop the dozen or so divisional sales managers. The VPs had all run sales operations before. *This is a structure that can continue to ramp*, Schwartz thought. *It's scalable. It's not dependent on me or Rob or Andrew.* Even though Solomon's revenue goals were ambitious, the sales team achieved them in eleven out of twelve months in 2010.

The key to harnessing the controlled chaos of Groupon was to create basic structures that could be replicated rapidly in other departments as well. "We're a lot like an assembly line," Solomon said. "You set up this editorial function where kids write funny stuff, and when you have to write more funny stuff, you hire more kids. You have a process and it works."

It was the same drill in rolling out new cities. Groupon would hire new sales reps eight weeks prior to launch. Two or three of them would begin calling local businesses there and setting up deals. "And then you roll it out," Solomon said. With the processes in place, Groupon just kept throwing more people at the machine, and it never seemed to break. Soon the results were improving along with the processes.

On the afternoon of May 5, when the Chicago staff was still a manageable enough size to fit into a function space, Solomon called an emergency all-hands meeting. After employees arrived, Solomon presented them with twenty bottles of tequila. It was an impromptu Cinco de Mayo celebration.

"I'm missing California," Solomon said. "Cinco's much bigger in California than Chicago, but all these twentysomething kids thought that this weird Silicon Valley guy was kind of cool."

It was just the kind of stress-relieving move that was needed in an environment that was quickly becoming a pressure cooker.

MAY 15, 2010

Two months after Andrew Mason's airport call with Oli Samwer, Groupon's CEO instant-messaged designer Steven Walker to tell him that the company was going to acquire CityDeal. It was a Sunday afternoon, and Walker was working from a café in his neighborhood. Mason was at a different café. Walker invited him to come over to his joint and hang out.

"Do they have food?" Mason asked.

"Yeah," Walker replied. So Mason tooled over on his green Vespa. Walker took a picture of him when he arrived to document the momentous day and still carries the photo on his phone.

While they were eating, Mason asked Walker to reprogram the city selector on Groupon's site. The company had just grown its footprint from two countries to fifteen. While the designer was getting started, Mason's phone rang. It was *The Wall Street Journal.*

Watching Mason give the nation's business newspaper of record an exclusive on the deal, Walker thought, *Is this what you deal with on a daily basis? You're twenty-nine!*

The headline the next morning read: "Shopping Site Groupon Buys Germany's CityDeal."

Groupon purchased the clone in exchange for equity that could add more than a billion dollars to the Samwers' portfolio if the IPO went well, though it was valued at around $125 million at the time. During a May 16 International Day celebration at Groupon, Mason donned a beret and a sari, while Solomon came to work decked out like a Swiss mountaineer to mark the closing of the deal. The Samwer brothers weren't interested in running the international business long term, but they agreed to stay on through 2011. It would turn out to be a very good thing for Groupon that they did.

FOURTEEN

The fact that Groupon was smaller than its European counter-part was a big laugh line for CityDeal employees when Mason addressed the Berlin office a couple of weeks after the purchase was announced.

"The ramp rate that you guys have been on has been like nothing I've ever seen, or even heard of, in my entire life," he told the young staffers as he stood next to a poster featuring hot-air balloons, a woman in a sauna, and the tagline "Wellness."

CityDeal's new leader, decked out in a dark-green T-shirt and rocking a full beard and shaggy mane that marked his persever-ance through another long Chicago winter, got a second laugh when he promised, "We don't plan to take the Iraq approach of American infiltration."

Ironically, infiltration soon would come from the German side into the U.S. operation. But this was a happy moment, and the CEO concluded it by saying, "I couldn't be more excited about the company we're going to build together. It really has the potential to be one of the great, iconic brands of the twenty-first century."

That meant continuing the international expansion push,

which Groupon did into 2011. Solomon ticked off the most important markets: "the big countries in Western Europe, the U.S., the big Asian countries, and Brazil. Brazil matters, Korea matters, Japan matters, and China matters—but if you don't win there you'll be okay. You gotta win the U.S. and you gotta win the U.K., Germany, France. And then there are a bunch of other countries that contribute."

To that end, the Samwers stepped in to help oversee Brazil, the rest of Latin America, and some of the Asian markets as well. "It's worked well from the perspective that if you get to the market early you have a pretty good chance of being the market leader," Solomon said. "The Samwers are fast and furious and they got us there. And things are good. If we didn't have them, we wouldn't have the footprint that we have everywhere."

As many a Western company has found, though, China was a special case. Groupon was setting up shop in every other major economy throughout 2010, though, so it was time to tackle that one as well. The leadership team had a choice to make: invest in or buy one of the two thousand or so Chinese daily-deals companies in the oversaturated market or find a suitable Chinese partner, such as the Internet commerce leader Tencent. It was a debate that would not be resolved until the end of the year.

The partnering option ultimately prevailed, which led to the creation of a joint venture that would launch at the end of February 2011, after a three-month, one-thousand-employee hiring spree. Groupon and Tencent were both 40 percent partners, with Groupon putting up $4 million for the stake, but Tencent held two board seats to Groupon's one. The other board seat was held by 10 percent partner Rocket Asia, owned by the Samwer brothers, and the remaining 10 percent was held by a private-equity firm. Because a Groupon.cn knockoff site was already in operation with some 7 million registered users, the joint-venture site was called Gaopeng, which translates roughly to "cherished friends sitting around the table."

"We can't go it alone," Solomon said. "Tencent's an amazing company, a leading innovative Internet company, and they work with the government"—a key factor in China. Still, this launch was one of Groupon's toughest slogs. Group buying had been popular in China since at least 2005, with crowds of shoppers entering stores and negotiating discounts on the spot, and the market was already saturated by the time Groupon entered it, with an estimated nine new clone sites popping up every day, according to a 2012 report issued by the Wharton School of Business.

With the number of competitors exploding to five thousand in China during Groupon's first year there and average deal margins in the 15 percent range—or worse—it didn't help matters that the company faced typical start-up struggles. Gaopeng went live in mid-February at Groupon's insistence—"We want to dominate the market in China," the company's Hong Kong CEO told the press—but Tencent quickly took the site offline over worries that it wasn't ready to roll.

Oliver Samwer was dispatched from Berlin to get the project back on track, and Gaopeng launched for good in Beijing and Shanghai on February 28. But by August Groupon had to get rid of hundreds of bad hires, and it ended up shuttering operations in more than ten cities, leaving it with offices in about twenty Chinese markets. If Gaopeng could get some traction, though, it would all be worth it. The market's top twenty performers generated some 90 percent of China's daily-deals sales volume, making the huge number of competitors more of a distraction than a threat. And the number of online shoppers in China was expected to explode from 140 million in 2010 to 520 million in 2015. Ultimately, even with low margins, China would be worth billions of dollars a year in revenues to the market leaders, and Groupon was hovering as high as number eight there by midyear.

But even though China was important, Solomon didn't see it as a make-or-break country for Groupon. "Whether we're successful in China or not doesn't matter," the COO contended. "It's gravy. Google's not in China and they're worth a couple hundred billion dollars. It's good to be in the biggest market; it just helps. If you can get it right, that's awesome. If you don't, life goes on."

In addition to gobbling up supersized clones and gallivanting around the globe, Groupon also saw its first big lawsuit in 2010—a state court case in Illinois over expiration dates that generated a lot of headlines but was quickly settled. The case went to the definitional heart of Groupon: Were the deals coupons, or were they gift certificates? Actually, they're both. The base value of a Groupon—the five bucks you pay for ten dollars at a sushi bar—is a gift card whose value never expires, per federal law. So customers can get five dollars' worth of *maki* for that Groupon even after the promotional value—the extra five bucks—expires just like a coupon does.

That distinction is made in several places on Groupon's site. But no matter how clear such statements read nor how often they're made, Groupon's such a phenomenon that it becomes a natural target not only for consumer lawsuits but also for state attorneys general to sniff around. With the company boasting up to 50 percent market penetration among adult consumers in some cities, officials "can't ignore Groupon; it's just too big," Lefkofsky said. "So if people are making any kind of noise at all, the attorney general has to kind of say, 'I'm going to look into it and figure out what's going on.' It's no different than [when] they might say, 'We're looking into Amazon's sales tax issue.'"

The company also faced legal review for potential violations of Prohibition-era alcohol laws in states that don't allow discounted liquor sales, and saw class-action suits filed by employees alleging they weren't paid for overtime when HR policies couldn't keep up with Groupon's hyper-growth. But nothing that happened in a courtroom seemed likely to slow the company down.

Not that the guys still didn't know how to blow off a little steam at the office. On an otherwise-normal Monday morning in August 2010, Andrew Mason stormed down a hallway at Groupon's Chicago headquarters, angrier than any of his employees had ever seen him. "Runnin' with the Devil" blared from behind the door of a studio apartment with which the company shared a floor, and Van Halen's power chords were disrupting operations.

Mason pounded on the door, but David Lee Roth kept yowling. "Michael, you have to turn it down!" Mason shouted. "And you owe me that money!" In a setup oddly par for the course at Groupon, there was apparently a lease arrangement between Mason and the mysterious man who lived there.

"Go away!" came the sharp reply from inside. But Mason kept knocking. Moments later, the seldom-seen resident erupted into the hallway, rocking a yellow jumpsuit that matched the bandages wrapped around his head. "Andrew's an idiot!" the man ranted. "I don't have your money. Daddy has your money!"

Before any of the hundred or so workers witnessing the spectacle could aid their boss, the man they knew only as Michael shoved Mason and made a break for the office entrance, running as fast as he could with a seemingly bum leg as he let loose a final taunt: "You will never get your money, and you'll never find me!" A stunned Mason gave chase, but Michael had too much of a head start. Soon, all Groupon employees received an e-mail from Michael that read, in part: "Please stay out my room and do

NOT trust andrew! I don't have any moneys. Do not try to find me." Mason later sent his own all-staff e-mail asking: "Can you help me find Michael?"

Several employees volunteered for the hunt, and although Michael remained at large, clues to his whereabouts kept turning up. Meanwhile, the apartment remained just as its unhinged tenant had abandoned it. An exercise bike was set up to play Sade's "Smooth Operator" on a connected turntable when someone pedaled it, and a glass terrarium sported a jagged hole in one corner where Michael's pet spider made a valiant escape. . . .

If this sounds like an elaborate prank, that's only because it was. "That's what's special about Groupon," Mason said. "We create these . . . little events. So much of what we do is about surprise—'What's the daily deal?' And who would imagine a room like that inside an office? As an employee, it shocks your system out of the monotony and says, 'This isn't like any job you've had before.'" The CEO believes keeping this irreverent culture intact will prove critical to its continued success.

As editor-in-chief Aaron With—who helped mastermind the Michael's Room bit with humor writer Cullen Crawford—put it, "The weird, stupid, ridiculous stuff is so important for us to do well."

For a slogan, it's not quite at the level of Steve Jobs' battle cry of "Insanely great!" But as the summer came to a close, some high-powered suitors started to see this collection of goofball misfits as a prime acquisition target—one that could generate a sale of potentially historic proportions—even as large online players such as Yelp entered the daily-deals space.

SEPTEMBER 4, 2010

September 4, 2010, was the chilly Chicago Saturday when Andrew Mason officially became more Internet famous than Steve Albini. Only seven years earlier, Mason had interned at Albini's Electrical Audio studios in a former pinball-machine factory on the city's near-northwest side. That summer of 2003, Mason had learned what it took to sustain a successful creative enterprise. Albini was one of the most respected recording engineers of the grunge era and beyond, having worked with such seminal acts as Nirvana and the Pixies. He and his colleagues had built Electrical Audio from scratch.

It was the first experience Mason had had with people at the top of their games who were absolutely committed to their craft. These were technicians of equal parts talent and integrity who rolled into the studio every day around noon and then poured themselves into their work until three or four the next morning. It was inspiring, it was rock 'n' roll, and it was exactly the education Mason needed to launch the start-up that would become Groupon.

Even as Mason's own company grew, Electrical Audio remained a touchstone for him. He liked to drop in on the studio's online message board, where his handle was "Intern_8033." For his part, Albini stayed in close contact with Mason as he ramped up the daily-deals site. The notoriously acerbic engineer had a rare soft spot for his former intern. "He's not a dreamer. He's a guy that actually pulls stuff off," Albini said. "When Groupon started to take off, it was obvious—and in the face of all the knockoff competition still is obvious—that it's the cock of the walk. Andrew is the reason why it can't be emulated successfully else-where: Nobody else has Andrew."

On August 18, 2010, just after Mason appeared on the cover of *Forbes* as "the next Web phenom," Albini launched a contest on Electrical Audio's site. The rules were simple: The first person to predict the day when Mason's name would generate more Google hits than Albini's would win dinner out with both of them.

"Those of you who have dinner with me or Andrew often enough not to give a shit are requested to shut the fuck up about it and not piss all over this fun idea I had," Albini added. That day, Albini's name generated 218,000 hits and Mason's a mere 160,000.

Less than three weeks later, Mason was up to 425,000, while Albini had slumped to 205,000. They would soon pay off the contest by taking the winners, local banker and music blogger William Ojendyk and his wife, to Alinea—a leader of the mo-lecular gastronomy movement and the most acclaimed restaurant in Chicago—where the twenty-four-course dinner was almost derailed because neither Mason nor Albini met the dress code's requirements, and they had to go home and change. Mason re-turned in a black suit, white shirt, and black tie that would have made the Blues Brothers proud. Albini, the poster child of be-spectacled, bantamweight Gen-X punk rockers, turned up in an all-black Johnny Cash ensemble.

During the wine-soaked meal, they talked about everything

from life at Groupon and Electrical Audio to playing in poker tournaments and the finer points of the band Insane Clown Posse. Every time Albini saw the young CEO those days, he'd ask him, "Are you a Republican yet?" Mason wasn't, and didn't plan on becoming one, yet he was learning that living well was a bipartisan construct.

During the unseasonably cold Labor Day weekend when Mason surpassed his mentor's notoriety on the Web, he was still a month shy of turning thirty. Little did Mason suspect that Yahoo! and Google soon would make him one of the most famous entrepreneurs on the planet by trying to buy Groupon. Forget Steve Albini: In a year's time, Mason's name would generate more search-engine hits than AOL founder Steve Case (though he'd likely never come close to Steve Jobs).

But could Mason the start-up wiz master the intricacies of running a large multinational company and successfully take it public by then? It would be like transforming a garage band into an arena headliner in just over three years. Given that U2 was the last act to have pulled off anything close to that particular trick—way back in 1980—the odds were decidedly against it. So, maybe it would be better to just sell out, declare victory, and walk away. . . .

FIFTEEN

In the near corner: a sixty-something woman who swears like a sailor and runs an aging Web giant like an old-school hard-ass. On the far stool: the brilliant, headstrong young man behind a runaway new e-commerce success. In this cage match, two moguls enter, but only one mogul leaves.

Okay, so no punches were actually thrown when Andrew Mason met then–Yahoo! CEO Carol Bartz in October 2010. But sparks certainly flew between them when Yahoo! took a surprisingly serious run at acquiring Groupon a month before Google jumped into the fray.

Why was Bartz discussing a purchase deal with Mason and Rob Solomon that fall? Yahoo! desperately needed a transformative hit, an acquisition that would vault it back into the top tier of Silicon Valley players. Where AOL, a Web 1.0 company whose luster had faded even more than Yahoo!'s, had placed its bet on content by purchasing the Huffington Post, Yahoo! started to explore the e-commerce space for opportunities.

Especially with former Yahoo! Shopping honcho Solomon in the president and COO role, Groupon looked like a potentially good fit—but Bartz only wanted it on her rather strict terms. For its part, Groupon was looking for ways to peg its true value in the market. Solidifying an offer from the fading giant would be a pretty useful benchmark, and when the final number came in it turned out that Groupon's board was very interested in selling.

Solomon had started a conversation with David Ko, head of Yahoo!'s U.S. media properties, in April 2010 about how Groupon might start feeding daily deals into Yahoo!'s content network. The two companies tested integrating Groupon deals into Yahoo! search results and local properties, but Solomon had also jokingly said to Ko, "You guys should just buy us."

Solomon couldn't see Yahoo! making an offer, but he underestimated how ready Bartz was to go all in on a game-changing purchase. As Groupon's sales continued to rocket throughout 2010, Yahoo!'s head of mergers and acquisitions, Andrew Siegel, started crunching the numbers. He reached out to Solomon in the fall and said, "We want to get to know you better and see if it makes sense to buy you." After a few more discussions, Siegel sent Yahoo! co-founder Jerry Yang and a couple of the company's key product guys to Chicago to meet with Groupon's management team.

Underscoring how this brash Chicago start-up was becoming almost a Silicon Valley outpost, the legendary Morgan Stanley analyst Mary Meeker, who was in the office to get a briefing from Mason and Solomon, happened to walk by the conference room where the meeting was taking place. Yang walked out to give her a hug. For Web geeks, that was a Hollywood moment. (Meeker soon left Morgan Stanley for Kleiner Perkins Caufield & Byers, where she and John Doerr helped guide the Valley VC firm's participation in Groupon's infamous $950 million investment round in 2011. They both then joined Groupon's board as observers.)

Though it has been downplayed in the business press to a footnote compared to the Google negotiations, the discussion between Yahoo! and Groupon was indeed a serious one, and the numbers quickly started getting significant. Siegel then invited Mason and Solomon to Yahoo! headquarters to meet with the team and kiss Bartz's ring.

The problem with Yahoo! from Mason's perspective was that beyond some additional resources and reach, it didn't provide strategic advantages that would supercharge Groupon compared to other possible mergers. For instance, Google boasted a search product so dominant that Yahoo! had actually ceded the field to it, and with its PayPal service eBay could offer a leg up on transactions. Yahoo! was ready to pony up a large amount of cash, but Mason didn't think Groupon needed it.

Still, the valuation question remained, and the board was intrigued. So at Lefkofsky's urging, the CEO traveled to Sunnyvale for a meeting with Bartz and Mike Gupta, Yahoo!'s senior VP of corporate development and finance, who has since departed for online gaming juggernaut Zynga. Solomon tagged along on the trip primarily to keep Mason and Bartz from getting into a fight. In that task, he failed miserably.

To keep word of the negotiations from leaking, Solomon was instructed to call when he and Mason arrived at the main gate so a Yahoo! handler could guide their car into the executive parking structure. That way, they wouldn't be seen walking across the corporate campus.

After they sneaked into the inner sanctum, Mason and Solomon, along with Groupon's product VP, David Jesse, and chief data officer, Mark Johnson, met with Blake Irving, Yahoo!'s head of product, and members of his team. Yang and Yahoo!'s other co-founder, David Filo, popped in to say hello. This was a big opportunity for Yahoo!, and Irving was spreading good vibes.

The Yahoo! team assured Mason that Groupon would remain a stand-alone unit after the sale. And with access to Yahoo!'s data, networks, engineering talent, and 690 million global users, the company would be able to grow even more quickly than it had as an independent operation. If Mason was still skeptical, at least the Yahoo! guys were making the right noises. The only thing that remained was for Mason and Solomon to meet with Bartz in a nearby seminar room.

In these situations, it's customary—and tactically smart—for the prospective purchaser to assure the start-up management team that they'll be given autonomy to run their business within the larger company as long as they hit certain performance goals. It's often a complete line of bullshit—just look at how Rupert Murdoch made *The Wall Street Journal* his bitch after famously pledging to let it remain independent as a ploy to seal the deal. But because Siegel and Irving had given Mason similar assurances, he went into the meeting with Bartz confident he'd still have a free hand in the event that Groupon was actually sold to Yahoo!

The stakes for Yahoo! were incredibly high. The $3 billion offer represented most of the company's remaining cash. But it just wasn't to be. After a bit of friendly opening banter, the cocky, quirky young entrepreneur and the battle-scarred boardroom general seemed to take an almost visceral dislike to each other. At that point, Bartz, who should have been wooing Groupon hard, didn't even bother to give Mason false assurances of independence. In fact, she directly contradicted what he'd been told in the previous meeting.

Mason stressed the importance to both companies of Groupon's operating independently and suggested it could make sense under such a setup for him to report directly to Bartz. But she told him that Groupon would take its place on the organization chart alongside every other business unit, run on a budget set by Yahoo!, and answer to the appropriate division head. Mason could forget the notion of running Groupon like his own business. Yahoo! would tell him what to do and when to do it.

A tense discussion ensued as it became apparent there was zero personal chemistry between the two executives. Bartz is such a force of nature and Mason is so sure of himself that Solomon, who was sitting at a table between the two of them, could do little more than watch the test of wills play out over the span of about ten minutes. At one point, he and Gupta caught each other's eyes. They both had "holy shit!" expressions on their faces. With billions of dollars on the line, all Solomon and Gupta could do was watch as Mason and Bartz completely failed to connect. When she suggested that Groupon could get rid of its entire editorial operation and use Yahoo!'s recently acquired Associated Content operation in its place, for instance, it was clear to Mason that she had no feel for the business and would likely prove to be a meddlesome partner.

This was one of the funniest scenes Solomon had ever witnessed in a career that had included its fair share of Web-culture craziness. Still, it put him in an uncomfortable spot; Solomon was supposed to be the grown-up in the room for Groupon. But forget courtship mode—this deal was all but fucked.

With a lot more sweet-talking, and perhaps a bit more financial sweetener, there was an outside chance the deal would have gone down. There was no rational reason for Bartz to preview the harsh realities that lay in store for Groupon under Yahoo! before an agreement was signed, but it seemed that she couldn't help but try to knock the headstrong young CEO down a peg.

With Bartz known for going from zero to F-bomb in a matter of seconds and Mason not known for hiding his disdain when he thinks he's being played, perhaps sparks were bound to fly. Solomon later was heard to say that Jesus Christ couldn't have facilitated a good meeting between the two. As often happens in such negotiations, the personality clash was the final proof that a deal didn't make sense. Mason and Bartz ended the meeting agreeing to disagree on the autonomy question, but it was clear the deal was hanging by a thread.

On the way back to Chicago, Mason laughed about the bizarre encounter; he was done with Yahoo! But with the deal still at $3 billion, which would be one of the bigger deals in Internet history, the board thought it was potentially worth saving. (Although one would be right to wonder whether Mason would have stuck around if the sale had gone through.)

Lefkofsky and Solomon swallowed their pride and apologized to Bartz for the way the meeting had blown up. But the Yahoo! honcho offered harsh terms in return, saying of Mason, "He's going to have to get on a plane and come apologize to me. He's going to have to convince me that he really wants to be part of Yahoo! and he really wants to work for me."

Groupon would also have to accept that it would not have autonomy under Yahoo! Since there was no way in hell that Mason was going to grovel, the deal was pretty much off as soon as the phone line went dead.

Solomon managed to salvage a global distribution pact with Yahoo! from the wreckage. Starting on November 16, Groupon deals would be served up via Yahoo!'s new Local Offers program, first nationally and then worldwide. "This partnership highlights Groupon's success in building a deep, global platform around local deals as we currently serve over 29 million subscribers in thirty-one countries," Solomon said in announcing the team-up. "We're excited to bring our unbeatable local offers to new users worldwide while providing Groupon merchants with this new platform of awareness and growth."

It was as if the COO was making an after-the-fact case for

why selling to his old employer Yahoo! wouldn't have been such a bad idea. Some board members also talked with Mason about not being so quick to derail the next offer that came along. He had to think of the company's duty to give early-stage investors a profitable exit at some point in the near future. But after the Google deal fell apart over the guaranteed-close issue, it became apparent that taking Groupon public with all due speed would be the best way to keep the VC crowd happy. No pressure going into 2011. No pressure at all.

In late December, Groupon threw a big holiday party—or, as it was officially dubbed, the Groupon Nondenominational Winter-time All-Company After-Work Semiformal/Drink-Too-Much-ebration—at Chicago's Field Museum of Natural History, home of Sue, the most complete *Tyrannosaurus rex* fossil yet discovered. (The "semiformal" part was key; the relaxed dress code helped Mossler spot a reporter who crashed the event wearing a tuxedo. She kicked him out.)

Speaking of fearsome ladies like Sue, just before the party Groupon held an all-staff meeting that featured a surprise appearance by Carol Bartz. Had the Yahoo! deal been salvaged somehow? Had Mason decided to play nice with the CEO from Sunnyvale? Actually, it was the opposite: Mason had hired a Bartz impersonator to appear at the event, but many employees, who'd been hearing rumors of a potential acquisition, believed she was the real deal.

"Hello, fucktards!" the fake Bartz shouted, immediately drawing everyone's rapt attention and doing nothing to dispel the notion that she was the trash-talking real deal. The ersatz executive then proceeded to say that she was buying Groupon (big pause) an order of fries at McDonald's! But she only had three seats available in her car out front, she added, and the offer was first-come, first-served.

As the phony CEO made her exit, stunned employees were given inflatable blue balls of the type sometimes used as ergonomic seating in progressive offices. Groupon had purchased them to give out as "Google balls" in the event that the search firm was to acquire the company, Mason said, because "our perception of Google was that it's a place where everybody sits on Pilates balls all day." But with that deal now off the table as well, at least the employees could get a little fitness boost from the balls.

SIXTEEN

Dancing with two potential multibillion-dollar suitors was a stressful way to close out the year, but Mason had devoted much of his time that fall to developing what he called Groupon 2.0. The development work for the mysterious initiative took place inside a tent fort on the sixth floor of the Chicago headquarters. And "tent fort" was no metaphor here: Sheets were draped over a section of workstations the way kids turn their rooms into pirate dens.

The project was aimed at keeping his company ahead of "everybody and their grandmother" starting competing discount sites, Mason said as he lifted up one of the sheets and stepped inside the fort, an overgrown kid playing Willy Wonka.

If Groupon was the emerging Amazon of services, doing what the Seattle-based online retail giant has done for products, perhaps the 2.0 version's social-media focus could end up making Groupon the Facebook of shopping as well. It was a potentially potent combination.

The new direction for Groupon grew out of a question Mason asked his team: If the company were able to launch with the advantages it had at scale—"a huge merchant community, operational machine, and customer base—would we build the same thing today?" The answer: Maybe not.

Groupon 2.0 planned to leverage those strengths in a way that "gets more merchants through the queue and extends the service," Mason said after he emerged from under the sheets and clicked through a PowerPoint presentation he'd set up in an adjacent conference room. "We're not dramatically increasing the number of deals a customer sees, but we are giving them something more relevant."

For businesses, 2.0 meant Groupon Stores. Any merchant that "claimed" its Groupon Stores page could use it to communicate directly with every Groupon member who had bought one of its past deals (if it had in fact done one before) or who chose to "follow" the merchant because they were interested in offers. Merchants vetted by Groupon also could set up self-service deals. All of those changes, Mason hoped, would help merchants develop a much richer relationship with Groupon customers: A onetime marketing hit becomes a long-term conversation.

"I keep seeing deals we would never run as a feature," Mason said of the beta self-serve option. Although they were worthwhile, they were too small to warrant a full-blown Deal of the Day. He cited examples such as knife-sharpening discounts and cheap hours of play at a video-gaming salon.

Groupon members would have a personal opt-in "deal feed" to include the daily feature offer selected for them by an algorithm using their location, age, past buying habits, and other data to understand what bargains were most likely to make them itchy to spend. In addition to that Deal of the Day, which was the core of Groupon 1.0, the upgraded feed would include recommended self-serve deals and messages from merchants the customers had bought from, as well as from others they'd chosen to follow. Consumers would even be able to alert Facebook friends when they bought a deal and see Groupons purchased by their pals. "By having people get different offers, they will have a bigger incentive to share," Mason said.

Merchants could send any kind of message they wished to their customer list, even offering discounts that avoided revenue sharing with Groupon. The standard split for traditional deals was 50 percent, while those rolled out under the self-serve plan earned Groupon 10 percent to 30 percent of each sale.

But if Mason was worried about losing revenue through back-channel communications, he didn't show it. In fact, he said, merchants should see a decent marketing payoff from deals pitched by Groupon to even small segments of its user base, at that point more than a million strong in Chicago.

And those official deals would reach well beyond the people who'd bought a store's previous offers or took the time to follow their page, Mason said, thus justifying a revenue split.

It sounded like a good idea at the time, but it landed with a big thud. With the daily deal, "we created this monster, this gargantuan thing, and it blew up," lead designer Steven Walker said later. "So there's this idea that whatever we create is gonna do that. But we quickly learned that's not the case with product development."

If there was a silver lining it perhaps could be found in the fact that the self-service deal model had not caught on with busy small-business owners—which suggested that Groupon competitors would have a hard time succeeding without ramping up a big sales force. And that did not bode well for the likes of Google, Facebook, eBay, and Yelp.

The failure underscored a key issue with the product team: It would send the developers and designers down a given path only to have Mason come in at a late stage and say, "I don't like it." And then off the team would go in a completely different direction. Groupon needed a product team leader with a strong vision, and one who saw eye-to-eye with the CEO.

Even Mason's whimsical tent-fort idea proved controversial. More than one high-level employee said it was a hated development, that it drove wedges between team members who were granted access and those who were shut out. One even complained about the fact that the tent-fort crew was fed catered meals, on the grounds that the last thing anyone needed during a sixteen-hour workday was another reason not to leave their computer and get outside for a meal break.

And yet this was a worthwhile detour for the company in some ways. "If you really believe in your product, you have to invest in it to a certain point," Walker said. With the Groupon 2.0 project, "we created a lot of technology that's still in our application." But just as they always say they do, when the Groupon team saw that the project had failed they learned what they needed to, mined what technology they could, and quickly moved on.

Still, there were rumblings among a few longtime staffers. "The daily deal is dead," they said. Rumors of its demise might have been a wee bit exaggerated, though, judging by the fact that sales were so far ahead of forecasts that the company went on an emergency hiring spree in November. Aaron With had to add eighty new writers in a month, for instance, so he turned three editorial staffers into recruiters overnight. And yet, with so many competitors popping up, it was past time to find the next big thing that would keep Groupon ahead of the game.

DECEMBER 10, 2010

This was the morning that Mason made his infamous appearance on *The Today Show*. The night before, he'd engaged in a low-key, in-depth conversation with Charlie Rose on PBS, which he enjoyed as a longtime fan of the show, and which anyone who considers Mason a lightweight clown should seek out on YouTube. However, NBC would provide Groupon with its biggest-ever media platform, its introduction to millions of potential customers, as the CEO made his first in-studio appearance on the show. But if you think Mason would take the opportunity to hang out with Matt Lauer on *Today*'s Christmas-bedecked set overlooking Manhattan's Rockefeller Plaza as seriously as he did Rose's show, you clearly haven't been paying attention.

"What if someone offered you billions of dollars for your start-up company—would you take it?" Matt Lauer asked by way of introducing Mason. After giving Groupon a dream pitch and saying of the site's users—young, educated, affluent—"these are the customers everybody wants," the host continued, "Let's get to the elephant in the room. The reporting of late on the business pages has been that Google offered you six billion dollars for this company, and the same reporting says you turned it down. Have you turned down a deal like that lately?"

"Unfortunately, Matt, I can't speak to that," Mason replied, laughing nervously, "but we're excited to have a cool company we're continuing to grow—"

Lauer interrupted Mason, hoping to pin him down: "Can you at least confirm that you were in the—I'm not looking for the specific number—will you confirm that you were in talks with Google for such a deal?"

"Let me tell you a story to answer that question, Matt," Mason said.

"I have a feeling I'm not going to get an answer here," Lauer interjected.

But Mason charged ahead: "My middle name is Divvens, and when I was in fourth grade, Josh Wilson, who was my friend—I was embarrassed of this middle name—Josh Wilson made fun of me on the baseball field, and I started crying and ran after him. And Mrs. Paddock pulled me aside and yelled at me. And then the next day, on the field trip to the pool, Kristin Flaherty made fun of me. She called me, 'Hey, Divvens,' and I tried to squirt suntan lotion on her—"

"This is answering my question how?" a bemused Lauer asked.

"I've got eight more of those," Mason said. "Every time you try—"

"You will stall any way you possibly can, right?" Lauer finished, breaking into a grin mirrored by Mason's.

Apparently satisfied that he'd taken a good shot at confirming the Google rumor, Lauer steered the segment back on track. He and Mason chatted about the business model for a couple of minutes, and Lauer was ready to tie everything up into a nice red bow that would match the set's cheery decorations.

"We are fascinated with guys like you, like the Mark Zuckerbergs and the Sean Parkers," he said. "You are the young guns, the pioneers in the digital world. What do you want to do with your clout, Andrew?"

"Um . . . ," Mason started. Viewers could see the wheels spinning as he locked into a riff: "I want to see if I can get more buildings to have 'laser' in their name. The word 'laser.'" After a beat, he added, "I don't know . . . what do I want to do with my clout?" He gestured to his blue jeans and untucked short-sleeve button-up shirt. "Do I have clout?"

"You do have clout, whether you realize it or not," Lauer said. "And you do realize it. You've got clout. You going to make the most of it?"

"I feel like clout is something that builds up on your teeth," Mason responded, cracking up the crew. "I can't even take the question seriously."

"Did I get one serious answer here?" Lauer asked, chuckling. "I'm not sure."

Here's what the audience didn't know: Groupon representatives had told *Today* producers that Mason would have fun with the host if pressed about the Google purchase rumors. In fact, the CEO tweeted that morning: "About to do TODAY show and beta test a new technique for dodging questions." So Lauer was in on the gag, and no one at the show was upset about how the segment turned out. But for the average viewer, what could have been a clean showcase for an exciting new service turned into a bit of a head-scratcher.

Vamping in front of the business press and at tech conferences had long been part of Mason's shtick. For instance, he'd told CNNMoney on December 1, "I'm hoping that McDonald's or ExxonMobil tries to buy us. . . . I want to be part of GE, or something like that."

Three months earlier, on September 29, Mason had appeared

at the TechCrunch Disrupt conference in San Francisco with greased-back hair, a face full of bronzer, and his shirt unbuttoned halfway down his chest to announce the Grouspawn initiative, which would provide up to two $60,000 college trust funds every year for babies born to parents who used a Groupon on their first date.

And, wonderfully, when the august *Wall Street Journal* asked for a picture of Mason upon which it could base one of its iconic hedcut stipple portraits, "he insisted [it] be drawn from his goofy driver's license photo," the paper reported in a caption beneath a hand-drawn ink-dot likeness of Mason displaying a hilariously hideous full-toothed grimace.

All of that can be great fun for people who are already aware of Groupon and its unorthodox CEO—as when the audience erupted in laughter during the D: All Things Digital conference the following June while Mason fixed journalist Kara Swisher with what she called a "death-ray stare" after she said she heard the IPO filing was around the corner when in fact they're clearly fond of each other.

But who would sabotage his company's big appearance on a top-rated network morning show watched by people who'd probably think TechCrunch was a brand of cereal if they ever heard of it at all? It was difficult to see the *Today* appearance as anything other than a missed opportunity.

SEVENTEEN

Something a lot less funny happened to Groupon in December 2010 as well: Amazon poured $175 million into LivingSocial. Would it become the Pepsi to Groupon's Coke, a formidable competitor but one that ultimately could be outpaced? Or, more ominously, would it become the Apple Macintosh to Groupon's PC, out-innovating the market leader and peeling off young, affluent customers by the bushel?

Either way, Jeff Bezos, the man who launched a company in Amazon that in some ways created the blueprint for Groupon's pell-mell, free-spending, land-rush rollout, was now interested in local commerce. All bets were off.

Why did Bezos jump into the fray? Rob Solomon put the move into perspective: "I think this is the biggest space that we've ever seen on the Internet. E-commerce is a big space, but it's only 4 to 6 percent of all commerce, so it's not even material in the grand scheme of things. What we're tackling is local commerce. It's a multi-trillion-dollar total adjustable market. So I think we'll end up as a big player, Amazon will probably be a pretty big player. Facebook and Google—we're talking about the best companies in the world—are going to play in this space because it's so big. So, yeah, I think Amazon investing in the number-two deals company suggests to me that it's a very big, important space."

Jeff Bezos ranks with the late Steve Jobs of Apple as a pre-eminent e-commerce visionary. So the fact that Groupon is following a market-expansion and customer-acquisition path similar to the one Amazon pioneered in its early days—and for which Bezos took plenty of arrows in the back—isn't necessarily a bad thing in the long run, even if it did open Groupon up to sometimes-vehement criticism that it was spending too much to make too little.

Bezos founded Amazon in 1994, launched the site in 1995, went public in 1997, and watched the company turn its first annual profit in 2004. During the decade it took for the Seattle-based retailer to slip into the black, Bezos focused on creating long-term value by expanding into new market segments (remember when everyone knew Amazon as simply an online bookstore rather than the everything-including-the-kitchen-sink retail powerhouse it is today?), acquiring new customers as fast as possible, and then satisfying those customers with dazzling innovations such as one-click shopping, Amazon Prime delivery, the Kindle e-reader, and personalization.

Guess what? None of those initiatives were cheap. Visitors to Amazon headquarters used to be greeted by a display cheekily honoring its $1.25 billion bond issue as "the largest convertible debt offering in history." Way back in 1999, when AOL was still mailing out dial-up Internet CDs, Amazon blew away its e-tailing competitors on the shipping front during the holiday season. Bezos, who was named person of the year by *Time* magazine in '99, understood that to compete with the shopping center down the road Amazon had to become known for stellar delivery service, which is why it spent $300 million that year building new distribution centers nationwide.

In fact, even while Amazon was still a long way from annual profitability in 2000, the company extended a free holiday shipping offer to anyone placing orders topping $100 that season. The Super Saver Shipping program turned out to be such a great customer-acquisition tool that the company made it a year-round option. In 2002, Amazon lowered the qualifying order threshold to $25, where it remains today. So when you buy that $23 book, you'll probably shop around for something else you need. After all, the shipping's free when you increase the spending by two bucks, right?

It's hard to imagine now that Amazon is such a dominant e-commerce titan, but before the profits started rolling in, the company took a terrible beating from the business press, short-term investors, and stock analysts. In late 1996, Bezos told CBS News, "If we make a profit any time in the next two years, I'd say it would strictly be an accident." In 1997, he told shareholders in his annual letter: "We will continue to make investment decisions in light of long-term market leadership considerations rather than short-term profitability considerations or short-term Wall Street reactions." It was a refrain he repeated to anyone who would listen.

But critics multiplied as the time to break even lengthened and overall losses approached $1 billion on paper by the turn of the millennium (although the brilliant James Surowiecki pointed out in the *New Yorker* in mid-2000 that the company's operating losses since inception were actually between $60 million and $130 million, hardly alarming given the company's size and growth prospects). In 1999, *Barron's* ran a cover story headlined "Amazon.bomb" and alleged "gimmickry" in the company's accounting practices. Some other critics dubbed the company "Amazon.con" and even "Amazon.toast." "And my own personal favorite over the years, Amazon.org, because clearly we are a not-for-profit company," Bezos joked. These critics also insisted Amazon was on the verge of running out of cash and needed to get its wild spending under control. An analyst at Lehman Brothers (*ahem*) famously announced that the more Amazon sold, the worse its financials would get.

Meanwhile, Amazon kept launching "stores" in new product categories, expanding its market share, adding loyal customers, making smart acquisitions (which over the years have ranged from Drugstore.com to online shoe store Zappos), and growing its top-line revenues, which shot from $500,000 to $3 billion in Amazon's first five years. In case you're keeping score, Amazon turned a net profit of $631 million in 2011 on revenues of $48.08 billion. Addressing those who decried the company's high burn rate in the early years, Bezos told *The Seattle Times* in 2000, "Our strategy hasn't changed at all, and it remains as it always was. This model does work. This is an investment phase in this model, and we're full steam ahead."

One of the biggest hidden differences between Groupon and Amazon is how their models affect local economies. In Washington, where its headquartered, and in the eleven other states where it had warehouses or customer-service call centers at the end of 2011, Amazon creates plenty of jobs and direct spending. But Groupon boosts sales at local merchants in every single city it serves. As a result, the direct local economic impact fostered by Groupon's model far outstrips that created by Amazon, which, like national big-box chains, funnels profits back to the mother ship. While as much as $68 of every $100 spent at a local business stays in that community, only $43 of each $100 spent at non-local businesses sticks around to create more local activity and, ultimately, jobs.

That's according to a study of Chicago businesses conducted by the firm Civic Economics on behalf of a neighborhood chamber of commerce. Similar studies completed by the firm in other communities over the past decade have found even more dramatic spreads between how much of that $100 spent at a locally owned business remained in a city compared to the C-note dropped at a chain store. In Maine, the split was $45 versus $14 in local spending between community-based businesses and chains; in Austin, Texas, it was $45 versus $13.

When the national retailer has only a virtual presence in the community, that spread would surely be even greater. So to the extent local merchants can harness Groupon as an effective marketing tool, the deals company could actually bolster a given city's economic development simply by driving more local purchasing. As Mason told Charlie Rose at the end of 2010, "For consumers, we want to reverse this trend of spending more and more time on the computer and help people rediscover their cities." "And generate more local jobs as a result," he could have added.

Amazon even angered merchant groups at the end of 2011 by offering customers discounts if they went to a local shop and uploaded a product price check via smart phone only to buy the item online. Groupon wisely took the opportunity to give customers a Buy Local discount for shopping hometown stores during the holiday season. "Buy Local is further proof that shoppers don't have to make the tough tradeoff of supporting local businesses and getting great prices," said Rich Williams, Groupon's senior VP of global marketing.

Even its model compares favorably to Amazon's, though that's not to say Groupon can't fail. There's a lot about Groupon's model that remains to be discovered; some of those discoveries will be good, and others inevitably will be bad. And the company's leadership might not turn out to be quite as visionary as Amazon's proved to be. As Bezos himself once said when the jury was still out on his business, "Most start-up companies do fail, but most fail slowly. It takes six or seven years for them to fail, usually."

So, what could kill Groupon? It's a fair question. After all, the business that used to occupy its headquarters building pioneered a revolutionary new sales concept only to get beaten at its own game. Montgomery Ward gave us mass mail-order retail in 1872 and led the world in the category until Sears started posting bigger catalog sales around the turn of the twentieth century. Sure, Ward's survived another hundred years, even giving us Rudolph the Red-Nosed Reindeer in a Groupon-like burst of whimsy, but the company had to adapt by opening department stores, and Sears outlasted it on that playing field as well.

If Groupon is overtaken by a competitor, it's likely to be none other than the Bezos-backed LivingSocial, which generated revenues of $245 million in 2011 and secured another $400 million in funding in April of that year, giving the company a $3 billion valuation. But awareness that an upstart rival could threaten its status as the leader of its market category is exactly what drove the company's aggressive expansion strategy. That was thanks in part to advice from Lefkofsky and Keywell, as well as key board members. "We didn't have any background in scaling a sales organization," Groupon editor-in-chief Aaron With said. "If those guys hadn't been driving us to do every city or you'll regret it for the rest of your life," the young leaders might have hesitated. And that could have been quickly fatal. "We invented the model, but a lot of these parts are easy to replicate," With noted. "It's important for us to be the first in every market. It is essentially a gold rush."

Of course, no one can know for sure if Groupon will follow Amazon's path to owning its commerce category over the long term. But Groupon's strategic plan—to expand to as many cities as possible as quickly as possible and to aggressively build its market share and customer base as a way of creating network effects in a business with low barriers to entry—certainly has a wildly successful precedent. And the company that showed Groupon the way was beaten up just as severely post-IPO as Groupon was attacked before it went public—sometimes by the same people and almost always using the same arguments. The critics were dead wrong on Amazon. Now that Groupon's gold-rush stage is near completion, at least in the daily-deals segment of the business, it's tempting to entertain the notion that the attacks on the company could prove to be just as far off base as they were when they were directed at the world's largest online retailer. But then retailers could revolt against the company, consumers could grow bored with it, or it could get crushed by the sheer size of its unprecedented marketing spend, and the critics would've gotten it right on at least one of the two behemoths.

EIGHTEEN

Mason has been known to send the occasional quirky e-mail blast to employees, but one in particular would land him and his company in hot water with federal regulators. He sent his most famous memo before that one to Groupon's global workforce on January 3, 2011. The e-mail likened the company to "Frodo climbing Mount Doom," but beyond the geeky *Lord of the Rings* imagery (and a final dig at Yahoo!), Mason gave the troops a grand overview of what had been a spectacular 2010 for the company and what he expected employees to achieve in 2011. Reporters clamored to publish the entire note, but only bits and pieces of it ever leaked out:

From: Andrew Mason
Date: Mon, Jan 3, 2011 at 4:57 PM
Subject: 2011
To: International Email List

Hi everyone,

It's hard to express what 2010 meant for Groupon. Maybe a few stats will evoke the appropriate sense of magnitude:

- $33M revenue in 2009 to $760M ($475M US) in 2010
- 2M subscribers in 2009 to 51M (22.5M US) in 2010
- 1 country to 35
- 30 cities to 565 (165 US)
- 120 employees in 2009 to 4,150 (1,150 US)
- Ran 3,100 deals in 2009 and 36,500 US deals (not sure of the global number yet) in 2010
- Launched personalization
- Launched self service / Groupon 2.0
- Opened offices in Palo Alto and around the world
- Completed 10 acquisitions
- Started running national deals, which accounted for 12% of Q4 revenue
- Grew from 0 to 1,345 Salesforce Balls
- Invested $215M in customer acquisition
- Struck partnerships with major brands including Yahoo, eBay, Twitter, Zynga, Tribune, McClatchy, Citibank, Bravo, Huffington Post, Angie's List, MySpace, Priceline, Fandango, Redbox, ESPN, MSNBC, and 7,000 affiliate partners.
- Landed major press recognition in *Forbes, Nightline, Charlie Rose,* Bloomberg, *Today Show, Good Morning America, CBS Sunday Morning, The New York Times, Wall Street Journal,* & named Best Place to Work by *Chicago Tribune.*

The earth is super old—thousands of years, some say—and no one has ever done anything like this. You should all exude a borderline-annoying sense of pride in what you've achieved. You should be wearing a big, toothy grin—the kind that makes people want to punch you in the face. No one deserves to be as happy as you are right now.

OK—now stop feeling proud. Forget everything we've accomplished, because it's nothing compared to what we need to do this year. Becoming a great company isn't that easy (you can't just do it in two years!). That's why there aren't many of them. If we are to become great, we must win one of the least fair fights in history: Not only must we continue to beat the thousands of clones who lifted our idea and began at roughly the same time as we did, but now we must also beat the biggest, smartest technology companies in the world. They are coming HARD.

If you feel a little like Frodo climbing Mount Doom, you can't be blamed. Is it hopeless? How can we avoid the fate of the Internet darlings before us—Yahoo, MySpace, Friendster, AOL—that crashed as magnificently as they rose?

My thinking about competition has changed over the last year—most dramatically, in the last month—and I thought I'd share a few observations with you.

Previously, when I thought about company strategy, I thought about moves designed to mutilate the competition. I listened to the Groupon skeptics who said, "Where are the network effects? What are the barriers to entry? How do you fend off competition?" and I conducted a deliberate search for strategic moves that could silence those questions.

But here we are, 2 years into our life, the most copied company in history with more than 500 clones, yet all but a handful of competitors are irrelevant. We remain more than six times larger than our closest competitor. So we either have network effects and barriers to entry, or network effects and barriers to entry simply don't matter. What actually matters? Something that's been at our core from the beginning: delivering an unmatched experience for our customers and merchants.

A quick lesson for those unfamiliar: "Network effects" refer to business models where scale makes the product more useful (and therefore defensible) against competitors. eBay is the classic example: Sellers attract buyers which attract more sellers which attract more buyers and so on—sellers won't go to a competing service because the volume of buyers deliver a higher price, and buyers won't go to a competing service because it doesn't have sellers.

Investors and pundits often search for businesses that exhibit strong network effects. But if you ask me, network effects are secondary—they're nice to have, but not core. There is only one thing that truly matters: customers must love your product. Social networking services have powerful network effects (do you really want to rebuild your social graph on another service?), but they didn't help Friendster beat MySpace (which had a better product), and they didn't help MySpace beat Facebook (which had a better product). Did people switch to Google because of network effects, or because it was a better search engine? eBay is perhaps the best example—they relied too heavily on its network effects, ignored customer experience (which began to suffer), and now it's losing market share to Amazon, which continues to "obsess over customers" (to use its language).

So here's the big thing I realized: Companies don't lose to competitors—they lose to themselves. MySpace lost to itself, not Facebook. MySpace essentially handed Facebook the keys to the castle by devolving into a service that wasn't delighting its customers. For whatever reason, it got stuck. It stopped innovating.

With that in mind, the recipe for Groupon's success is beautifully simple. I've distilled it into three simple values that we should all live and breathe every single day:

1. Make People Happy.

Simple language for a simple concept. We must constantly exceed the expectations of our customers and merchants and make them feel like Groupon is magic.

2. Never be Satisfied.

Whatever you're doing, you can do it better. Don't be like MySpace. Don't start to suck. Continue innovating. Question your assumptions. When you see Groupon on the cover of *Forbes*, the response shouldn't be celebration, but a reminder that the stakes just got all that much greater. The higher we go, the harder we can fall. We are competing against ourselves—we must be better today than we were yesterday.

3. Don't be Boring.

This motto was suggested to me by a reporter; I think it's what makes Groupon Groupon. Think of it as a modifier that flavors everything we do, including our other values. Don't just make people happy—surprise them with unusual kindness. So much of what we do is rooted in surprise. Surprise people with the daily deal. Surprise people with the writing. Surprise people with our marketing, with our customer service—give people something fun to remember us by. Don't be boring. Life is too short to be part of another cookie cutter company. Surprise reminds people that they are alive, that they haven't seen it all. Let's make Groupon the reason that people wake up every day.

So that's it—if we do these things well, we will be a great company. If we don't, we won't. Every single one of you play a role in making this happen. Salespeople: How does each merchant feel after they're done working with you? Like we're the arrogant gorillas of the space, or like they're our most important customer? City planners: Are your cities' customers constantly surprised by the quality of businesses being featured, or are they disappointed and bored by lackluster deals? Customer service: Are customers amazed by your speed and willingness to go further to solve their problem than any company they've ever encountered, or do you leave them feeling frustrated and impotent? Editorial: Do customers run to their computer every morning to check the Groupon because they know that even if they don't love the deal they love your writing—or do they tolerate the deals in spite of the ungrammatical and pointless writing? Product/Engineering: Is the site experience fun and simple to use? Are you finding new ways to delight our customers and merchants? Or is it starting to feel like MySpace?

I could go on, but you get the idea. . . . winning is dead simple—we must always have the best customer experience, hands down. Yes—we must be aware of what the competition is doing—but it should be so we can understand if they're making customers as happy as us. If we win this battle, we win the war.

I'll leave this train of thought with a few choice words by Jeff Bezos I recently came across: "I constantly remind our employees to wake up every morning terrified. Not of our competition, but of our customers."

2011

Having the best customer experience is easy to explain, but difficult to execute. With that in mind, here are a few things we hope to achieve in 2011.

Growth: 150M subscribers by end of year, and billions in revenue.

Customer Satisfaction: We will start measuring the happiness of our customers and merchants and hold ourselves to global standards with the same discipline we use to measure revenue.

The Best Talent: Great companies are made of great people—we must be ruthless in ensuring we only have triple-A talent at Groupon.

New Revenue Streams: At least $1B in revenue from new products we launch in 2011, not just the current daily email.

One Global Platform: Run all International sites from the same technology platform so we can leverage our shared innovations.

Change the Game: How do we make consumers think about Groupon every time they leave the house? How do we deliver merchants customers on demand, whenever they want them? How do we get customers to buy from Groupon not 6, but 60 times per year? Build this.

Call For Ideas

It's going to take our complete collective effort and brainpower to succeed in 2011. I certainly don't have all the answers—but together, I bet we do. To win, we need everyone's ideas—so please email your thoughts to ideas@groupon.com by the end of this week. We will organize and read everyone's submissions, and report back with the best stuff.

By this time next year, we will either be on our way to becoming one of the great technology brands that define our generation, or a cool idea by people who were out executed and out innovated by others that were smarter and harder working. That said, there's no group I'd rather be in this fight with—I know it sounds cliché, but it's the great privilege of my life to work with you people. I don't know what exactly we did right to attract such a dedicated group with an unrivaled passion towards the company they're building . . . but for it, we are lucky. It is 100% of the reason we've made it this far.

Happy New Year!

Andrew

Not everything in the memo panned out. The self-service initiative Mason referenced fizzled out, even though some of the underlying technology was used in other, more successful products, such as the mobile Groupon Now! The revenue figures Mason cited were eventually revised downward, so change the dollar amounts in "$33M revenue in 2009 to $760M ($475M US) in 2010" to $14.5 million, $313 million, and $299 million U.S., respectively. Before adopting a new accounting method at the SEC's request in late 2011, Groupon had reported its gross billings as revenue—which included the merchant's portion of each Groupon sale. The revised figures remove that portion, as Groupon essentially acted as a middleman, passing it along from consumers to merchants.

Toward the bottom of the note, Mason's call for products that would lead customers to buy from Groupon sixty times a year wasn't even close to materializing, but most of the other audacious goals he set forth were substantially achieved. All in all, it's about as inspiring a corporate memo as you're likely to read—though the bar's been set pretty low in that department over the years. You may even have experienced such classics as "Pilfering employee lunches from the office fridge will NOT be tolerated" in your own workplace.

This was, in short, a shining moment for Groupon. It wasn't to last.

NINETEEN

Things began to go south on the public-perception front right at New Year's as Groupon Japan made national headlines for offering a deal on traditional January 1 *osechi* meals that the merchant was unable to deliver adequately or sometimes at all.

It was a sad rerun of problems the U.S. operation had encountered. But, as Rob Solomon put it, "We've had shitty deals that have gone awry. But we're running about thirty thousand deals a month now. And even if you only mess up ten of them—what's that, like, maybe .01 percent or something?—the blogosphere's gonna be all over that. And that's gonna make it to *The Washington Post* and *The Wall Street Journal*."

Groupon Japan said it would follow the parent company's lead in training merchants on "capacity management"—in other words, not agreeing to sell more deals than they could hope to fulfill in a timely fashion. Mason issued a video apology, subtitled in Japanese, promising that such a customer-service snafu would not happen again. In the wake of the tsunami and ensuing nuclear disaster that hit Japan two months later, it is unlikely many customers remember what was in comparison an insignificant customer-service failure, but the soured deal set the tone for the rest of the year.

The business press, smelling blood, began heaping on the critical stories, often aided by missteps from members of Groupon's management team who were as green as the company's logo. If 2010 was the company's magic moment, 2011 was Groupon's hazing year.

In the month following its $175 million investment in Groupon's most dangerous daily-deals rival, Amazon helped LivingSocial make another huge splash with a deal giving subscribers the opportunity to buy a $20 Amazon gift card for $10 on January 19. The move was the online commerce version of the Soviet Union's proxy war against the United States in Korea.

LivingSocial purchased the gift cards from the retailer at terms that were never disclosed but were presumably favorable. Moving from behind-the-scenes investor to active deal participant proved a smart move for Amazon, as the "once in a lifetime" offer sold more than 1.3 million gift cards and generated almost as much media attention as consumer interest. "LivingSocial creates frenzy" was how the *Los Angeles Times* characterized the deal. *The Washington Post* said it "evokes the dot-com boom." Only *The New York Times* played it somewhat cool with the headline "LivingSocial Gets Attention for Amazon Discount."

The deal—which far outpaced Groupon's earlier $50-for-$25 Gap offer on gift-card numbers (445,000 Gap Groupons were sold), if not revenues—came just nine days after Groupon closed a massive $946 million investment round, with cash coming from Andreessen Horowitz, Battery Ventures, Fidelity, Greylock Partners, Kleiner Perkins Caufield & Byers, Mail.ru Group (formerly DST), Maverick Capital, Silver Lake, and Technology Crossover Ventures. In a triumphant press release, the daily-deals company proclaimed, in what may have been the finest expression of its self-mocking humor shtick, "Groupon Raises, Like, A Billion Dollars."

The brief release continued in a jokey vein: "In the last year, Groupon has been called 'the fastest growing company ever' by *Forbes* Magazine and 'America's best website' by one of Groupon's television commercials." But the biggest gag in the release was hidden in the subhead: "Investment to Continue Rapid Growth of Global Social Commerce Platform."

In fact, nearly $810 million of the round went directly to insider payouts—including an eye-popping $398 million for Lefkofsky and entities controlled by him and his wife—with only $136.2 million held back for working capital and "general corporate purposes." The VCs knew about and signed off on the terms of the round. But the unprecedented size of the cash-out would fuel a huge backlash against the company from analysts and the business press when Groupon released its financials.

Although Groupon faced one trumped-up controversy after another throughout 2011, the size of the insider cash-outs from this investment round prompted the most sustained outcry against the company from the business press and investment community. After the billion-dollar round, Solomon said, the June disclosure of the resulting cash-out had transformed the company from phenom into "the most hated company in Internet history. They went from being the darling, like this love child, to the most demonized company in really a short amount of time. It's frickin' amazing how that happened."

Lefkofsky, by far the largest beneficiary of the cash-out, made no apologies. "When people ask me, 'Does you selling stock mean you don't believe in the company,' I say if we didn't believe in the company we would have sold the whole company," he said, referring to the Yahoo! and Google offers. "We had the chance to cash out entirely and sell 100 percent of our stock, so the fact that we sold 15 or 20 percent of our interest is, relatively speaking, pretty small."

Corporate chieftains such as Microsoft's Bill Gates and Berkshire Hathaway's Warren Buffett are romanticized for holding large stakes in their companies over the long haul, but Lefkofsky argued that approach isn't healthy in general—and it isn't realistic for entrepreneurs who want to diversify their investments and take out enough money to live well. "I'm a huge proponent of selling off a small amount of your interest on a regular basis," he said. "You may end up holding a stock, even after it's public for ten or twenty years—I'm still one of the largest shareholders in InnerWorkings and that business is ten years old, and I'm the largest shareholder of Echo, and it went public four years ago. But when people are holding their stock until the end, it makes me really nervous because at some point they're going to want to sell. And then what happens? They're dumping all the stock and creating even more disruption."

Groupon's chairman does agree with Solomon that the cashout sparked a backlash. "People just hate it," Lefkofsky said. "They think, 'Oh, that guy made all that money and it's easy money.' Nobody wants to say, 'You know, Mark Zuckerberg, you're worth $10 billion; that's awesome, you must have worked really hard.' They just want guys like him to go down. But without the Mark Zuckerbergs of the world, the economy doesn't move forward. What's great about America is every once in a while a twenty-five-year-old can make all that money in such a short amount of time and change the world."

Solomon called that line-in-the-sand defense "absurd," adding, "There's no way that it isn't viewed as just a pure greedy thing to do. I think you have to do it in a less egregious way than the way we did it." Solomon buys into the "school of thought where entrepreneurs shouldn't have to worry about buying houses and paying bills—let them take some off the table and then just let them focus on what they're good at, which is building companies." But for him, the scale of this cash-out was just too large to pass the smell test.

"The backlash might have come anyway," Solomon said. "But Andrew's attitude, the irreverence, the cash-out, all of that sort of conspired to make people hate us."

Mason does not dismiss the cash-out critics quite as readily as Lefkofsky does. And it's worth pointing out that the CEO took a comparatively modest $10 million off the table from the $950 million round, after selling about $18 million in stock after an April 2010 investment round that brought in $135 million.

"It's in the class of criticism that I understand as opposed to stuff like 'Groupon is running out of cash,'" Mason said. "I think the reason that the criticism exists is our growth has been so fast that everything just seems like funny money. If you take a zero off all of our numbers, then everything we're doing seems pretty normal."

When it was pointed out that the very size of the numbers—the existence of that extra zero—was exactly what stoked the backlash, Mason agreed. "But in terms of percentages the behavior is fairly typical," he said. "And you can credibly make the argument that the cash-out was in the best interest of the company.

"Now obviously Eric and I weren't cashing out to be altruistic, but what it allowed us to do was bring in new shareholders who add a lot of value in different ways without diluting the rest of the shareholders" by issuing additional shares, Mason explained. That round alone enabled Groupon to enlist top-tier advisers, such as John Doerr from Kleiner Perkins, Marc Andreessen, and Mary Meeker.

"It also allowed us to bring in some of these mutual funds that buy into IPOs, which is going to prove to be invaluable because they are already familiar with the story," Mason said. "If we didn't have people like T. Rowe Price and Fidelity and Capital World and Capital Global that already knew the Groupon story and had already seen the numbers and were already investors, then we would have to work a lot harder to get them to buy in this IPO."

Besides, the firms that ponied up nearly a billion dollars in the final pre-IPO investment round knew what was coming. "Remember who we're screwing," Mason said. "If we're screwing someone, we're screwing really sophisticated investors, the most sophisticated investors in the world. So we're cashing out to people who knew that we were raising that money to put in our pockets, and it wasn't a problem for them." In fact, the round was dramatically oversubscribed, and the selling shareholders could have unloaded twice as much stock as they did.

Solomon acknowledged that the cash-out was "a very pragmatic thing to do. If you're Eric, you can take hundreds of millions of dollars off the table. If you're Groupon, you get to bring on the all-star cast of investors, one of the best crews of all time."

But the breathtaking scale still bothered him. "It would have been really easy to take in three or four hundred of that and give out four or five or six hundred of it," Solomon said. "It wouldn't have looked so bad."

That opinion was shared by some employees lower down on the food chain as well. Mason did discount them, at least. "We're a three-year-old company and a lot of these people have been here for less than a year," he said. "Their time will come. If their options had vested then, they could have sold off equity in those earlier rounds as well. Everybody had that opportunity."

If everything turned out well for Groupon over the next several years, it would be a case of no harm, no foul, in terms of the money the founders took out up front. But if Groupon were to go south after facing a cash crisis, a lot of loyal employees could see their options evaporate and a lot of venture capitalists might end up second-guessing the fact that the company's leadership had left Groupon with no margin for error.

Meanwhile, the SEC was taking a hard look at all the investor cash Groupon's senior leaders had stuffed into their pockets, and questioning what it saw.

TWENTY

Two days after Amazon fired its big salvo through LivingSocial, Mason jetted to Munich, Germany, for the start of his European tour. He stayed at the Bayerischer Hof, where he and CityDeals co-founder Marc Samwer met up to talk business. In the glass-domed lounge of the elegant 1841 hotel, Mason's usual dot-com uniform of tails-out button-down shirt and casual pants looked decidedly out of place

But he was a rising star, one set to be interviewed onstage by *The Wall Street Journal*'s Kara Swisher at the DLD conference that was about to start in a trade hall around the corner from the hotel. He'd be joined by such luminaries as his recently spurned merger partners Eric Schmidt and Nikesh Arora of Google, Arthur Sulzberger of the *Times*, Sean Parker of Napster and Facebook infamy, and mind-body health guru/spiritual futurist Deepak Chopra.

The conference, whose acronym stands for "Digital, Life, Design," is kind of a Davos or Sun Valley conference for tech visionaries, and it was a challenge for Mason to be goofier than his surroundings. At one moment Donovan—yes, the "way down, below the ocean" Donovan—would be onstage, and then the next it was the German actress and physician Dr. Maria Furtwängler-Burda. You'd go grab a coffee only to find upon your return Chopra delivering a gee-whiz PowerPoint presentation. This would be followed by Parker claiming he's not nearly the shallow douche bag he was made out to be in *The Social Network*, though his narcissistic tour de force onstage did little to support that assertion. And, oh yeah, Parker for some reason was paired, in an oddball "disruption talk," with Portuguese novelist Paulo Coelho, who had the wit to tease him about how he was portrayed in the movie.

Wandering the halls, you could chat up Madonna's manager, Guy Oseary, who served as an informal adviser to Groupon and gave Mason his first taste of Hollywood living, and then exchange pleasantries with several journalists who wrote frequently about the company, including Swisher, the delightfully acerbic queen of Groupon scoops; Felix Salmon of Reuters, who soon would write one of the few thoughtful post-backlash takes on how "Grouponomics," as he dubbed it, could succeed; and Henry Blodget, the dashing, fair-haired founder of online muckraker *Business Insider*, who looked far too young to have been the central figure of one of Web 1.0's biggest scandals.

L'affaire Blodget focused on his actions as a senior analyst of Internet companies for Merrill Lynch from 1999 into 2001, just before and right after the online bubble burst. Then in his early thirties, the banker with the decidedly Dickensian name got caught in the crosshairs of the New York attorney general's office. Investigators uncovered internal e-mails from Blodget denigrating companies his research reports publicly praised.

The problem arose from a major conflict of interest: Merrill Lynch's investment-banking unit wanted to secure business from some of these firms, so the analysts, who were supposed to be giving independent investment advice, were under pressure to rate the companies highly regardless of their actual prospects. The analysts also sometimes shared their ratings before publication with Merrill investment bankers and the companies themselves, in violation of the bank's own rules designed "to avoid the misuse of market-sensitive information and the appearance of impropriety."

The SEC filed a federal securities fraud suit against Blodget on April 28, 2003, alleging that he issued a fraudulent "buy" rating on online advertising services company GoTo.com, which now operates as the Yahoo! Search Marketing Division, while telling an institutional investor that the only thing interesting about the company was the fees it could generate for the investment-banking unit. It was only after GoTo took its underwriting business elsewhere that Blodget pulled the trigger on a downgrade. The SEC backed up its allegations with smoking-gun e-mails that were breathtaking in their disregard for ethical conduct.

For his misdeeds, Blodget paid $4 million in fines and dis-gorgements of ill-gotten gains and accepted a lifetime ban from the securities industry. He had risen to fame in 1998 when he correctly projected that Amazon's stock price would soon top $400. By 2001, both Web 1.0 and Blodget's bubble had burst, with the analyst taking a buyout from Merrill Lynch before facing the SEC charges.

After returning to the journalism career he'd abandoned in the mid-nineties, Blodget published as much juicy material about Groupon as *Business Insider* could get its hands on. At the height of the 2011 backlash, the site hit every would-be Groupon scandal of the day. But during the SEC-mandated quiet period that started after the June IPO filing, Groupon was barred from re-sponding to negative stories posted on *Business Insider* or any other media outlet. That was when Eric Lefkofsky began noticing something that alarmed him about the questions coming from the SEC each time the agency re-reviewed the prospectus.

"You can't speak to the media" during the quiet period, he said. "But when you look at the SEC's questions, the regulators are reading everything and reacting to it. So the media is driving at least part of the process. If the media says that we are doing something wrong, the SEC starts asking questions about those stories that they didn't ask before. You want to say, 'Wait a minute. This is crazy.' Right? Don't talk to the media, but when someone writes a bad article, you've got to respond to questions from the SEC because they're reading every word. The SEC really is paying attention to the coverage."

So in effect, Henry Blodget, who has been banned for life from the securities industry, was part of the media scrum that helped delay Groupon from going public. "It's completely nuts," Lefkofsky said.

The situation's crazy enough to indicate it's probably time for the SEC to revisit quiet period rules that, in an age of online pack journalism, enable brutal hazing of companies trying to go public. For every Kara Swisher, Felix Salmon, and *New York Times* DealBook doing solid original reporting and analysis on a company like Groupon, there are dozens, if not hundreds, of sites amplifying every rumor into a narrative so heightened that it would be comical if the stakes weren't so high.

Gotcha stories, however thinly sourced, on hot companies generate page views. It's the flip side of the analyst ratings that were trumped up to solicit investment-banking business in the first dot-com era. A Google search of "Groupon" and "Ponzi scheme" in October 2011, for instance, yielded 980,000 results. On August 23, Sam Hamadeh, founder and CEO of financial research firm PrivCo, appeared on Bloomberg Television's *Bloomberg West* and likened Groupon to a Ponzi scheme as well. Vivek Wadhwa, research director at Duke University, appeared on the same program September 1 to call on the SEC to significantly delay Groupon's IPO as punishment for what he deemed Mason's "childish" behavior in sending employees an internal memo defending itself against charges hurled at it. In neither case did host Emily Chang question those assertions.

But although giving voice to such critics is core to journalism's public-service mission, when the echo chamber's as big and unprofessional as it is now, barring company officials from publicly responding to such incendiary assertions seems fair neither to the start-ups under attack nor to potential investors trying to find the truth with only a prospectus in hand to address the escalating crescendo of outrage. As smart and charming as Henry Blodget may be, an SEC rule that gives him backdoor input into a company's IPO approval process would seem to be a rule the SEC itself would be racing to revise.

By the way, Blodget's official bio for the Munich DLD conference identified him as "a former top-ranked Wall Street technology analyst," which, when you think about it, is every bit as true as identifying Mel Gibson as a beloved action-movie star of the 1980s. Of course, many of us could improve our public image by simply cutting a few unfortunate years out of our biographies.

Mason showed up for his big day at DLD wearing a green-checked shirt, blue jeans, and black loafers. When he wasn't presenting, much of his time was devoted to interviews with international reporters. As the day ground on and more questioners appeared for their audience with the CEO, one had to wonder if this was the best use of his time. He clearly wasn't enjoying himself, but he hit his talking points well.

"People who have scars from bubbles have taken a good look

at the business and invested," he told one reporter. Deals in the Chicago area were up to around ten a day; the company was in forty countries and five hundred markets; it was still examining "how we can best serve the Chinese people"; he still purchased Groupons for personal use—"It's about discovery, and once the deal is there, you might as well buy it."

Lunchtime passed, and he barely scored a small salad. Reporters asked him how being rich had changed his life. "I upgraded my toothpaste to whitening," he cracked. "I'm more reckless in my purchase of video games, yet I don't have time to play video games. . . . I'm either at my cubicle at work or at home. I'm usually working there." Continuing along that more serious line of thought, he added, "There's no consequences to your actions anymore. You don't have to think about buying a cup of coffee. It's something I'm consciously trying to stay conscious of."

Finally, Mason shook his head and smiled. "Maybe if Groupon is going well in five years, I'll walk around with little toy dogs and sign autographs," he said.

He riffed on something the late Steve Jobs used to talk about a lot at Apple: the intersection of art and technology. "Building Web sites satisfies the same creative impulse for me as creating music," Mason said. "It's been immensely satisfying to me. I wish more musicians or people who grew up in the arts got into business. I think more people should do what they weren't meant to do."

The idea of creative disruption holds tremendous appeal for Mason. "Most of the really great entrepreneurs that I've met and admire are deeply creative," he said. "Solving a business problem is often a creative enterprise and great people in the arts can do that as well."

In the next room, reporters watched presentations on video monitors and filed online reports. More of them began to rotate behind the partition to grab whatever wisdom Mason was prepared to offer. On ramping up globally, he said, "A spa in Turkey is the same as a spa in Munich or Chicago," but there are cultural differences that local partners can help Groupon navigate.

Moving to a new interview spot, he rode an elevator one floor down, which took just long enough for Mason, clearly feeling squirrelly, to offer an outrageously funny idea for a bachelor party service for which he'd charge $10,000. "I might buy that," a reporter next to him said. Successful elevator pitch.

He moved to the Lufthansa Lounge. "They're like stewardesses," Mason said of the hostesses in jaunty orange scarves and smart blue skirts and jackets, with their hair pulled back tightly into buns under their pillbox hats.

The latest German journalist asked, "Have you used Groupon today?"

Mason grinned, thinking perhaps there was a language barrier. "Do you mean have I used Groupon literally today?"

"Yes," the reporter replied.

"Well, no," Mason answered. "I have not used Groupon today. I got out of bed and came here to talk with you."

In the middle of a sentence, Mason found himself hustled onto the interior balcony to do a television stand-up. He carefully placed the microphone pickup in his back pocket, disentangled his feet from the wires, and, as a cacophony of voices rose up from the floor below, sent some text messages. After the lighting was set, he stood, hands deep in his pant pockets, and stared into the lens. Most of his public life is lived in that centered stance. He's there, but he's also detached. With the earphone in place, he started answering questions, gesturing in a calmly enthusiastic way.

All day it was the same questions, and he met them by preaching the same gospel, smiling that toothy, squinty smile, hands diving into his pockets as he listened, and then coming back out as he reengaged long enough to answer. He came across as disarmingly unself-conscious. But in fact, the grind of having to address the same queries over and over while big issues weighed on him—while he was in fact leaving important work undone—was starting to be too much.

Soon, he was back in the Lufthansa Lounge to finish with the "have you used Groupon today" guy. They talked China and mobile, about how 97 percent of merchants who do deals want to be featured again ("but we prefer variety"), and then the conversation turned to workload. "I sleep seven hours a night, typically," Mason said. "I can't function well with less than that, but the other seventeen hours I spend working, or with my fiancée. I'd love to have a life where I play video games all the time." But in addition to Groupon, he added, he had ideas for at least eight Web sites he'd like to launch. When you're on that kind of roll, how do you slow down?

He ducked questions about Google and pushed aside talk of an IPO. "Whatever we do, we'll think about what's best for the company ten years from now," he said. Marveling at how far Groupon had already come, he added, "There was no moment where we said, 'When do we start an iconic, multi-billion-dollar company?'"

Next up was an onstage session with Dennis Crowley, the founder of social check-in service Foursquare, through which Groupon had begun offering some on-site deals—though there was some question about how valuable it was for merchants to offer bargains to customers who were already checking into their establishments. Still, the partnership was important as a precursor to the Groupon Now! product, delivering immediate deals to customers primarily through their mobile devices.

Marc Samwer kicked off the local markets session by sharing

some of Groupon's mind-blowing growth numbers: 2 million subscribers in 2009, 51 million in 2010; one country in 2009, thirty-five countries in 2010, and five more since the start of 2011; thirty cities in 2009, thousands of cities globally in 2010; 120 employees in 2009, more than four thousand at the start of 2011; three thousand deals in 2009, more than one hundred thousand to date; more than 650 deal offers per day globally; $1.5 billion in savings for consumers; more than 32 million Groupons purchased worldwide. "And Groupon is profitable," Samwer concluded, incorrectly, before bringing on moderator Kara Swisher, who found both Groupon and Foursquare significant debuts even though she claimed Groupon sent her deals on stripper-pole lessons every week.

Mason described the company's all-hands meetings as morbidly fixated on everything that could go wrong, contrary to the popular view of a carefree Groupon corporate culture. Swisher imagined his mother calling after the company turned down Google and saying, "Andrew! What the hell were you thinking?" and said, to applause, that Mason's non-answer about the rejected acquisition sounded like the *wah-wah-wah* sounds of the adults on *Peanuts* cartoon television specials.

When Mason claimed that the decision to go public was juicy for the business community but in reality would be "so uninteresting" compared to where the company might be in five or ten years, Swisher responded, "Money, sex, and power are interesting to humanity, just FYI." She then shared a choice anecdote about how Facebook's Mark Zuckerberg once asked her why people were interested in a $15 billion valuation. "I'm like, 'Are you an idiot?'" Swisher said. "Of course, immediately after, three really hot women came up to him apropos of nothing and started to pay attention to him. I'm like, 'It's because of your fine looks and obvious bod.'"

So all was going along somewhat normally. Mason said at one point, "What Amazon has become for products, we want to be that for local. We want to be something that people think about every time they go out to do something in their city. . . . If we succeed, then what we're doing today is just one small part of what we will become. I think there's an opportunity for a company to bring offline transactions and offline commerce online, and we're well positioned to do that."

But then Swisher made the mistake of asking Mason what he'd be doing if Groupon didn't exist. And there in all its glory came Mason's comic elevator pitch: "I'm having a bachelor party at some point in the next six months because I'm getting married later this year . . . and at a certain point you need to find new kinds of thrills, especially if you'd had a lot of success." He paused, then added, "The ultimate thrill is killing things, but there's not many opportunities to do that." Amid nervous laughter, Mason laid out his plan:

"Imagine you go to Las Vegas, you go to a casino, you're with like four of your friends, and you start playing cards. And then there's someone at your table, and he's sweating and he's sick, and it's like, 'What's wrong with that guy?' And he goes, 'Excuse me,' and then he goes to the bathroom and he's gone for ten minutes and then he comes out a zombie. And he bites somebody else and then somebody else says, 'Hey, guys, over here!' And then you and your friends go into another room and there's paintball guns. And you spend the next two hours shooting your way out of this casino, killing all the zombies. Then the coup de grâce is at the end, when you make it out . . . there's like one hundred zombies right behind you, and there's a military chopper and they're like, 'Come on, guys, get on!' And you get on, and as you're flying away, there's a paintball Gatling gun and you shoot all the zombies down."

Cheers and applause ended the session. For a minute, Mason had been able to let his freak flag fly, but now it was late afternoon and getting dark. Snow had started to fall and there was concern that the late flight to Berlin would be canceled because of the weather, and Mason was scheduled to visit the former City-Deal office, now Groupon's European headquarters, there the next morning. Samwer quickly worked his smart phone to rebook and whisked Mason away in a waiting car. Julie Mossler followed in a taxi and flew to London to set up the next leg of the trip.

Early the next morning, January 25, Mason e-mailed to say he would be at the Berlin office as scheduled. But thirty minutes later, he wrote: "I may not actually make it over there for a while."

Mason was staying at the Radisson Blu, two blocks from Groupon's European stronghold, a third-floor loft space at 17 Rosenstrasse in the former East Berlin, a stone's throw from the famous onion-bulb spire overlooking Alexanderplatz. Only a small sign next to the buzzer identified the place as a Groupon office from the street. On the main entrance wall, a sign still called out City-Deal.de. Inside the office, the CEO was nowhere to be found, but visitors were welcomed by a black-and-white laminated sheet of paper on the door sporting the Groupon logo.

A quick tour of the operation revealed young employees working elbow to elbow on tables arrayed with computers, prospecting for, setting up, and executing deals for all of Germany. Finance, IT, and some other functions had offices one floor below. The company would soon take over three more floors in the modest building with a cobblestone courtyard.

A row of clocks on one wall confirmed Mason was running late across multiple time zones. One clock displayed Chicago time, while another showed the same time in Mexico. An hour later, after a walk around Alexanderplatz turned up a theater, restaurants, bowling alley, and menswear store boasting "sizes from XX–XXXXXXXXL," word came that Mason had decided to skip the office entirely.

The CEO had flown to Berlin, stayed two blocks from his company's European headquarters, and then blown off the visit. It was extraordinary even for him.

"I have too much to do in the U.S.," he confirmed in a cordial note later that day. Meanwhile, Mason had sent a not-so-cordial text to the home office canceling the remainder of the trip. It was unfortunate that some of the newer employees missed a chance to meet him, but he'd heard the same questions repeated enough times by reporters to trigger his rebellious streak. He had a company to build back home. It was simply time to go.

Unfortunately, Mason was about to trade those distractions for an exponentially larger one.

FEBRUARY 6, 2011

When Groupon, feeling its oats after a stellar 2010, decided to step onto the national television stage in 2011, it started right at the top, purchasing multiple Super Bowl slots. It was a big leap, and Andrew Mason believed the cutting-edge ad shop Crispin Porter + Bogusky would stand the best chance of effectively introducing both Groupon's business model and its zany culture to the football-loving masses.

CP + B had been making creative waves for years: They were behind the stark anti-tobacco Truth campaign and produced memorably bizarre television spots for Burger King. But the agency's "Whopper virgin" ads, which showed actual villagers in remote areas of the world trying Burger King's signature sandwich for the first time, were deemed culturally insensitive by critics.

Unfortunately, the main Super Bowl spot Crispin Porter crafted for Groupon's "Save the Money" campaign, a commercial that many people took as mocking the persecuted people of Tibet, cranked the insensitivity dial all the way up to eleven. That was only fitting, given that the ad was directed by Spinal Tap's own Nigel Tufnel, aka Christopher Guest.

It all started when Groupon's senior leaders convinced the

board that the company should do some offline advertising. They decided to debut on the biggest stage in the world, feeling the same itch that Web 1.0 stalwarts such as Pets.com scratched on their way to the scrap heap. The concept was to do mock public-service ads that would start by talking about rain-forest depletion, endangered whales, and persecuted peoples only to segue into a pitch for saving money via Groupon. The spots would also generate donations for partner charities. In theory, that would immunize Groupon from charges of callousness.

A group of brand and marketing staffers, including Groupon PR head Julie Mossler and site editor Aaron With, traveled to Los Angeles on a January day when Guest was set to film Groupon's Super Bowl commercials with actors Timothy Hutton, Elizabeth Hurley, and Cuba Gooding, Jr., as well as singer-songwriter Sheryl Crow.

Mossler was supposed to spend all day on the set, but she fell so ill after ten minutes that she was taken to the nearest emergency room and missed the shoot. The plan was to make her as comfortable as possible so that she could return to Chicago and see her doctor the next day, and although she was released a few hours after being seen, she was still woozy from the anesthetic.

A friend sent a car to pick her up, and she headed to dinner with a couple of other Groupon employees who wanted to celebrate what they felt was a successful commercial shoot. Mossler's colleagues didn't know the extent of her treatment in the emergency room—including Percocet and Dilaudid, or "hospital heroin" as the strong narcotic painkiller is often called. Though she seemed tired but coherent, the painkillers left her on autopilot with little memory of the evening. After dinner, the group met up with Aaron With at a nightclub, where bottle service ruled and a man who looked familiar to Mossler was holding court. In her state, though, she couldn't place him.

The next day, With solved the mystery: The man was Miami Dolphins running back Reggie Bush. With and his colleague had ended up going to a party at Bush's L.A. home, which was swarming with gorgeous models. Although With didn't have any luck chatting them up, he did drunkenly tell Bush he was sorry Miami had been eliminated from the play-offs. The running back proved a genial host. This was the Hollywood high life, and With's second run at Groupon just kept getting better.

But Mossler had a story from the same night that easily topped that one. After a few hours at the club and noticeably sticking to water as her drink of choice, she blurted, "Let's go get my tattoo right now," to two female employees still at the table. This request sounded perfectly reasonable in the context of Groupon's fun-loving culture, so the women accompanied Mossler to a nearby tattoo parlor.

There she had the word *briefly* inked in cursive below her right wrist. It's the title of a song by Mossler's favorite band, Better Than Ezra, and "briefly" is dear to her because it evokes the song's message, which is that life is short, so you'd better make it count. Years earlier, Mossler had tucked into her wallet a sample of the font she wanted for the tattoo, but she ended up with a different script style on her arm. Still, it's a subtle, elegant tattoo that reminds the hard-charging twentysomething to get the most out of life and feel grateful for what she has achieved.

That attitude helped Mossler cope with Groupon's stressful ramp-up period, during which a consultant told her she should have a staff of fourteen to support the work she was doing solo. Like Google employee number twenty Marissa Mayer, another woman who's carved out a powerful place for herself in the boys'-club world of tech start-ups, Mossler's blond hair and striking blue eyes sometimes distract people she meets from realizing just how talented and effective she is. Mossler's remarkably patient with those who underestimate her, though, which is a crucial trait since it happens so often.

All in all, her tattoo adventure had a happy outcome. Except for the fact that Mossler had to piece that sequence of events together the next day. She has no recollection of actually getting inked. "I didn't discover it until I was on the 8:00 A.M. flight taking off the bandages from the hospital and realized that one of them had a tattoo under it," she said. Soon, she had a hazy recollection of sitting in the chair at the parlor. Her colleagues filled in the rest of the blanks. So Mossler's surprise may only have lasted, well, briefly, but at least she has an unforgettable story to tell, now that she's remembered it.

If Groupon's ad campaign had stuck to non-human-rights issues, the controversy would have been minimal. But Mason insisted on airing the Tibet ad. "Eric thought it was hilarious," Solomon said. "Andrew thought it was hilarious. We just ran something we shouldn't have. We overestimated how willing people would be to connect the dots and realize it was us making fun of ourselves. There were a few miscalculations."

Groupon's infamous commercial, which aired late in the game's fourth quarter, parodied a standard charity commercial. It started with shots of a snow-covered peak, a large temple, and natives in colorful dress as a voice intoned, "Mountainous Tibet, one of the most beautiful places in the world. This is Timothy Hutton. The people of Tibet are in trouble; their very culture is in jeopardy . . .

"But they still whip up an amazing fish curry!" Hutton exclaims as the ad cuts to a Tibetan man walking toward the camera and reveals that he's a server in an American restaurant.

Only then does Hutton deliver the pitch: "And since two hundred of us bought a Groupon.com, we're each getting thirty dollars' worth of Tibetan food for just fifteen dollars at Himalayan

Restaurant in Chicago." The spot ended by showing a simple graphic of "save the money" in black text on a Groupon green background. A different announcer told viewers to "save the money. Unlock great deals in your town . . . Groupon.com."

Two other spots in the campaign aired that night: one in which Elizabeth Hurley compared Brazilian bikini waxes with deforestation in Brazil and another in which Academy Award winner Cuba Gooding, Jr., segued from saving endangered whales to taking a discount whale-watching cruise. All three of the ads were designed in part to help raise money for a charity: The Tibet Fund, Rainforest Action Network, and Greenpeace, respectively.

Unfortunately, Mason decided that including the charity information in the television spots would confuse the brand message and undercut the parodic punch lines. He figured enough people would see the campaigns when they checked out Groupon .com that the company would raise plenty of money for the nonprofits and everyone would come out a winner.

Unlike her actor counterparts, singer Sheryl Crow avoided embarrassment when her ad, the final one of the campaign, was pulled before it aired. It was promoted online with the words "coming soon" superimposed over a screen capture of Crow and a reference to a buildOn campaign to "construct four new schools in some of the world's poorest villages." That one was never even released online.

I happened to catch the other three spots on Groupon's site a few hours before the game. Seeing that the commercials did not include the charity information, I told my wife, "This Tibet ad is going to get them into trouble."

It wouldn't have been clear to anyone outside Groupon that this campaign's primary goal was to introduce a brand still in its infancy to tens of millions of people who had never heard of it. To really get the running gag and be comfortable with it, viewers had to know that Groupon had emerged from a site designed to foster collective good works, that it infused its every action with goofy-yet-well-intentioned humor, and that the spots had the full support of the charities working on the featured issues. In short, you almost had to work at Groupon to understand the subtext of the jokes.

Even though Crispin Porter never raised a red flag about those problems, some Groupon employees who reviewed the ads told Mason he was on the wrong track. Solomon sent the CEO an e-mail flatly stating: "We will be slaughtered if we run Tibet."

"Slaughtered" turned out to be an understatement. Almost before Hutton's face faded from the screen, Twitter exploded with outrage directed at Groupon's alleged insensitivity. The jaw-dropping reaction was akin to that of the audience seeing "Spring-time for Hitler" in *The Producers*. If you had been watching Twitter that night you would have seen the following choice commentary cascading through the service:

"The next Groupon commercial will have something about small pox, blankets, and a great discount for Bed Bath and Beyond." . . . "Turmoil in Egypt got you down? Come to @ groupon where we have half off rooms at the Luxor Las Vegas." . . . "Groupon CEO offices: 'It's Dolly somebody for you. He sounds mad.'" . . . "I'm just as angry about Groupon as everyone else—Ethiopia would have been WAY funnier." . . . "Thousands of Jews died at Auschwitz, but thanks to Groupon our tour of the camp was practically free!" . . . And, finally, "A bunch of people died on Sept. 11, but thanks to @Groupon, we got half-priced airfare."

Amid the carnage, user @ischafer tweeted: "If you go to Groupon.com, they are raising money for the causes they use as comedy in their spots." But there was no way to know that without visiting the site, and it wasn't letting people log in at that point. After an avalanche of negative comments slid by, Groupon tweeted: "Support Tibet's largest charity here: http://savethemoney.groupon.com."

"If we had inserted the URL and prompt to donate in the ad, some people would still have been upset," Mossler said, "but I think we might have even gotten away with keeping the ads up because people would realize that the charity component was always built-in. It's our bad for not properly telling the story, making sure viewers knew we were poking fun at celebrity cause campaigns, and also that we have charity in our DNA as The Point, but it really pissed me off that people thought we did that as a PR fix afterward."

By then, big-name tweeters had joined the masses in ripping the company. The account for news site Salon.com tweeted: "Groupon exploits Tibetan plight for giggles? Why?" Humor writer Andy Borowitz quipped: "I guess Groupon decided to do a funny commercial about Tibet because Darfur would be in bad taste?" Nor was Hollywood comedy director Judd Apatow amused: "Best commercial was the Dorito's finger sucking one. Worst was that Timothy Hutton commercial. Bizarre use of Tibet. Wasted 3 million." Famed venture capitalist Guy Kawasaki added, simply: "Groupon, you suck."

After the celebrity pile-ons, suggestions of additional grotesque scenarios, and even the real Himalayan Restaurant piping up on Twitter and Facebook from the Chicago suburbs ("We are hoping people didn't take that commercial the wrong way! Hope you know that groupon is supporting The Tibetan Fund. . . . You can donate here!"), Twitter commentators began assessing the damage to Groupon's reputation. One choice insight: "That Groupon commercial may actually inspire the Dalai Lama to give up a lifetime of non-violence to kick the CEO in the nuts."

Thousands of users pledged to quit Groupon, sending out

tweets such as: "Groupon login and registration is down right now. That's the only thing keeping my wife and I from deleting our accounts." Other salient comments included: "Groupon seems to have achieved the unique feat of paying $3M to lose customers who previously loved them"; "After their Super Bowl commercial, Groupon's valuation has gone from $15 billion to $15"; "A brand's first Super Bowl commercial helps introduce their personality to the masses. Groupon chose selfish, materialistic and douchey"; and, most presciently, "Future News: Groupon seeks new agency after Super Bowl flop."

Mason was in fact taking the first steps toward firing Crispin Porter that very evening. When his Pittsburgh Steelers had fallen behind the Green Bay Packers early in the game, the CEO had left Groupon's Super Bowl party at Chicago's LaSalle Power Co. nightclub. So he was on his computer at home when Twitter erupted with vitriol toward his company.

As he watched the hatred build to a fever pitch, Mason reached out to a contact at the agency to ask if this type of reaction was normal. Sure, he was told, an envelope-pushing ad like that would always spark some controversy, with negative comments making up as much as 50 percent of the online conversation. But this felt more like 99 percent negative, and quantitative research conducted by social-media analytics provider MutualMind indicated that sentiments expressed on Twitter about the Tibet ad ran at least 80 percent against Groupon, making the spot suicidally edgy.

Mason was incredulous that the agency he had hired to push the company's message right up to the line had instead shoved Groupon well into the land of damaging controversy. While the CEO took responsibility for ignoring internal requests to include the charity messages and always said the buck stopped with him on evaluating and green-lighting the campaign, he said Crispin Porter was tone-deaf about how the spots would be received.

"I went to Crispin and I said the reason we're working with you is because in theory you understand how to help us do a commercial that is going to be more than just something funny and wacky, but is going to help get the story of Groupon across, one, which is just you as a marketer," Mason said. "And then number two, with the stuff that you have done before, you will know how to push us up to the edge, but not take us beyond that edge. . . . They didn't serve us well in that role. They should know when something is going to be universally despised."

Back at the party, Mossler watched employees' jaws drop not because of the commercial itself but because of the reaction to it. Kool-Aid had not been served that night, but they had apparently drunk enough already.

Immediately after the Tibet spot showed on the big screens, employees were elated, cheering and raising glasses to their debut on the world's most watched broadcast. But when people started checking out the Twitter reaction on their smart phones, their euphoria turned to shock: "Why is everyone mad at us?"

In the coming months, it would become painfully clear to even the biggest cheerleaders in the company that a growing number of people hated Groupon.

To Crispin Porter's credit, the agency shouldered its share of the blame and apologized to Mason, who remained shocked by how badly the agency had misread what the public reaction would be. But Solomon and others who saw the spots before airtime didn't need an expert opinion to know they were toxic.

This was one case where Mason's management inexperience proved a liability for the company. "I totally understand why people were so pissed off," he said with the benefit of hindsight. "We got a little too close to the sun with that one."

And it wasn't just the public that Groupon had to worry about. The Tibet ad not only appeared to use the struggles of an oppressed people as the setup for a cheap gag; it also raised the ire of the Chinese government, which is hypersensitive to any discussion of its human-rights record. And that posed a potential problem for Groupon, which had just entered the Chinese market. Fortunately for Groupon, the issue blew over quickly, but Mason and Groupon's PR team had more than enough damage control to do Stateside.

First, the ads were modified to include the charity information, and the campaigns ultimately raised about half a million bucks. "We made sure each organization received the full amount we promised when they agreed to participate," Mossler said. Next, Mason issued a couple of apologies, one somewhat grudging and, when that one didn't fly, a more heartfelt version. Finally, the ads were pulled from the air altogether, though the first three are still available on YouTube.

Solomon put the incident in perspective, noting that taking such a big hit was a kind of coming-of-age ritual for Groupon. "The backlash is part of the cycle in Silicon Valley," he said. "When you're a new special thing, people adore you. And then over time familiarity breeds contempt. EBay was the most special company in the world, and then they started favoring the power sellers and the small guys said, 'Fuck you, eBay. You're the worst thing in the world.'

"Yahoo! was the greatest company in the world—so much fun," Solomon continued. "Everyone would yodel all over the place. Then they started fucking around with Chinese dissidents and Jerry Yang gets called before Congress. . . . So Yahoo! got beaten up. And Amazon got bashed badly for being a horrible investment, the stupidest company in the world. Google—same thing. Facebook went through their shit."

Like everything else with Groupon, Solomon said, "we went through our love cycle very quickly. And then we went through our hate cycle very quickly because we fucked up."

But here's the kicker: After all the negative headlines, tut-tutting cable news coverage, late-night parodies, like Conan O'Brien's where he had Groupon using the Trail of Tears to sell a Trail of Beers deal at T.G.I. Friday's, and blustery outrage spewed on social media, Groupon actually gained members in the week after the Super Bowl. Most of the complainers were never customers in the first place, and those who were largely chose to keep saving money over closing their accounts.

End result: The deals site enjoyed its best sales week ever. Well, perhaps "enjoyed" isn't the right word. "We've never promoted that because we never want people to think that was the motivation for the ad," Julie Mossler said. "It wasn't." But sometimes the law of unintended consequences just comes down in your favor.

In addition, Solomon said, "Tibet was pretty happy [with the controversy] because it elevated the dialogue. Nobody had talked about Tibet in a really long time—so the charities were pretty excited. And we support charities like crazy. Had we done a more innocuous Super Bowl campaign, we wouldn't have gotten a real pick-up I don't think."

Having the last word on the ill-fated campaign, Mason said, "While I wouldn't do it again, part of me will always be proud that we made the decision to run those commercials. There's no way you can really push things forward unless you get slapped from time to time."

Okay, so maybe "enjoyed" was the right word after all. . . .

TWENTY-ONE

Mason's desire to refocus on what was a critically important moment in Groupon's development led him to skip a March 13 speaking engagement at the 2011 South by Southwest Interactive Festival in Austin, Texas, on the topic of "Strange Business: Corporate Creativity That Doesn't Suck," leaving editor Aaron With to pick up the slack. It turned out to be a good panel to blow off, as the after-session featured a public spanking from an unhappy client.

Travis Kalanick is a well-known Silicon Valley entrepreneur who mentors start-up founders at his home, nicknamed the Jam Pad, and he likes to tell the story of how he was written out of the film version of *The Social Network*. Although Kalanick was at the New York City dinner where Napster's Sean Parker first met and wooed Facebook's Mark Zuckerberg and Eduardo Saverin (you may remember it as the appletini scene), he didn't make the cut as a character. "I was replaced by a pretty Asian woman," he said at SXSW. At any rate, Kalanick was largely complimentary about Groupon's innovative chops and rapid scaling at the session's outset, but most of the conversation was dominated by his negative experience with marketing his Uber car service through Mason's company.

"The big issue that Groupon has isn't on the marketing side— they're frickin' killing it," Kalanick said. "I think their major issue is that they're not connecting the actual experience of using a Groupon to that brand, and that promise, and that marketing message. . . . Anybody who's actually been a vendor to Groupon knows it's probably one of the worst experiences you'll ever have working with someone that's an aggregator of consumers. All that great stuff you see on the copywriting and marketing side is completely disconnected from the operations side."

After noting that his choppy merchant experience could have been due to Groupon's growing pains, Kalanick pointed out that the marketing and copywriting functions had scaled just fine, calling into question the company's commitment to the merchant and consumer experience. "When marketing is disconnected from operations, then promises are made that aren't kept," he said. "From the moment a salesperson gets on the phone with you and says, 'Do this, do this, do this,' to the moment these Groupons are being redeemed, that entire experience has many points of brokenness, and they have to work on that on the operations side."

At that point, Kalanick was challenged from the audience by Darren Schwartz, Groupon's head of sales, who said it wasn't fair to generalize. So the Uber honcho got very specific:

"It started with the sales guy who got us on the phone who said, 'We really want to do something with you, Uber, we love you guys, and we want to associate our brand with yours.' We said, 'Look, this is a big step for our brand. We've got to have primary placement.' And he said, 'We'll make sure you get primary placement. We'll make sure we do it on this date.' There were, like, five different promises, all of which were broken. We didn't get primary placement, didn't get it on the date. They disappeared for two weeks, then came back begging us to get back on it."

From there, Kalanick said, the marketing copy and fine print were full of errors, coupon codes went live before they were supposed to, and customer data was sent to Uber in unwieldy spreadsheet form that revealed customer names even though that wasn't supposed to happen. Ultimately, Groupon's sales projections were wildly inaccurate and Uber sold only 10 percent of the deals it thought it would.

Schwartz grabbed a microphone and apologized for problems with the Uber deal. "It's not a unique experience, though," Kalanick countered. Calmly plowing forward, Schwartz promised to look into the specific sales issues and then explained that Groupon had recently created merchant manager positions designed to take the handoff from sales and improve the experience. Again, Kalanick was unimpressed. "There was that handoff" with the Uber deal, he said. "But the merchant manager we had didn't understand the process she was managing. At all."

"It's likely because we've just ramped this program up," Schwartz responded. "Thirty days ago we had none, and now we have sixty."

Finally, Kalanick began to relent. "I understand," he said. "There's a lot of amazing things about Groupon. My point is, I don't think this is a specific sales rep thing or a specific merchant manager thing. I think it's a disconnect between a powerful, well-oiled marketing machine and an operational environment that is not even close to as tuned as that marketing machine. And if that operational environment can get up to snuff comparable to that marketing machine, Groupon is going to be killing it." He then added that Uber would be open to doing another deal with Groupon if they got their merchant-services act together. And, in fact,

Uber later used Groupon to promote its service in new markets, including Chicago.

At the end of the day, a high-profile client, respected in Silicon Valley, not an in-over-their-head mom-and-pop coffee shop, had called Groupon out for paying too little attention to the merchant experience during a live webcast from a prominent digital conference during a session moderated by a journalist from *Fast Company* and attended by other reporters.

The damage had been done.

MARCH 14, 2011

After the Uber fireworks, Mason ultimately did show up at SXSW—for the music festival—the next day as a favor to Harry Weller, a key early Groupon backer at investor New Enterprise Associates. "Walking around Austin by myself at sxsw carrying a book of Billy Joel keyboard music—no one has asked me to join their band . . . yet," he tweeted that evening. He'd come by the songbook honestly, as he'd once played in a Billy Joel tribute act. Soon, Mason, in black T-shirt and jeans, was parked behind a keyboard at a downtown club, where audience members were given glow sticks and chorus lyric sheets, the better to sing along with the parody of Joel's "Honesty" that Weller had turned into a Groupon song that made Mason squirm when he heard it for the first time that night:

> *"Honesty" is such a lonely word.*
> *Everyone is so untrue.*
> *Originality is hardly ever heard.*
> *Copycats, I'm crushing you-oooo.*
> *Honestly, Groupon is just a fad.*
> *I must tell you that's so very true-oooo,*
> *My apology, for that silly Super Bowl ad.*

I admit it was long overdue-oooo.
"Honesty" is such a lonely word.
Everyone is so untrue.
Lefkofsky, why must you be heard?
It was my idea, buddy, not you-oooo.

Accompanied by a drummer and guitarist, Mason played keys creditably, even while trying to make out the sheet music in the dark club. Meanwhile, the fortysomething Weller, who had left Groupon's board of directors that February to make way for Starbucks founder Howard Schultz—belted the song to a packed house, after saying up front, "This is the result of a very bad bet gone wrong."

In announcing Weller's departure from the board a month earlier, Mason had said, "Without the support of Harry Weller from NEA, we might have never received the funding we used to conceive and grow Groupon—he's also been our most prescient adviser, predicting trends like the rampant cloning of Groupon far before the rest of us." Also, thanks in part to Weller, NEA stood to clean up in the IPO.

Well before Mason got to know Weller, NEA had entered Lefkofsky's orbit in October 2005, when he and Harry Weller's colleague Peter Barris met following an all-too-common University of Michigan trouncing of Northwestern University in football at NU's stadium in the Chicago suburbs. Barris was a Northwestern alum; Lefkofsky had gone to Michigan; a friend of Barris' introduced them. NEA went on to invest in Lefkofsky and Keywell start-ups and later invested in Groupon as well. As Bloomberg headlined the manly meet-cute, "NEA's Barris Turns Football Loss into More than 150-Fold Gain from Groupon."

But tonight, Weller and Mason were simply two guys in a bar, finding catharsis in cheesy music. Call it karaoke therapy.

TWENTY-TWO

As Groupon grew increasingly popular, it started to draw a fair share of celebrity visitors. Perhaps the most prominent was New York City mayor Michael Bloomberg. He came to the Windy City on April 15 to join nearly one thousand local movers, shakers, socialites, and swells in sending off Chicago mayor Richard M. Daley as he ended his record-setting twenty-two years in office. A photo taken that evening on the terrace atop the Art Institute of Chicago's stunning new $300 million Modern Wing shows a mirthful Bloomberg, perhaps suppressing a laugh, flanked by a chuckling Daley and a slyly smiling Chicago mayor-elect Rahm Emanuel, with one of Daley's signature accomplishments, Millennium Park, stretching out behind them. What was so funny? That's lost to time. But the gathering might have turned somber if Mayor Bloomberg's visit that day to Groupon headquarters had played out as Andrew Mason originally planned it.

For Bloomberg, the Groupon whistle-stop was a way to underscore his commitment to nurturing the next wave of high-tech firms sprouting up in his city. In fact, the mayor had visited NYC-based Foursquare earlier in the week and proclaimed April 16 Foursquare Day to promote the online social check-in service.

The official @NYCMayorsOffice Twitter account even shared a photo of Bloomberg talking to Mason and Eric Lefkofsky in Groupon's reception area, along with the caption "exactly the kind of tech company we're trying to grow in NYC." The main sartorial difference between Mason and Lefkofsky that day was that the chairman bothered to tuck his shirt into his blue jeans while the unshaven and perennially disheveled CEO went wrinkled tails out.

Vanity Fair memorialized this visit in the opening scene of a major Groupon profile that August, but the magazine was only let in on half of the story. A plan to give Bloomberg a pony was aborted at the last minute, as the piece noted, but the pony plot was actually Plan B, and a much tamer one than Plan A had been. Before we get to that, though, it's worth taking a quick trot through the pony tale.

Mason has long been fond of giving "inconvenient gifts," as founding employee Joe Harrow put it. In Groupon's early days, "Andrew used to buy us all turkeys on Thanksgiving," Harrow recalled. "But when he bought us turkeys on Thanksgiving, it wasn't a nice gift. I think half the office is vegetarian, and half of us also bike to work. So he bought us all the cheapest frozen turkeys possible, the Butterballs, and they were delivered frozen on Wednesday afternoon," too late to thaw for the big meal even for those who managed to muscle one home on their handlebars.

The pony stunt was similar in concept, except that the target was much more prominent and the animal in this case was a rental—a $300 prop. The whimsy kicked into gear at 7:00 A.M., when Groupon PR head Julie Mossler awoke to a chat message from Mason's assistant saying: "FYI, pony in the office today." But Mossler didn't find out what the cryptic note meant until she arrived at work.

Just as Bloomberg was entering the building, Mossler Googled

"Bloomberg and horse" only to discover that the mayor's daughter Georgina, a top-rated show jumper, had suffered a concussion and spinal fracture the previous November when she fell off her mount. Her saddle had come loose while she rode in a speed-jumping event dressed, in a Groupon-worthy twist, as a witch. At that particular event, all the riders wore costumes. Shocked by the story, the PR pro caught Mason on his way down to the building's lobby and said, "Andrew, you can't do this, the thing with the horse; you just can't." After she explained the problem, the CEO agreed that it would be best to hide the pony.

She e-mailed everyone in the company who might come into contact with Bloomberg: "Don't tell anyone that we have a horse here." Mason's assistant led the pony into a freight elevator and kept it there until Bloomberg left. All that survives of the scrapped mission is a picture Mossler tweeted of herself standing in the break room next to the black-and-white animal with a green bow tied around its neck. "Introducing Groupony," she wrote. The shot was taken mere seconds before Bloomberg rounded the corner, but by the time he arrived the kitchen was empty.

If the pony presentation would have created an awkward moment, the other stunt Groupon almost set in motion for Bloomberg's visit would have generated negative national headlines. Believe it or not, Mason thought it would be a great idea to parade the mayor of New York City's security detail past an employee wielding realistic-looking fake weapons. The gag played up the idea that this was just a normal day at work, while something obviously off-kilter was going on without anyone mentioning it.

The gestation of the idea illustrates Mason's reflexive need to subvert convention and flout authority, a trait that often, but not always, serves him well. Before the big visit, Groupon was told Bloomberg's security detail would scan the premises and make sure that everything was safe. That announcement was actually what triggered Groupon's crazy plan: to have someone in customer service sitting at his desk in fatigues and cleaning a rifle during the pre-visit security sweep. The patsy in question, a humor writer named Andrew Smreker, wore a full camo suit and black ski mask. He toted a fake plastic assault rifle and also had fake munitions cases on his desk, wood boxes, with military white spray paint on the sides.

"He was all dressed up and ready to go," Mossler said, "but we realized that although we thought it was funny and Bloomberg probably has a really good sense of humor, if you see the photo in the wrong context, the average customer isn't going to get the joke."

Not to mention that the poor guy in the fatigues would have experienced a real-time demonstration of the threat-neutralization plan developed for the mayor of a city that suffered the worst terrorist attack in U.S. history. Groupon employees, used to bizarre office happenings, barely registered the supposed gunman practicing his act. In fact, Sean Smyth, Groupon's VP of business development, was interviewing a woman for a senior-level position at the company when Smreker arrived to conduct a dry run.

When he saw a guy walk by the glass-walled conference room in fatigues while waving a gun around, Smyth's first reaction was, "Who's fucking around?" The job candidate simply continued with the interview until Smyth told her, "You can't ignore that. You can't."

But Groupon employees are so immersed in prank culture that they might not believe it if someone literally went postal in the office and started shooting people. If the bodies started falling, Smyth predicted colleagues would say, "You're not really dead. Who is fucking with us today?"

After finding out what Smreker was up to, Smyth stepped out of the conference room and flagged down Rob Solomon as he walked by.

"Rob, this is irresponsible," Smyth said. "That guy is going to die." Thinking he had perhaps saved Smreker from a violent end, Smyth finished the interview. But when he emerged from the conference room, there was the employee, sitting at his desk and playing with a huge camouflage grenade launcher. And he was still wearing the mask.

Thankfully for all concerned, sanity finally prevailed and the stunt was scrapped. But if Bloomberg ever returns to the Groupon office and encounters what appears to be a terrorist cantering by on a Shetland, he should probably tell his security guards to keep their weapons holstered. After all, as the famous adage reminds us: Dying is easy. Comedy is hard.

TWENTY-THREE

The daily-deals space was getting harder to compete in as well, with Facebook announcing it would launch Facebook Deals in San Francisco on April 26, followed by Atlanta, Austin, Dallas, and San Diego. First LivingSocial, then Yelp, and now Mark Zuckerberg's social-networking giant were looking to eat Groupon's half-priced lunch.

By late summer, though, the threat would fade. Facebook pulled the plug on its Deals on August 26, and Yelp laid off half its Deals staff three days later, effectively throwing in the towel. That left plenty of competition—including Amazon, which rolled out a mainly LivingSocial-powered deals service under the Amazon Local name in Boise, Idaho, on June 2; and eBay, which jumped into the offers market in late December. But Groupon and LivingSocial still commanded 80 percent of the U.S. sector, and the game suddenly didn't seem quite as easy for interlopers to master as so many analysts had believed.

With every competitor except LivingSocial struggling to scale, Groupon was able to keep its deal margins around 40 percent. Critics had predicted Groupon's standard deal cut would prove to be unsustainably high, but so far it had been fairly resilient. Part of that probably had to do with the fact that merchants did not pay any fees up front, so that sharing a big chunk of the deal revenue wasn't as psychologically difficult for them.

But something else was at play here, something familiar to any business owner who had ever mounted expensive direct-mail campaigns only to see dismal returns: Offering a guaranteed minimum threshold of consumers via a robust new marketing channel was pretty much worth its weight in gold, if businesses could convert them into long-term customers. As Silicon Valley entrepreneur Sramana Mitra put it in a June 2011 blog post, "Whatever happens to Groupon in the IPO market, it has shown us something important: merchants are willing to pay heavy channel fees to acquire customers."

That's why "any time something's described as a Groupon killer, I'm like, 'You have no clue what you're up against,'" designer Steven Walker said. "It's such an irresponsible thing to say. I just don't buy that you're gonna kill us."

During one particularly intense company meeting, Mason had told his employees of the clones, "It's going to get tougher and tougher with competitors, and we've got to put our foot on their necks." Walker took the sentiment to heart. "I just keep repeating that," he said. "Whenever these people try to compete with us, I'm just going to keep going."

So at the moment it seemed that Groupon's biggest problems were internal ones, and they were substantial. The company trudged through three months of flat sales growth in the United States to start 2011, and Groupon continued to struggle with scaling its operations efficiently. Solomon saw the writing on the wall: "My worst day, and maybe my best day, was when Andrew and I had a conversation about the fact that we needed a different type of operator and it's time for me to go."

It wouldn't be easy for Solomon to step off the ride so soon.

He'd figured on having another year in the saddle, but everything at Groupon always happened faster than they thought it would. It turned out his wife had been right not to rent out their California home for more than a year.

"I feel like Brett Favre," he said. "I'm in the limelight. This is the sexiest company on the Internet. Well, it's not Facebook—maybe they're a little sexier, but not much. And I'm leaving. What do you do after that? I don't know what the fuck to do next. So that's a little bit of a sad day."

The prospect of leaving Groupon behind was also liberating. Solomon was a big-picture strategic thinker. The process-oriented job of a COO was not in his DNA. And leading a historic corporate ramp-up was no easy thing for a guy in his forties with a wife and young kids. He might go home for dinner, but soon he'd be back on e-mail closing a deal. He was working on or thinking about Groupon all day, every day. It was grueling. That's why the day he talked with Mason about leaving was both his worst and best one with the company.

"It's the most stressful thing in the world to be on the hook to make this thing work," Solomon said. "Giving me time to get back into my California life with my kids and my wife—that's a good thing."

If someone had told him in 2008 that Groupon would be the second-fastest company in history to reach a valuation of a billion dollars, that it would take only three years to be in markets representing 90 percent of the world's GDP, that it would grow during his fourteen-month tenure from around two hundred employees to nine thousand, "I would've said it's not possible," Solomon admitted.

"If when Eric interviewed me, Andrew had said, 'Hey, come in here and we'll go into forty-six countries. We'll hire a few hundred people every month. We'll start at $10 million a month in gross sales and we'll exit at over $300 million,' I would say, 'Oh, no, I can't do that. You gotta find some other sucker.' I'd be lying to you if I told you we could do it. What you do is you condition your brain and your body to thinking much bigger than you ever thought possible. And then you just do it."

When he'd set a goal during his first staff meeting of growing Groupon's subscriber base to 25 million from 3 million, people had shaken their heads in disbelief. Yet the company had hit that milestone within nine months. In 2011, they were on track to have 125 million subscribers globally.

"When you go to one of these start-ups, it usually takes a few years to scale it up to a place where you can be ready to go public," he said. "We did in a year what typically takes three to five or even seven years at the best Internet companies in the world, Google or Yahoo! or eBay or Amazon."

After a year of hyper-growth, though, further refinement was needed, and Solomon wasn't the guy to put in what he described as a "rigid, rigorous, process-oriented, and metric-oriented" system. "I'm a little bit more of a move fast, use the gut, and rally the troops guy as the number one," he said. Solomon would stick around until midyear to break in the new COO, and he'd always be available to advise Mason as needed, but it was time to step back.

Solomon had been one of the first outsiders brought into Groupon to be an adult in the room. But now Jeff Holden, an Amazon veteran, was running the product end of the business. Another Amazon hire, Jason Child, came in as CFO. Brian Totty, who built Inktomi's search platform, was leading the technology team as SVP of engineering. Solomon had helped pave the way for this team, but the gig was getting to be a lot less fun.

"It's a tough job," Solomon said. "What we did was very hard. And then when I think about the next years, it's much harder."

He'd be leaving with more than 4 million shares of Groupon stock. But the memories were priceless. Solomon thought back in particular to a board meeting he'd attended in February, shortly after Groupon had turned down Google and secured its billion-dollar funding round. Looking around the table at the caliber of the directors assembled, he'd savored the moment.

"Eric's a stud in his own right," Solomon said of Lefkofsky. "And he'll be one of the hotshots over the long term. And then Ted Leonsis is sitting in there. He's kind of a medium mogul—owns the Washington Capitals and the Wizards—but he's a mogul. And then the king of the nerds is down at one end of the table, that's Marc Andreessen. Marc invented the browser, and he's gonna become probably the most legendary VC of all time—or one of them.

"At the other end of the table are John Doerr and Mary Meeker. Doerr is the Google guy and the Amazon guy and the godfather of all venture capital. And Meeker was the analyst who ushered in this whole crazy Internet thing. They're board observers. And then Howard Schultz is a board member who just joined—the guy who brought the latte to America in a big way.

"I'm this kid who had my first job in tech testing video games and answering phone calls for Electronic Arts. I was making twenty-four grand a year. I'm not a technologist—I'm lucky. I've achieved some success, but I chalk it all up to being more lucky than good. For me, sitting in that room with that crew was surreal."

Another impressive investor, LinkedIn co-founder Reid Hoffman, wasn't in attendance that day, but director Kevin Efrusy was there, and Solomon had a story to tell about him. "He's the guy who found Facebook for Accel," he said. "He'll end up being pretty legendary for discovering Facebook and making the Groupon investment."

Yes, it was an impressive cast, but Lefkofsky was sometimes wary of the Silicon Valley crew. When Meeker was joining Kleiner Perkins, she'd called Groupon and said, "I want to get in this deal; can we get John Doerr talking to Andrew and Eric?"

Lefkofsky's initial reaction was to turn down the offer. His response was similar when Hoffman reached out to connect the company with VC firm Greylock Partners. In such situations, Lefkofsky would say, "We have enough people in the syndicate."

Solomon couldn't believe a tech start-up wouldn't want to have Doerr, Meeker, and Hoffman investing and advising. "But then when Eric stops to think about it, he does want those guys," Solomon said. "Because Eric likes to control the process, his knee-jerk reaction is to distrust Silicon Valley and do it his own way." Lefkofsky quickly came around to the notion of assembling an all-star investing team, though, and Solomon was pleased to make some of the introductions.

TWENTY-FOUR

If Google was annoyed with Groupon for turning down its $5.75 billion purchase offer in December of 2010, the tech titan must have viewed it as insult to injury when Groupon announced the hiring of Margo Georgiadis as its new COO on April 21, 2011.

The day Groupon plucked Google's VP of global sales operations from the search giant's Chicago office happened to be the same one on which Google Offers, which had been announced way back on January 21, finally launched to compete with Groupon in New York City, the San Francisco Bay Area, and Portland, Oregon. But Google would soon take its revenge for being upstaged.

When Andrew Mason began looking for Rob Solomon's replacement, he knew he needed someone who could ratchet Groupon's operations, which had grown wildly under Solomon's watch, under tighter control. If Solomon was more of a natural CEO—good at developing strategies, setting big goals, rallying the troops, and tapping his strong Silicon Valley network for board members, partnerships, and advice—the company now needed a detail-oriented operator who would further overhaul the sales process, bring down Groupon's enormous marketing spend, and help put the place on a glide path to profitability just in time for a monster IPO performance.

Mason believed he'd found the person he needed in Georgiadis. At forty-seven, the Harvard MBA had extensive experience at management consulting firm McKinsey & Company, an expense-slashing, process-tightening machine. But Georgiadis also had run Google's huge advertising business as well as its commerce and local operations. And even though Google was the very definition of a mature Web company, Mason hoped some of its innovation-focused, employee-friendly culture had rubbed off on her. Besides, she had helped champion Google's offer to purchase Groupon the previous year. It seemed like a good match.

A product of Kenilworth, Illinois, an exclusive community on Chicago's suburban North Shore that was ranked by *Forbes* in 2011 as America's second-most-affluent neighborhood, and a graduate of nearby New Trier High School, the academic powerhouse featured in several John Hughes movies, Georgiadis impressed Mason with her keen intellect and incredible poise. When she was hired, though, a joke went around the office in true Groupon style asking why the company had hired Rob Solomon in a dress. Georgiadis' hairstyle was in fact a close match for Solomon's nearly shoulder-length brown shag.

That was about the only thing the two COOs had in common, though. Solomon thought it was a mistake to hire someone with so little start-up experience, and he worried that Georgiadis would make wrenching changes so fast that she would endanger the freewheeling culture that had helped Groupon become an overnight success.

Solomon's last day on the books as president and COO was March 22, but he stuck around until midsummer to help with the transition. Mason called an all-staff meeting in May at a church down the street from Groupon headquarters to introduce Georgiadis, who briefly addressed the employees.

There were no tequila shots this time, but while Mason was singing Solomon's praises—"This is Rob's last all-hands; we want to thank him"—the pride of Berkeley water polo bounded onstage, hugged the CEO, and grabbed his microphone.

Solomon proceeded to share one final piece of wisdom with the troops: "Don't fuck it up."

MAY 6, 2011

In the midst of the latest upheaval, Neil Young visited Groupon headquarters and talked business for a spell with Mason in one of the glass-walled conference rooms while everyone found an excuse to say hi to their colleagues at nearby desks. Young was brought in by one of Groupon's vendors, who's also a friend of the musician's.

At the time, there was talk of dropping Groupon's iconic cat mascot from the site. But thanks to Young, the plump brown feline sporting a thick gold chain earned what appears to be a permanent reprieve. As Groupon copywriter Daniel Kibblesmith, who became a minor celebrity after Mossler booked him on an episode of *Millionaire Matchmaker*, tweeted at the time, "The actual Neil Young stopped by to tell us he was a fan of Groupon the Cat."

The next month, the cat, now firmly entrenched as the company's "official voice of reason, settler of moral disputes, and head of HR," posted "The Groupon Guide to the 'Quiet Period'" on the company blog. "The 'Quiet Period' is the time right before a company 'goes public,' during which it is legally prohibited from saying anything to the press that may make the company look 'good,' 'successful,' or 'not currently on fire,'" the not-at-all-bitter feline wrote. "During this sensitive time, it is the duty of the press to force the adolescent company through a series of brutal hazing rituals, designed to desensitize it to public criticism. This tough love helps the naively optimistic company to thicken its skin, atrophy its soul, and finally grow up into a real corporation."

The SEC declined to bring Groupon the Cat in for questioning.

TWENTY-FIVE

With U.S. sales of daily deals—called G1 deals in-house—flat early in the year, Andrew Mason started pushing hard for the company's next big innovation, Groupon Now! This would be Groupon's mobile play, giving consumers an app through which they could find nearby food and entertainment deals instantly when they were out on the town. As with the original Groupon site that had succeeded with code from a failed reboot of The Point, Now! was built in part on the abandoned Groupon 2.0 platform.

The shift in strategy came as an unpleasant surprise to Darren Schwartz. On April 4, the head of Groupon's U.S. sales was in San Francisco meeting with a disgruntled merchant when Mason called to tell him the board had signed off on aggressively ramping up Groupon Now! and that from here on out the sales team would be selling these instant deals along with daily G1 features. Upon his return to Chicago, Schwartz met with Georgiadis, who'd just come aboard. He told her he was freaking out about the shift in focus because he still had big sales numbers to hit on the daily-deals front. But the course of action was set. Not only would some of the existing sales force be shifted to selling Now!

deals, but the remaining G1 reps would have to sell instant deals on the side.

Mason and Schwartz convened a meeting of the sales team. "We were like Mussolini from the balcony," Schwartz recounted.

"This is the next thing," reps were told. "Get on board. It's real."

Partly as a result of the shift in focus to ramping up Groupon Now! for its May 20 launch, G1 sales continued to take a hit. Schwartz wanted to see a bigger marketing push to get consumers in the habit of checking Now's instant offers whenever they were out and about. "It's under-performing versus this grand vision that I think Andrew and Eric had in the spring," he said later in the year. "It's not the ramp-up that happened with G1." Still, he believed the concept could prove to be very powerful once consumers made it part of their routine.

"Part of me also thinks that maybe Groupon was lightning in a bottle and the core business will always be the core business," Schwartz said. "We just have to tweak G1 and make it more special. Version one was you get a deal and then a side deal, and now it's version whatever and you get some targeted kinds of deals. But maybe it gets really sexy when I get the e-mail and it's exactly right—it's the stuff that they know I want and I'm being informed that my friends are buying stuff and it's social. It might be that Now! will be incremental and help, but daily deals will always be the core business."

Beyond the drag on G1 sales created by the Groupon Now! ramp-up, Schwartz attributed poor numbers in June and July to a standard seasonal slump. LivingSocial had taken an even bigger hit, he noted, and Groupon had actually picked up market share during the slowdown as a result. Whatever external factors might have contributed to the soft G1 sales, Georgiadis did not like what she was seeing, and Schwartz knew he had a target on his back.

Meanwhile, product diversification continued to be the order of the day. On May 9, GrouponLive launched in partnership with Live Nation Entertainment to sell discount tickets to concerts and other live events. Groupon Getaways, a travel deals offering in conjunction with Expedia and its 135,000 worldwide hotel partners, debuted on July 12, selling fifteen thousand deals in its first three days. With the IPO hopefully coming up soon, it was all hands on deck to roll out the new sales vertical, as marketing SVP Aaron Cooper's launch-day e-mail to Groupon's North American staff indicated:

> The massive effort from sales, planning, product, dev, marketing, editorial . . . including full weekends and days and nights of war rooms . . . all came to fruition this morning with the public launch of Groupon Getaways with Expedia.
>
> Between us, things were coming down to the wire into this morning - but ~4AM Suneel [Gupta, Groupon's first VP of product] blasted the Thompson Twins (Hold me Now) and got back his Mojo, called in reserves and finished it out.
>
> For Travel lovers: Groupon Getaways delivers handpicked premium travel experiences - And running today you see truly awesome deals on great properties and experiences.
>
> For Revenue lovers: Getaways is poised to quickly become the fastest growing "division."

In its first three weeks, Getaways generated about $9 million in revenue, and Lefkofsky believed it could be a billion-dollar-a-year business for Groupon. That's a lot of revenue to love.

Brad Keywell and Sean Smyth had helped lay the groundwork

for the Getaways partnership with Expedia and the Live partnership with Ticketmaster Live Nation when they'd flown to Manhattan for a meeting with Barry Diller, chairman of both Expedia and Ticketmaster, earlier in the year.

The duo ended up spending an hour with the mogul. Smyth found Diller to be enjoyably eccentric. "He has pencils on the conference room table, superfat pencils that are well sharpened, and I guess if they're not sharpened or they're broken he yells at people," Smyth said.

"Listen," Diller had told them, according to Smyth's account. "I'm not going to compete with you guys; you've already won."

But with half of concert tickets going unsold, on average, he thought Groupon could help Live Nation manage its inventory, filling seats with last-minute discounts as needed. After twenty minutes on that topic, the conversation turned to forming a travel partnership with Expedia.

"That's when I really understood if you just start at the top, it's so much faster than trying to come up from the bottom," Smyth said. That was triply true in this case, as Guy Oseary had introduced the company to Live Nation, while Solomon knew the Expedia crew from his Kayak days.

Yet another new niche offering was set to be imported from Groupon U.K. shortly after the launch of Getaways. On September 21, Groupon sent a test e-mail to 3 million U.S. subscribers, or about a twentieth of the subscriber base, with the header "Great deals on Ray-Ban Sunglasses, Golden Tee Arcade System and More."

The stealth Stateside rollout of Groupon Goods, the company's direct product-sales play, was spectacular. Offerings included Ray-Ban Aviator sunglasses for $77, a twenty-piece flatware set, a home edition of the *Golden Tee* video game, fashion watches, and $499 memory foam mattresses. The products sold out in less than six hours, generating gross revenue of $1 million, suggesting that Groupon Goods could generate $20 million a day in turnover in the U.S. market. Dealing with resellers kept the margins low, but at high volumes, it looked like a real business.

"It's going to be massive," predicted Chris Muhr, who had recently come to Chicago from running Groupon U.K.

The company next test-launched Groupon Reserve on October 27 in New York City, via reserve.groupon.com. Customers had to receive invite e-mails to join the new "select premium service," which would feature customized deals at high-end restaurants and the like. Gone was Groupon green; these offers would be presented inside black-framed pages with sophisticated lettering and write-ups that eschewed Groupon's absurdist humor.

"As a member of Reserve, you will occasionally receive exclusive offers for premium experiences," the introductory note from Mason read. The first Reserve deal was $70 for a three-course prix fixe meal for two at the Manhattan outlet of upscale Italian restaurant chain Bice. As with so many of the company's initiatives, Reserve had a humorous precursor in Groupöupon, a 2010 April Fool's Day joke billed as "An exclusive, invitation-only premium marketplace designed to enhance your status" and offering such deals as a $250,000 Money Collage "formed of authentic U.S. currency." (Reserve morphed in early 2012 into Groupon VIP, which gives subscribers early access to deals and other perks for $30 a year.)

Perhaps inspired by Montgomery Ward's example of creating the mythology of Rudolph the Red-Nosed Reindeer as a Christmas sales tool, Groupon also started its own holiday complete with silly traditions and an animal mascot. Grouponicus, as the "age-old wintertime Groupon holiday" was known, happened to start right around Thanksgiving when holiday shoppers flocked to the Web. Groupo The Bargain Bird, a furry blue creature with arms, legs, and a green serpent for a tail, began promoting Grouponicus on November 22, 2010, but the celebration and its attendant online storefront really kicked into high gear at the end of 2011. By bringing together special deals from its key new channels—Groupon Goods and Groupon Getaways—along with above-average G1 gifts, the company generated more than half a billion dollars of revenue in the fourth quarter. If Groupon could become a top online shopping destination during the all-important holiday season, the payoff would be phenomenal. Remember, Amazon really started to take off only after it offered free holiday shipping. Grouponicus might have been Groupon's silliest-sounding initiative yet, but it was deadly serious for the bottom line.

At this rate, if 2011 ended with Groupon rolling out a national chain of dollar stores it wouldn't have been a shock. But could the everything-but-the-kitchen-sink approach hobble the company's core daily-deals business?

JUNE 2, 2011

Even as Groupon was launching a flurry of new sales channels—another case of mirroring Amazon's early land-grab expansion strategy—the company decided it was ready to go public. Andrew Mason was in New York City on the big day, but Rob Solomon was still in Chicago, just days away from the end of his transition period.

He was polishing off an order of calamari at a windswept outdoor café a few blocks from Groupon headquarters at the exact moment the IPO filing was announced, and he took the opportunity to deliver a clear warning about his successor in the COO role.

Georgiadis, who had served as chief marketing officer at decidedly old-school Discover Card before moving on to Google and then Groupon, was "a very big-company, non-start-up person," Solomon said. "It'll be interesting to see how the place changes."

He didn't seem to think Groupon was changing for the better. In terms of restructuring the sales function and other core operations, "The big question mark is do you have to do it incrementally or right away?" he said, squeezing some lemon onto the golden-fried rings. "In a thing like this, you have to be careful because there is magic to how it all works. There's the culture thing. They have to get it right. I'm not the right person to put in that structure. But Margo is probably the right person two years from now. She's going to have to do it not like she's trained to do it, but do it more incrementally, in a way that works for Groupon. Andrew will push her to do that. And Eric will make sure of that. He has a very firm grasp on what happens and what doesn't happen. And if she screws it up, she won't be here long."

Solomon swiped a crispy clump of tentacles through a dish of spicy cocktail sauce, popped the squid into his mouth, and grinned. Groupon was somebody else's problem now. But he was going to enjoy watching how it all turned out. The Dude abides.

Meanwhile, Andrew Mason was delivering a refreshingly unorthodox letter to prospective investors in the company's S-1 filing:

> On the day of this writing, Groupon's over 7,000 employees offered more than 1,000 daily deals to 83 million subscribers across 43 countries and have sold to date over 70 million Groupons. Reaching this scale in about 30 months required a great deal of operating flexibility, dating back to Groupon's founding.
>
> Before Groupon, there was The Point—a website launched in November 2007 after my former employer and one of my co-founders, Eric Lefkofsky, asked me to leave graduate school so we could start a business. The Point is a social action platform that lets anyone organize a campaign asking others to give money or take action as a group, but only once a "tipping point" of people agree to participate.
>
> I started The Point to empower the little guy and solve

the world's unsolvable problems. A year later, I started Groupon to get Eric to stop bugging me to find a business model. Groupon, which started as a side project in November 2008, applied The Point's technology to group buying. By January 2009, its popularity soaring, we had fully shifted our attention to Groupon.

I'm writing this letter to provide some insight into how we run Groupon. While we're looking forward to being a public company, we intend to continue operating according to the long-term focused principles that have gotten us to this point. These include:

We aggressively invest in growth. We spend a lot of money acquiring new subscribers because we can measure the return and believe in the long-term value of the marketplace we're creating. In the past, we've made investments in growth that turned a healthy forecasted quarterly profit into a sizable loss. When we see opportunities to invest in long-term growth, expect that we will pursue them regardless of certain short-term consequences.

We are always reinventing ourselves. In our early days, each Groupon market featured only one deal per day. The model was built around our limitations: We had a tiny community of customers and merchants. As we grew, we ran into the opposite problem. Overwhelming demand from merchants, with nine-month waiting lists in some markets, left merchant demand unfilled and contributed to hundreds of Groupon clones springing up around the world. And our customer base grew so large that many of our merchants had an entirely new problem: Struggling with too many customers instead of too few.

To adapt, we increased our investment in technology and released deal targeting, enabling us to feature different deals for different subscribers in the same market based on their personal preferences. In addition to providing a more relevant customer experience, this helped us to manage the flow of customers and opened the Groupon marketplace to more merchants, in turn diminishing a reason for clones to exist.

Today, we are pursuing models of reinvention that would not be possible without the critical mass of customers and merchants we have achieved. Groupon NOW, for example, allows customers to pull deals on demand for immediate redemption, and helps keep merchants bustling throughout the day.

Expect us to make ambitious bets on our future that distract us from our current business. Some bets we'll get right, and others we'll get wrong, but we think it's the only way to continuously build disruptive products.

We are unusual and we like it that way. We want the time people spend with Groupon to be memorable. Life is too short to be a boring company. Whether it's with a deal for something unusual, such as fire dancing classes, or a marketing campaign such as Grouspawn, we seek to create experiences for our customers that make today different enough from yesterday to justify getting out of bed. While weighted toward the measurable, our decision-making process also considers what we feel in our gut to be great for our customers and merchants, even if it can't be quantified over a short time horizon.

Our customers and merchants are all we care about. After selling out on our original mission of saving the world to start hawking coupons, in order to live with ourselves, we vowed to make Groupon a service that people love using. We set out to upturn the stigmas created by traditional discounting services, trusting that nothing would be as crucial to our long-term success as happy customers and merchants. We put our phone number on our printed Groupons and built a huge customer service operation, manned in part with members of Chicago's improv community. We developed a sophisticated, multi-stage process to pick deals from high quality merchants with vigorously fact-checked editorial content. We built a dedicated merchant services team that works with our merchant partners to ensure satisfaction. And we have a completely open return policy, giving customers a refund if they ever feel like Groupon let them down. We do these things to make our customers and merchants happy, knowing that market success would be a side effect.

We believe that when once-great companies fall, they don't lose to competitors, they lose to themselves—and that happens when they stop focusing on making people happy. As such, we do not intend to be reactive to competitors. We will watch them, but we won't distract ourselves with decisions that aren't designed primarily to make our customers and merchants happy.

We don't measure ourselves in conventional ways. There are three main financial metrics that we track closely. First, we track gross profit, which we believe is the best proxy for the value we're creating. Second, we measure free cash flow—there is no better metric for long-term financial stability. Finally, we use a third metric to measure our financial performance—Adjusted Consolidated Segment Operating Income, or Adjusted CSOI. This metric is our consolidated segment operating income before our new subscriber acquisition costs and certain non-cash charges; we think of it as our operating profitability before marketing costs incurred for long-term growth.

If you're thinking about investing, hopefully it's because, like me, you believe that Groupon is better positioned than any company in history to reshape local commerce. The speed of our growth reflects the enormous opportunity before us to create a more efficient local marketplace. As with any business in a 30-month-old industry, the path to success will have twists and turns, moments of brilliance and other moments of sheer stupidity. Knowing that this will at times be a bumpy ride, we thank you for considering joining us.

Andrew Mason

TWENTY-SIX

As analysts and journalists pored over Mason's letter and the rest of Groupon's prospectus, they raised more red flags than a Soviet May Day celebration. For instance, the filing revealed for the first time that the company had used 86 percent of its last two investment rounds to cash out Eric Lefkofsky, Brad Keywell, Andrew Mason, and other insiders to the tune of, like, a billion dollars.

Many commentators shared Rob Solomon's view that the size of the insider payday was unseemly for a company with an unproven business model. And by setting aside just $151 million for acquisitions, working capital, and general expenses, Groupon left itself vulnerable to a cash crisis if deep-pocketed competitors rapidly drove down deal margins or other operational speed bumps arose.

And then there was the fact that Groupon had never turned an annual profit, despite past public statements to the contrary from Mason, Marc Samwer, and other executives. According to the company, Groupon was profitable in some quarters in 2009 and 2010, which made these statements technically accurate when made. But there was another reason why leadership had painted such a rosy picture of the financials: Groupon was using a non-standard accounting metric called "adjusted consolidated segment operating income" that made its bottom line look much healthier than standard measures would have.

ACSOI—pronounced like someone spitting out overly salty Chinese food ("Ack, soy!")—broke out Groupon's marketing expenses related to acquiring subscribers, under the theory that once the company reached full scale, it could radically reduce that outlay. But critics doubted the costs of signing up new customers would ever be negligible, and they viewed the creation of such a metric outside of generally accepted accounting principles, known as GAAP, with suspicion. Even though the total ACSOI expenses were in the SEC S-1 filing for all to see, removing them from the top-line equation led some analysts to believe the company was trying to pull a fast one on unsophisticated investors who might not look beyond the deceptively rosy figures.

Speaking of which, the S-1 reported Groupon's top-line revenue in another non-standard way by using gross sales figures that included money simply passing through the company's hands on the way to its merchant clients. In other words, if Groupon split half of the proceeds from a ten-dollar offer with a merchant, it would still book the entire ten bucks as top-line revenue even though five dollars would be paid directly to the client. Again, the net figures were included in Groupon's filing as well, but news reports suggested that the company's top-line revenue figures were too good to be true.

If the gross sales issue seems confusing, think of an example from childhood: When your favorite uncle handed you two five-dollar bills and told you to give one to your sister, how much trouble would you get into with your parents if you claimed you'd just made ten bucks? Even if you planned to slip your sister her fiver after dinner, it'd look like you were trying to pull a fast one, wouldn't it?

It turned out that the Securities and Exchange Commission didn't like those aspects of Groupon's S-1 filing, either, and regulators promised to ground Groupon's IPO until the company addressed all of their concerns.

"We note your use of the non-GAAP measure Adjusted Consolidated Segment Operating Income, which excludes, among other items, online marketing expense," the SEC told Groupon in its June 29 response to the S-1 filing. "It appears that online marketing expense is a normal, recurring operating cash expenditure of the company. Your removal of this item from your results of operations creates a non-GAAP measure that is potentially misleading to readers. Please revise your non-GAAP measure accordingly."

Regulators then asked why Groupon would record its gross sales as top-line revenue, since "a Groupon is a means for the customer to purchase a product or service from a merchant at a discounted price," and thus not all of the bucks stopped with Groupon.

The SEC also trained its sights on the insider cash-outs, writing: "You disclose . . . that you raised net proceeds of $1.1 billion through the sale of common and preferred stock and that you used $941.7 million of these proceeds to redeem shares of your common and preferred stock, with the remainder being used to fund acquisitions and for working capital and general corporate purposes. Please explain why you used most of the proceeds of these stock sales to redeem stock rather than to fund your aggressive growth strategy."

In language equally dry, the SEC added: "Please balance the discussion of Mr. Mason's belief that 'Groupon is better positioned than any company in history to reshape local commerce' by noting the company's net losses and competitive landscape. Provide the basis for Mr. Mason's belief. Also disclose that

Mr. Mason's belief may not translate into investment returns for potential purchasers in the offering."

Translation: You've gotta be kidding.

As if Groupon's attorneys didn't have enough problems tap-dancing their way through this minefield to get the IPO approved, both Lefkofsky and Mason made statements during the SEC-mandated quiet period that were so ill considered the company had to amend its S-1 form twice to walk them back.

Lefkofsky got the ball rolling with Cory Johnson, a hard-charging Bloomberg News reporter. Johnson reached Lefkofsky on his cell phone while he was driving on the Kennedy Expressway to his home in Chicago's north suburbs the day after the IPO filing, when the clock had started ticking on the quiet period designed to let the company's prospectus do all the talking to investors.

The reporter—who later made his personal views on the company clear when he tweeted, "Groupon's massaging of numbers makes Kobe beef look taut"—informed Lefkofsky that Bloomberg soon would run a story looking at his sometimes-controversial early business dealings with his companies Starbelly .com, Echo Global Logistics, and InnerWorkings. Lefkofsky, who's excitable on the best of days, was pissed.

"There was an article coming out," he said. "The reporter was going to talk about lawsuits I had been in ten years ago. So my attitude was, 'What are you doing drumming up stuff that's totally disconnected to Groupon and old news to begin with?' And at this point I had talked to Bloomberg quite often, so for some reason I felt compelled to talk to him."

The lawsuits in question were connected to a firm Lefkofsky and Keywell had run that collapsed in the dot-com bust, but only after they had sold the company. That sequence of events drove some of the harsh critiques of Lefkofsky's big pre-IPO Groupon cash-out. He's been asked about the situation often enough that he addressed it on his personal blog at Lefkofsky .com in a post headlined "Early Years" that starts with an account of a carpet business he started during his freshman year at the University of Michigan. He then writes:

My second business was Mascot Sportswear, a company that made t-shirts with college logos. We focused on school mascots and developed a $4 circular t-shirt program for JC Penney stores in the Midwest. The company grew, and I sold it shortly after I started law school at U of M. When I graduated, I joined up with my friend Brad Keywell and bought a Wisconsin-based company called Brandon Apparel Group which made children's licensed apparel. We bought the company when it was doing about $2 million in annual sales and we leveraged it up to about $20 million. Along with our sales growth came lots of debt which eventually crippled the company when fashion trends changed in the late 90's.

In the midst of trying to save a dying business, Brad and I decided to switch industries altogether and jump on the Internet bandwagon that was raging at the time. In March of 1999, we started a company called Starbelly.com, which used the Internet to dis-intermediate the promotional products market. In May of 1999 we raised $1.5m, in July we raised another $8m, and in December of that year we sold the company for $240 million in stock just before the Internet bubble burst. Unfortunately the company that acquired Starbelly, HALO, was itself a failed roll-up and the stock they gave us became largely worthless. After a year as HALO's COO, I left and a few months later started my second technology company, InnerWorkings, which sought to make the printing industry more efficient by finding open capacity. Unlike Starbelly, InnerWorkings was a company with lots of revenues and profits, and it eventually went public in 2006. Around that same time, Brad, who had been working for Sam Zell, joined me to start a company called Echo, which used technology to disrupt the transportation space by finding the right truck moving in the right direction at the right time. Echo grew even faster than InnerWorkings, and it too went public a few years later. In June of 2006, Brad and I started MediaBank, which is a software-as-a-service (SAAS) business using technology to route media in real time. MediaBank has also grown rapidly and today, approximately $50 billion of advertising is routed through its systems.

It's an unapologetic account by someone who doesn't feel responsible for the dot-com bust and isn't going to lose a lot of sleep over the fact that he and Keywell exhibited perfect timing in selling Starbelly for a huge payday just before the bottom dropped out of the technology market. Still, they later faced a HALO shareholder lawsuit settled in 2004 that reproduced an e-mail Lefkofsky had sent about the company: ". . . lets start having fun . . . lets get funky . . . lets announce everything . . . lets be WILDLY positive in our forecasts . . . lets take this thing to the extreme . . . if we get wacked on the ride down-who gives a shit. . . . THE TIME TO GET RADICAL IS NOW , , , WE HAVE NOTHING TO LOSE. . . ."

The highly caffeinated e-mail provided color for skeptical profiles of Lefkofsky, including one that ran in *Fortune* in June 2011 under the headline "The Checkered Past of Groupon's Chairman."

Lefkofsky knew the Bloomberg story was heading down a similar path, but he was under the impression that the five-minute conversation with Johnson was confidential: "The reporter said, 'Let me interview you.' And I said, 'I don't want to be interviewed until I see the piece.' I thought it was clear to him that the conversation was off the record, and he apparently decided that it wasn't off the record."

When the story ran on June 6 over Groupon's request that it be killed, it quoted Lefkofsky as saying, "I'm going to be in technology for a long time. I'm going to start a lot of companies. These are not sham companies. These are great businesses. InnerWorkings is profitable. Echo is profitable. Groupon is going to be wildly profitable."

Adding to what he viewed as the reporter's failure to treat the conversation as off the record, Lefkofsky believes he was misquoted. "The comment I think I made was, 'What company would go public that doesn't think it's going to be wildly profitable?'" he said. After pausing a moment, he added, "That's what I think I said. I mean, it's hard to remember given that I was in a car, but I don't recall saying, 'Groupon's going to be wildly profitable.'"

The conversation wasn't recorded, so it's impossible to know exactly what was said, but Bloomberg and the reporter stood by the story. Regardless of the wording of Lefkofsky's statement, or if the chat was confidential, he later called the exchange "a huge mistake by me for even talking to him in the first place." The report helped fuel a snakebit run of bad publicity that would last well into the fall.

Mason was overseas when the story broke. "I don't remember it being that significant," he said. "There was a lot of press, but internally I think it was like a day of, 'That's annoying, we shouldn't have said that.'" So, if there was one painful lesson

Groupon learned in 2011, it was to keep bad press in perspective and soldier on as the business continued to explode.

"At that point it was just one more thing in the circus of IPO," Mason said.

As quickly as the controversy blew over inside Groupon, Lefkofsky's statement certainly caught the SEC's attention. In the agency's June 29 letter to Groupon, regulators cited the Bloomberg story and said: "Please provide your analysis of how this statement is consistent with the disclosure in your prospectus about the company's financial condition and prospects."

On July 14, Groupon refiled its prospectus with the SEC, saying of the infamous quote: "The reported statement does not accurately or completely reflect Mr. Lefkofsky's views and should not be considered by prospective investors in isolation or at all." In a letter that day to the agency, Groupon's attorneys added: "Mr. Lefkofsky's disavowal of the reported statement as an accurate and full assessment of his views and his good faith intent to avoid any publicity relating to the Company is evidenced by the Company's request that Bloomberg not publish the alleged statement."

Groupon proposed only a partial retreat on the ACSOI question, however, telling the SEC that the company found it an important internal tracking measurement. It suggested keeping the metric in the S-1 but modifying the prospectus to "advise investors that Adjusted CSOI is an internal performance measure and should not be relied upon as a valuation metric."

Regulators' response to that position was, essentially: Why don't you just remove ACSOI from the revenue statement altogether? Groupon's attorneys, knowing when they were licked, wisely agreed.

The company similarly pushed back on the gross revenue

question, arguing that since the Groupon Promise obliged it to refund the full deal purchase price to unsatisfied customers even after merchants were paid, the full amount should be booked as revenue. The company had received advice to that effect from its accounting firm, Ernst & Young. Groupon's attorneys also pointed out that a "gross profit" line farther down on the prospectus "reflects the gross revenue less the cost of the vouchers (that is, the payments to the merchants), and therefore, is essentially the same as a 'net' revenue figure."

When the unmoved regulators told Groupon to just stop booking the merchant payments as revenue, the company again complied. This was a particularly painful change, however. In a September 16 letter to the SEC, the company's attorneys acknowledged that the change would need to come in the form of a revenue restatement. As a result, Groupon's 2010 revenues officially dropped by more than half, from $745.3 million to $312.9 million. And talk about gross: The number for the first nine months of 2011 fell from $2.8 billion to $1.1 billion. Of course, the gross billings were still readily available in Groupon's S-1 filing, but making that definitional change in the top line, which Mason said corrected a mistake "equivalent to putting your fork on the wrong side of the plate," led to another round of scare headlines and a huge headache for a leadership team eager to get the IPO done.

Finally, Groupon addressed the nagging cash-out question by telling the SEC that "the decision to use such net proceeds to redeem shares was made by management and the board of directors based on an assessment that the Company's projected cash flow from future operations would be sufficient to support the Company's growth strategy."

Translation: Who needs a rainy-day fund when there's nothing but blue skies ahead?

* * *

"The beating surprised us," Mason said after Groupon made all of the S-1 changes, including restating the revenue. "Nobody anticipated that ACSOI would be a problem. Looking at it now, I can completely understand why people would be skeptical.

"The public has a healthy skepticism for companies that make up metrics just because there is a history of correlation between making up metrics and shady companies," he continued. "So I guess looking at that it's like, 'Okay, I can see.' It was just my naiveté. I'm surprised that other people, like our bankers, didn't say, 'Hey, usually making up metrics doesn't work out so well.'"

Mason was a stand-up guy. He always took responsibility for Groupon's missteps. And yet, when it came to the stumbles that generated the biggest backlash, he tended to suggest he'd been victimized by bad advice. The ad agency should have put the brakes on that Super Bowl campaign. Those bankers should have warned Groupon not to insert a made-up metric into their IPO prospectus. The accountants were the ones who'd said to book merchant payments as top-line revenue.

That was all true, as far as it went. The problem is, it didn't go very far. In each of those cases, an experienced leader would have rigorously questioned the advice Mason so readily accepted, sometimes even as senior executives were urging him to reject it. Seasoned CEOs know it's always their ass—and their company's reputation—on the line. After they get burned a few times by inept advisers, their bullshit detectors get better. Just because Mason had not foreseen these events did not in any way mean they were unforeseeable. One of the tricks to enjoying a good long run as CEO is separating the good advice from the bad, and Mason hadn't mastered that yet.

TWENTY-SEVEN

Not six weeks after Lefkofsky got called on the carpet by the SEC, Mason bought himself and Groupon a passel of trouble when he sent a lengthy all-staff e-mail on August 25 rebutting the negative press that had been heaped on the company. The memo was immediately leaked to Kara Swisher of *The Wall Street Journal*, who regularly out-scooped everyone when it came to Groupon. Henry Blodget of *Business Insider* flat-out stated what many in the press were thinking: "Groupon Tries Sneaky New Way to Get Around SEC 'Quiet Period' Rules—Think the SEC Will Notice?"

Interestingly, the story Mason cited in the opening of his letter wasn't from one of the usual suspects in the tech press; it was written by Nicholas Jackson, an associate editor of *The Atlantic*.

Dear Groupon,

This weekend, I did a Google News search on our company—my first in a while. The first story that popped up was called "The Fall of Groupon: Is the Daily Deals Site Running Out of Cash?" I laughed when I read the headline (in the car by myself, weirdly). First—with this article, the degree to which we're getting the shit kicked out of us in the press had finally crossed the threshold from "annoying" to "hilarious." Second, I was struck by the irony—I had just finished a board meeting last Wednesday saying this to myself: I've never been more confident and excited about the future of our business.

I realize that this sounds like the kind of thing that CEOs say when they're trying to pep people up. First of all —I'm all about not pepping people up. If you don't believe me, just ask my fiancée, Jenny "why don't you ever say anything nice about me" Gillespie. Want another example? Look at the magazine covers in our lobby, which are there to make you sad by reminding you of the impermanence of success.

I'm going to spend the rest of this email explaining why I'm so excited. You need some ammo to argue back against your blog-reading "friends" (silently argue in your mind, that is—you can't actually say any of this yet), and I've been told that the "what have you ever done with your life that's so great?" rebuttal isn't working as well for you guys as it has for me.

While we've bitten our tongues and allowed insane accusations (like in the article above) to go unchallenged publicly, it's important to me that you have the context necessary to brush this stuff off.

I'll summarize my excitement with four points: 1) Growth in our core business is strong, 2) Our investments in the future—businesses like Getaways & NOW—look great, 3) We are pulling away from competition, and 4) We've built a great team that I would pit against anyone. In other words, all the stuff that one would want to look good? It looks good.

Many of the long-term unknowns of our business are becoming known, and we like the answers. I will now elaborate in a level of financial detail that will give [CFO] Jason Child a stomach ulcer.

1. GROWTH IN THE CORE BUSINESS

Thanks to a tremendous effort by our sales team, August in the U.S. is shaping up to be a pivotal month. It appears that revenues will grow by about 12% over last month (which is a lot), while we cut our marketing expenses by 20% in the same period.

Beyond their obvious goodness, these numbers are important because they answer one of the main criticisms thrown at us in the past few months, relating to a metric we put in the S-1 called ACSOI (adjusted consolidated segment operating income) to help people understand how we think about marketing expenses. The reason everyone in the world seems to hate ACSOI is that it makes us look magically profitable by subtracting a bunch of our customer acquisition marketing costs from our expenses. The reason we didn't realize everyone in the world would hate ACSOI (no, it's not the same reason we didn't realize everyone in the world would hate our Super Bowl ad) is that we think it actually does a pretty good job at describing our marketing expenses in a steady state—we just didn't realize there would be so many skeptics. I think it's worth going deep on this one more time—brace yourself.

Our internal forecast shows two different types of marketing: what I'll call "normal marketing"—which is NOT excluded from ACSOI—and "customer acquisition marketing," which is. The way Groupon spends on marketing is unique in three ways:

1. We are currently spending more than just about any

company ever on marketing—in Q2, we spent nearly 20% of our net revenue on marketing, while a typical company spends less than 5%. Why do we spend so much? The simple answer is "because it works." But that's only part of what makes our situation special.

2. Our marketing—at least the customer acquisition marketing that we remove from ACSOI—is designed to add people to our own long-term marketing channel—our daily email list. Once we have a customer's email, we can continually market to them at no additional cost. Compare this to Johnson and Johnson, McDonald's, or most other companies. If I'm a Johnson, and I'm trying to sell you a box of Band Aids, I have to keep spending money on commercials and magazine ads and stuff to remind you about how sweet Band Aids are, even after you've bought your first box. With Groupon, we just spend money one time to get you on our email list, and then every day we email you a reminder of the sweetness of our metaphorical Band Aid. There is no cost of reacquisition—that's unusual (and we created ACSOI to point that out). If Johnson wanted to follow the Groupon strategy, he would have to start a free daily newspaper about bandages and then run Band Aid ads in it every day.

3. Eventually, we'll ramp down marketing just as fast as we ramped it up, reducing the customer acquisition part of our marketing expenses (the piece that we remove in ACSOI) to nominal levels. We are spending a ton now because we're acquiring as many subscribers as we can as quickly as we can. We aren't paying attention to marketing budget (just marketing ROI) in the way a normal company would, because we know that even if we wanted to continue to spend at these levels, we would eventually run out of new

subscribers to acquire. So our customer acquisition spend drops severely to reflect the fact that eventually we'll run out of people we can add to our email list. We view this internally as a very large one-time expense and then our job forever after will be to continually convert these subscribers into customers and to make sure our customers keep buying from us. Ongoing, the normal marketing dollars we spend are not something we would remove from our internal calculation of ACSOI.

I tried my best to explain this simply, but it's not lost on me that if you actually understood this, you probably had to read it three times. It's not easy stuff. It's much easier to assume that we're goons. So people can be forgiven for being suspicious. In fact, feel a little bad about how downhearted the critics will be when we don't turn out to be a Ponzi scheme—those are good impulses for journalists to have, and I hope our non-evil ways don't destroy their spirits.

Anyway, there's a reason that I just went on about ACSOI. One of the questions that skeptics ask is, "when you ramp down marketing, won't revenues stop growing as well? Aren't you just buying growth?" Over the past several months we've been consistently reducing our marketing spend and yet revenues are still increasing at a significant pace. In Q1 of this year, marketing represented 32.3% of our net revenues. By the end of Q2 it had fallen to 19.4%. And it has continued to fall over the past several months all because we've been investing in our own long-term marketing channel—our email list.

Internationally we see the same trends—marketing is down, but revenues are up—every country is either losing less or making more. Even in young markets like Korea, where we're still making massive investments, we're seeing unprecedented growth. We started building our Korean team this January, despite the presence of two competitors that were larger than any we'd previously battled from behind. Thanks to the brilliant execution of the Korean team, we are set to be the market leader within months. We've never had a country grow as fast as Korea!

What about our joint-venture with Tencent in China? Did you read the article that Gaopeng's CEO has kidnapped the first born children of all our employees and is putting them to work building a laser beam he'll use to slice the moon in half? It turns out that that one isn't true either. China is definitely a different market, but every month we inch closer to profitability. As has been our strategy in launching other countries—Germany, France, and the UK included—our China growth strategy was to hire quickly and manage out the bottom performers. So far, that strategy has improved our competitive position in China from #3,000 to #8. Will we one day reach the dominant status we enjoy in most (come on, Switzerland!) other countries? It's too soon to tell, but there's no question in my mind that we're building a business that will be around for the long haul.

2. NEW BUSINESS LINES ARE BOOMING

Travel and Product are enormous opportunities. After only a few months, they're already making up 20% of revenue in some countries. We sold $2M worth of mattresses in the UK—in one day! Groupon Getaways will do $10M in its first calendar month—which you might think is awesome, but we're actually disappointed with those results because we know how much better we'll be doing soon.

While there's still a ton of work to do, Groupon Now!

continues to see weekly double digit growth. The model works and I believe it will play a major part in the future of our global business as more merchants and customers join the marketplace.

3. WE ARE PULLING AWAY FROM COMPETITION

If there's a question I've received from Groupon skeptics more than any other, it's, "how will you fend off the competition—especially massive companies like Google and Facebook?" I could give a dozen reasons to bet on Groupon, but it's impossible to predict the future or the actions of others. Well, now the sleeping giants have woken up—and the numbers are showing that what was proven true with literally thousands of other competitors is just as true with the incumbents of the Internet: it's kind of hard to build a Groupon. And since anyone with an Internet connection can track the performance of our competitors, I can be more specific:

Google Offers is small and not growing. In the three markets where we compete, we are 450% of their size.

Yelp is small and not growing. In the 15 markets where we compete, our daily deals are 500% of their size.

LivingSocial's U.S. local business is about 1/3rd our size in revenue (and smaller in GP) and has shrunk relative to us in the last several months. This, in part, appears to be driving them toward short-sighted tactics to buy revenue, like buying gift certificates from national retailers at full price and then paying out of their own pocket to give the appearance of a 50% off deal. Our marketing team has tested this tactic enough to know that it's generally a bad idea, and not a profitable form of customer acquisition.

Facebook sales are harder to track, but are even less significant at present.

My point is not that our competitors will fail—some may actually develop sustainable businesses, or even grow—after all, local commerce is an enormous market. The real point is that our business is a lot harder to build than people realize and our scale creates competitive advantages that even the largest technology companies are having trouble penetrating. And with the launch of NOW, I suspect our competition will have an even harder time in light of the natural barriers to entry that are needed to build a real-time local deals marketplace.

4. OUR TEAM

This is the fluffiest of the four points, but maybe the most important—we've built a global team of hungry entrepreneurial operators and seasoned executives that rivals any team I know of. Almost every day, I find myself in a scenario where I silently think, "I can't believe I got this person to work for me—that failure of judgment is perhaps their single flaw."

I point out the team because while today the business is strong and it appears we must endure success for awhile longer (despite its impermanence), we will inevitably be challenged with issues we didn't predict—and when that happens, the quality of our team will be a deciding factor in our ultimate long-term success.

FINAL THOUGHTS

I wrote this email because when I read some of the press this weekend, I realized a rational person could read this stuff and wrongly conclude that we're in trouble. The irony is hopefully clear: We've never been stronger.

And while we've refrained from defending ourselves publicly, you've continued to create our best defense, with every department innovating new practices that are taking our business to the next level. Thanks for staying tough, determined, and agile throughout this process. For now we must patiently and silently endure a bit more public criticism as we prepare to birth this IPO baby—a breed for which there are no epidurals. If there's a silver lining, it's that we're almost on the other side, and the negativity leaves us well-positioned to exceed expectations with an IPO baby that, having seen the ultrasound, I can promise you is not one of those uglies.

I've been as candid as possible—hope this sheds some light on things. Reply with your questions if anything remains unclear. Amidst all this, I hope you remember what we're doing here—we are making history together. I guess you don't get to build something that reshapes the local commerce ecosystem without getting a few bruises. I'm so proud of the work we're doing, and I feel extraordinarily lucky to work on what I think is the best thing that's happened to small businesses since the telephone. We've invented something that is catalyzing millions of dollars of local commerce every single day in 45 countries and fills the lives of millions of customers with unforgettable experiences—it's pretty remarkable.

Looking forward to getting this behind us!

Andrew

P.S.: I almost forgot to address the nonsense about us running out of money in the article above. If you apply the same logic used in the article, you'd have concluded long ago that companies like Amazon and Wal-Mart were running out of cash too. Both have often had payables far in excess of their cash. Finance geeks call this a working capital deficit. It's normal, manageable and a lot of folks actually believe it's a good thing and would kill to get paid from their customers long before they have to pay their suppliers. We are generating cash, not losing it—we generated $25M in cash last quarter alone, adding to the $200M we had before. In other words, we're doing the opposite of running out of money.

Mason drafted the memo shortly after running into an employee at a local bar. She wanted to know what was going on with the company's financials because her parents had expressed concern. She was worried about her job security.

"I was like, 'Jesus Christ!'" the CEO said. "It was just affecting people internally in an absurd way, in a way that wasn't fair. I have to be able to communicate with my employees. The costs of not communicating with them are greater than the risks of communicating."

Noting that his all-staff e-mails are not uncommon, Mason insisted he never intended for the memo to be leaked. "I probably should have considered the possibility of it getting out to the public more than I did," he said. "But if I had wanted it to get out to the public, I wouldn't have written it in that way. It's kind of weird and crazy in a lot of ways."

The SEC certainly wasn't crazy about it. Only after the agency's questions about Groupon's S-1 filing were made public at the end of December did it become clear how seriously regulators had taken the memo leak.

In phone calls to Groupon's outside counsel on August 31 and September 6, SEC staffers expressed their displeasure. "Provide an analysis of whether Mr. Mason's e-mail constitutes a violation of the Securities Act of 1933," the regulators demanded.

"The public dissemination of Mr. Mason's e-mail was an isolated incident outside of the control of the Company and was not intended to evade the requirements of Section 5 of the Securities Act," Groupon's counsel responded, in part, two days later. "The Company believes that Mr. Mason's e-mail appropriately balanced the Company's need to provide information to employees with its quiet period restrictions."

Not good enough, the SEC said in its follow-up call. Asked to provide more in-depth analysis of why Mason hadn't broken federal securities law, Groupon's attorneys danced as fast as they could. "Mr. Mason's e-mail was not a publication or a publicity effort," they wrote. "It was a confidential communication not intended for public release, and it contained reminders to refrain from discussing any aspects of the Company's business. Further, the e-mail was not part of any 'selling effort' . . . no part of the offering will be directed to employees, and the e-mail did not discuss the terms of the proposed offering."

Groupon agreed to additional disclosures in the prospectus to warn potential investors not to rely on the CEO's e-mail when making their decision. The attorneys' nearly eleven pages of analysis also contended that there was no violation because "Mr. Mason's e-mail was limited to factual business information . . . and does not contain projections or other forward-looking information."

Groupon's counsel sidestepped the part where Mason said the IPO was "well-positioned to exceed expectations." Certainly, "Our investments in the future—businesses like Getaways & NOW—look great"; "I believe [Groupon Now!] will play a major part in the future of our global business"; and "Eventually, we'll ramp down marketing just as fast as we ramped it up" all seemed a little projection-y. But having sternly made its point, the SEC chose to drop the matter.

If regulators truly had wanted to go after Mason, they likely would have interviewed Swisher, the journalist who obtained his memo and posted it on her *Wall Street Journal*–owned digital-news site, All Things D. But when the pre-IPO corre-spondence between the SEC and Groupon was released on De-cember 28, Swisher saw the controversy her story had caused and tweeted: "Yipes. I am in an SEC lawyerfest and did not even know!"

Swisher confirmed to me that she was not approached by regulators about the leak. "Never once," she said. "Then again, I never return my phone messages." Later, the reporter added, "Their issue was with Groupon, not my talent at getting inter-nal memos."

Even though Mason's e-mail necessitated yet another revision of Groupon's prospectus and generated an additional round of brutal headlines, Lefkofsky insisted the CEO had needed to write it to shore up employee morale. Even the new COO, Georgiadis, backed the play.

And Mason didn't just dash off the letter on the back of a bar napkin. He drafted it over the course of a day and got input from Lefkofsky and CFO Jason Child, as well as his PR team. Despite the joke about giving Child an ulcer, the CFO signed off on the financial details included in the memo.

Ultimately, Mason did not regret sending the note. "We have to stay true to who we are through all this," he said. "We're go-ing to take a certain degree of criticism right now, but the busi-ness is strong and when we get through it we'll be glad that we endured the criticism."

Groupon's attorneys put a less optimistic spin on the situa-tion. "In the face of an extraordinary level of unbalanced specu-lation and negative commentary in the media, including media reports that brought into question the integrity of management and the Company's ability to continue as a going concern, the Company acted in a manner it believed to be responsive to the needs of its employees and consistent with applicable securities laws," they told the SEC. In other words, as the media kept piling on, Groupon's knees were finally starting to buckle, and it needed to push back.

One other shoe dropped around this time as well: Bradford Williams, the VP of global communications who'd come over from VeriSign, left on August 22 after only two months at Groupon. Publicly, Williams and Groupon said it was a joint decision. As Williams put it, "We mutually decided it wasn't a fit."

But, mysteriously, a source identified only as someone "familiar with one view of the situation" told *Business Insider* that Williams had walked because he objected to Mason's quiet-period communication strategy.

"Andrew and . . . [Williams] didn't agree on a lot—[they had] different views on lots of things," the mysterious source said. "Do the math. . . . [Williams] walked out of there last Wednesday. The first thing . . . [Mason] did was send out that memo . . . which . . . [Williams] would have advised strenuously against."

Anyone who actually did do the math would have found problems with the equation. A source familiar with a different view of the situation said early in Williams' tenure that the PR pro worried Mason didn't like him and he was struggling to fit in. Also, whenever you read about a "person close to the situation" commenting on a mid-level departure, odds are good that the anonymous source is in fact the "person who was pushed out the door." In this case, it's unlikely an insider would go to bat for Williams after two months. It doesn't add up.

When asked what had happened, Williams replied, via e-mail: "I'd only want to comment to the extent I'm part of the story, which, considering I was there for about 8 weeks, I have to question." He refused further comment. Williams truly was a blip on

Groupon's radar screen, but stories criticizing the company that fall invariably threw in his departure as evidence of a troubled workplace, when it likely resulted from nothing more than a run-of-the-mill bad cultural fit.

There seemed to be a lot of that going around at Groupon.

TWENTY-EIGHT

I like to make things happen," Margo Georgiadis told *Crain's Chicago Business* for a "women to watch" brief heralding her appointment in May. Unfortunately, despite her impressive credentials, she soon became known around Groupon as a drag on the process.

But she was onboard for Groupon's rapid, comprehensive restructuring of its U.S. operations. As Georgiadis described the steps the company had taken, it was easy to see why she had wowed Mason when he met her.

She saw her job as preserving Groupon's essential DNA even while creating more structure around it. And in fact, more than one person who had regular interactions with Georgiadis that spring and summer saw her as a much-needed mature presence. She called Groupon's need to tighten up its processes typical of a company going through explosive growth. Although Groupon was bursting with energy when she arrived, it too often threw bodies at problems instead of pausing to create scalable operations that would first help it go public and then deliver consistent profit growth.

Of course, this was still Groupon, so the overhaul came with a few twists. When it was time to recruit an SVP of operations whom Joe Harrow's customer-service team and Aaron With's editorial crew would report to, for instance, the company hired Hoyoung Pak, whose résumé included work as the stunt double for Donatello in the film *Teenage Mutant Ninja Turtles II: The Secret of the Ooze.*

As soon as Georgiadis came aboard, she started making sense of a system that now sold deals in 580 categories and subcategories. "There was a huge learning about the best deals that you could possibly close in each one of those areas," she said. "The right price points, the right structures, how to present them—and being able to codify all that so we could repeat it over and over and over again."

Using past sales data, Groupon began crafting merchandise plans to maximize the profitability of daily deals. "You have to say, 'In this market, on Monday, we're running a health and beauty, and on Tuesday we're running an activity, and on Wednesday we're going to run a restaurant, instead of just, Close whatever you want and we'll figure it out,' " Georgiadis said.

Across all product lines, Groupon wanted to focus more on the curation end of its business—opening people's eyes to cool and unique experiences instead of just emphasizing the discount aspect. That could mean working with a top restaurant to create a prix fixe menu, as with the Groupon Reserve test. "We want to get away from this concept of being a discount and really focus on this idea of the experience that we're providing, how we put it together," the COO said. The approach could work just as well in Groupon's travel and event-ticketing businesses as in the core daily-deals unit.

But many of the salespeople chafed under this more scientific approach. That was understandable, if frustrating, Georgiadis said. "If you think about the first year, you had these wonderful young, emboldened salespeople that were basically the pioneers of each city. Just go close a bunch of great deals and run them. Every offer was new and different; no one else did it. So they felt like they were independent entrepreneurs; I've built my own book of business, I've put my flag in this city, and I've launched the company. They often did that over and over and over and over, in multiple cities. The issue is, once we get to a different stage in our evolution we don't need just independent entrepreneurs; we have a customer with expectations that we need to satisfy."

After telling salespeople which types of deals to sell when, Groupon worked to sync the product team's focus with the company's operational needs. In late 2010, during the doomed Groupon Stores phase, "the product team started to kind of work in its own silo," Georgiadis said. "People thought, 'Well, if I come up with this new Now product or I do Smart Deals or all these new innovative features, that's going to be what propels us to the next level.' But what we lost sight of is that we're as much sales driven as we are technology driven. It's about a balance, an integration of those two things." Bringing in Amazon veteran Jeff Holden to run the product development team was key to that effort, as was hiring Rich Williams, also from Amazon, to head up global marketing. "We've all existed in those worlds where you get the best of technology and business coming together," Georgiadis said.

This was a time of near-constant reorganizations as the company struggled to scale its processes. "When you grow this fast you realize that what you're doing worked two months ago, but it doesn't work right now," said Steven Walker, the lead designer. "We're constantly doing that. One of the most important things is just realizing when something works and when something doesn't and not waiting to throw it away."

By mid-September, Groupon had already undergone so much

restructuring that some seventeen hundred of Groupon's two thousand U.S. employees "are doing something different than they were five months ago in a material way," the COO said, dubbing the shift of resources from stagnant areas to critical initiatives as "re-gluing the organization back to itself."

With the new roles came new reporting structures designed to cut the gridlock created by Mason overseeing too many managers directly and lessen interdepartmental squabbling. "When I came in, the sales guys were fighting with editorial and editorial was fighting with customer service and city planning was fighting with all of them," Georgiadis recounted. "I spent half my day refereeing. And I said to myself, 'Look, this has nothing to do with being an operator. I'm just a human being. We all need to play on the same team with the same rules.' It's a heck of a lot more fun to win as a team, but it was hard to feel that sense of winning as a team when nobody was really focused on that. The enemy is outside the building."

Workforce quality was a problem as well: Some early hires were no longer suited for their roles, and the newbies often lacked the core crew's entrepreneurial drive. Walker met with Mason one evening that summer. Now that he was managing a large team, Walker asked, "How do I get people to feel how I feel?" When the designer had come aboard as a contract employee, he billed forty hours a week but vowed never to leave the office before Mason.

"How do you get people to walk in and have that kind of ownership, that same feeling that you do about this company after you've been here forever and watched it grow from nothing?" Walker wondered. It was one of the toughest questions faced by any organization moving from infancy to adolescence. Finding the right answer would be essential if Groupon was to enjoy long-term success.

Weeding the workforce also was core to Groupon's restructuring plan. During the IPO road show in October, Andrew Mason would get dinged by headlines claiming that he was about to lay off 10 percent of Groupon's sales force en masse. The truth was, all the process changes finally set up Groupon to cut loose low-performing salespeople on a regular basis and the CEO had simply estimated that the annual turnover could be around 10 percent. In mid-September when I asked Georgiadis how many sales staffers wouldn't make the transition, she said it was still too early to tell—score one for a seasoned corporate hand.

She would say, however, that "our turnover in the first two years was like eight percent. A typical outbound call-center environment is fifty-plus percent. So not everybody is going to be here forever and not everyone's going to make a gazillion dollars and not everybody's going to be a pioneer, and that's hard."

The COO then fired her first salvo at Groupon's office environment: "That's the downside of having a little bit too freewheeling of a culture. International has always been very disciplined in their operations. Here, it was do your own thing, make your own hours. There was not a lot of measuring of performance, not a lot of metrics."

The revamping of the U.S. sales operation was only radical "compared to everyone beer drinking every night and coming whenever they want and no sense of a minimum standard of contribution—it's just such an extreme," Georgiadis lamented. Other members of Groupon's leadership team vehemently disagreed with those characterizations of the workplace culture.

"For a lot of these people it's their first job, so they have no reference point," the COO continued. "The high-performing people are still high performing. They're doing better than ever because they feel empowered. 'Someone's telling me this is the deal to run and this is the opportunity and I can make as much or even more than before.'"

Employees grumbling about the new order stuck in Georgiadis' craw. Coming from McKinsey, Discover Financial Services, and Google, she said, "I've had the privilege of always working for exceptionally high-performing companies that manage their people well. So I personally really care about it. But it's a massive cultural shift of expectations. Sometimes you have to work late and sometimes you have to follow directions and sometimes you can't just do what you want."

Georgiadis to Groupon staff: Grow the fuck up. But not really.

"You have to inspire people that this is why we're doing this, and you have to be really open and transparent," she said. "But in a business of our scale and with the level of maturity of a lot of the people that are working here, it's tricky. It's really tricky."

She bristled at any suggestion that her early experiences at McKinsey had turned her into a classic cost-cutting operator out to impose her ideas on a staff sorely in need of discipline. In customer service, Georgiadis noted, simply sharing industry standard call-answering times had led the staff to improve on its own.

"The sales side is probably the most tricky," she said. That was in part because the compensation structure had gone out of whack. People churning into new territories in the early days could rack up easy sales and outsize paydays. It's tough to roll those habits back.

"There's always that risk of a real entitlement culture," Georgiadis said. "And employees have very high expectations, given how quickly this business has grown and how much money some of them have made. What is a realistic expectation? Most of these people are making four, five, six, seven, eight, nine, ten times what we ever told them they would make in their job. So when it was that fast and easy for a lot of people, how do you keep them realistic? They don't leave because if they compared themselves to any other job they could do they're vastly doing better by orders of magnitude. So they know they need to stay, but they need to change their mind-set."

To that end, Mason and Lefkofsky embraced the idea of bringing in Marc Samwer and his London team to shake up the sales function and harmonize the U.S. and international processes. "The company I think until the spring was two different companies," Georgiadis said.

Unlike Web 1.0 titans such as Google and Amazon, where creating a global template was difficult because the U.S. business had scaled far bigger than the international operations, Groupon had a unique opportunity to adopt a worldwide operating platform early on. This was because the business was rolled out from city to city rather than nationally and overseas clones purchased by Groupon had been ramping up right along with the core U.S. business.

One big stumbling block: "The international business had been much, much more focused on the city-by-city development," Georgiadis noted. "The U.S. had kind of gotten away from that as we scaled, and that loss of focus on winning in New York, winning in Chicago, winning in L.A., had taken us away from the roots of loving and owning each market."

The daily deal, it seemed, was adrift.

TWENTY-NINE

Owning—and mercilessly dominating—markets was a specialty of the Samwers and their top European managers. When Chris Muhr, the hard-charging German head of CityDeal's London office, had announced the company's sale to Groupon to his employees on May 17, 2010, he got a big laugh out of the 150-person-strong British crew by starting off, "I'll try to make this as less emotional as I can."

Certainly, the standard casual dress in the office that day—Muhr himself wore an unfortunate pair of acid-washed jeans—mirrored what you'd encounter at Groupon's Chicago headquarters, and the London staff was just as young. But Muhr and his team were focused relentlessly on one thing: selling as many daily deals as humanly possible. They didn't wait for an editorial team to deliver humorous write-ups. They didn't place a premium on office antics. For instance, the best Muhr could come up with for examples of Groupon-style employee fun in the United Kingdom was that there had been designated high-five days, when staffers were encouraged to slip each other some skin, and a Canada day, when they had to wear Canadian shirts. The London crew simply prided themselves on being CityDeal's top-performing city.

Overall, the CityDeal system, with its city managers owning the performance of each local market, was much more efficient than the Groupon system. In addition, where the U.S. sales organization had one manager for every twenty-five to thirty reps, the European operation kept the number of direct reports per manager to fifteen.

In the United States, a sales manager could oversee one large city, a couple of medium-size ones, and five or six smaller cities. It was too much. In Europe, said Jens Hutzschenreuter, one of the founders of the U.K. team, "we have a very clear model of who is actually responsible for a certain group, preferably one city, and you hold yourself accountable for that city."

Added Marc Samwer, "With the management team the U.S. had in place, they could manage maybe fifty reps but not the eight hundred they had. They couldn't scale. And it's not because they weren't smart enough or good enough; it was simply the sheer number of direct reports."

When it became clear in the summer of 2011 that Groupon needed to raise its sales game and drive the company toward profitability before the IPO, Eric Lefkofsky called Samwer.

"Marc, I spoke to Andrew and he and I agree, you need to come over," the chairman said. "We need to turn it around."

At that point, talk centered around having Samwer come in as a consultant, not the embed he soon became. "In the beginning they thought, if we just explain the model a little bit, how it works, after four weeks we can go home again," Samwer said. "It turned out that, because they just don't have enough managers, it's not just about explaining." It was time for fundamental change. Samwer brought along Muhr and his top London team—which consisted of two other Germans and a Canadian—to supercharge the U.S. sales force.

That did not sit well with SVP of sales Darren Schwartz.

"We don't want to do things like they do," he said. "They're real harsh and they hammer people. So we tried the program that Rob led and we just didn't probably do it right."

Samwer and CityDeal U.K. co-founder Emanuel Stehle had recently introduced the city manager model to Groupon's Brazil operation and had learned a few things about how to export the model beyond Europe.

"When we came to Brazil, we were irritated that the structures weren't as implemented as they should have been," Stehle said. "But in hindsight, I think they did a pretty good job. We came in there and we were expecting them to follow our advice within two or three days. It didn't happen that quickly. But we saw that just by teaching and preaching the principles, you don't achieve much. It's all about the execution. The culture is slightly different in Brazil. They care a lot about empathy and interpersonal relationships, so that's something that we had to take into consideration."

Not a bad tip for the U.S. offices, either, but empathy was not on the agenda for the first Chicago trip. The structural problems with the U.S. approach were apparent to Samwer and Stehle within an hour after they arrived. "The company was going in the wrong direction; that was very clear," Stehle said.

Samwer did not sugarcoat what he perceived as the failings of the Chicago team. "When he got here, within three minutes he was telling me and Andrew we should do some things their way, the right way," Schwartz said. "He laid it on the line."

The meeting soon erupted into a yelling match between Samwer and the sales executive. "He was telling us that we sucked," Schwartz said. "He was really harsh, and the key thing is they have the deal structure that we weren't doing." Where the European operation put the sales function above everything, the U.S. unit had set up city planners in "a separate ivory tower from sales and we always fought with them," Schwartz said. "So Marc came in and within a week he had unraveled everything."

"The company needed that change to get to the next growth phase," Samwer countered. "And it wasn't really a fight with Darren; it was more that we said, 'Listen, a lot of things have to change,' while I think here people thought a little change would be okay."

In fact, Stehle was shocked when he and Samwer arrived at the Chicago office to find Mason in one of the glass-walled cubicles surrounded by twenty-five people going through a complex PowerPoint presentation.

"The key takeaway of that big, big master deck was: Increase deal counts regardless of their quality," Stehle recalled. "When we read this, we couldn't believe it."

Samwer and Stehle excused themselves to grab a bite to eat, but they chewed over the damning sentence from the presentation more than the actual meal.

It turned out, though, that the "deal quality" metric meant something different in the German operation than it did in the United States. The point of the presentation was that a higher density of deals is better for the company assuming high deal quality as a constant—not that Groupon should sacrifice deal quality for density. So, it was a big misunderstanding, one that had the Germans ready to chew some scenery. After lunch, the hard discussions began.

"You have to communicate a lot" to pull off a restructuring, Samwer said. "You have to overcommunicate. You have to repeat. You have to explain and explain and explain. You have to win ambassadors within the organization. For no organization is it easy for change to come from the outside. And since we had built the international business based on CityDeal, we were basically two companies under one umbrella. And I think for the

U.S. it's always not easy. You're used to being the world power. It's not easy for people from International to come and tell you, 'We have developed a much more successful model.' "

The U.K. innovations included "the Glasgow pitch," a sales technique straight out of a David Mamet play that Raj Ruparell, a Canadian who was the only non-German on the core team, developed to help close deals with high-quality merchants. The team also developed the concept of the Perfect Pipeline.

"We said, in a perfect world, how can you keep a certain story line in the deal flow?" Stehle recounted. "You want to have a cool restaurant on a Monday, for example, and you have a spa deal on a Tuesday, you have a go-kart on a Wednesday, and what else can you feature to not bore your subscribers and to not break that story line? That's the concept of the Perfect Pipeline. We brought all these innovations in the U.K. together, and because we executed these ideas that helped you get better deals all the time, the revenue followed. That's exactly what we tried to explain here in the first week as well. There was a lot of skepticism, obviously, but to be fair, the American way is that someone's always embracing change: We want to do better and so we listen to ways of improvement."

Samwer agreed that "the majority said, 'that is great, that is exactly what we were waiting for, finally there's structure for a far too big sales organization.' Of course, there were some people who didn't like change because they felt like either what they're doing is great or they felt threatened by us changing the status quo." But the fact that the Samwers had sold CityDeal in exchange for equity meant the brothers could only score if Groupon became a big public company. So they were committed to spending as much time as necessary to tighten up the North American operation.

This would be no short-term consulting gig; the turnaround

would take as long as a year. Muhr would come in with Stehle, Ruparell, and Hutzschenreuter, who had recently helped Groupon's South Korea operation reach a dominant position.

City planners would now report into sales just like in Europe. The German team was tasked with teaching the Chicago sales leaders the CityDeal system, with its focus on closely managing the sales reps, selling experiential deals, and creating the proper flow of different types of offers from day to day. The idea was that the Germans would then hand the reins back to the local team, but as the months wore on and the results began improving, the consultants became provisional leaders. A lot of what the Germans implemented Schwartz described as "Sales 101—it's not like it's too difficult." Although he felt he had been told to run things differently when he'd come aboard, he also felt willing and able to lead under the new system.

But as Muhr settled in, "very quickly everyone realized he should become SVP of sales because he had done this before," Samwer said.

That's when Mason and Lefkofsky eased Schwartz out.

One day in August, Schwartz came into Lefkofsky's office and asked, "What is going on here? Are these guys actually going to leave?"

"Listen, dude, you don't want this job," Lefkofsky replied. "You've taken us from a million a month to one hundred and twenty million a month, but this job is going to be tough moving forward. It's going to be shit that these guys are good at, and you are not. It's going to be all about operations and execution and scale. Even if you can learn it, you don't want to have to learn it; you don't want to do it. You've done your thing. Raise your hands, declare victory, and help us somewhere else."

Mason gave Schwartz a similar pep talk. "If Eric Lefkofsky was the head of sales at Groupon and these guys came in, they would take over because they are that good, because Marc is that good," he said.

At the time Schwartz thought, *You know what, that's great. I'll do something else. There are plenty of other things to do.*

It's a testament to Schwartz's character and dedication that he was kept on to help run Groupon Live and later the company's "epic deals," such as a $12,500 trip to explore the wreckage of the *Titanic.* A couple of months after their shouting match, Marc Samwer spoke of him with admiration.

Schwartz ultimately accepted that Lefkofsky and Mason's analysis had been shrewd. "Listen, Rob lasted for a year," Schwartz said. "I lasted in that position essentially for two years and I'm still here. If these guys can really do it, then great, let them do it." He was proud that the people he'd installed as regional vice presidents and divisional sales managers were, for the most part, given a chance to execute the new system.

"The one thing that mattered way more than anything about me was that they saw that the people I put in place had value and they didn't just throw the baby out with the bathwater," Schwartz said. "That's what I feel good about."

A transition that started with a couple of U.S. cities in July was fully in place by mid-August. The improvement was immediate. "We are seeing results," Schwartz said in September. "August was up. It was a big step forward and our numbers look great, so it seems like it's working. Chris Muhr is really talented. He also has the people perspective and he is very thoughtful."

With Muhr at the helm, Schwartz felt confident that the only salespeople being driven out of the organization were those who weren't performing. "It's time for them to go," he said. In terms of top sales talent walking because of the change in leadership, "we haven't seen that," he added. The turnaround was well under way.

THIRTY

Under Chris Muhr, Groupon U.S. had indeed enjoyed a spectacular August. Some cities had increased sales 300 percent in five weeks. There were big gains in big cities, including Atlanta and Boston, which also happened to be the company's most mature market outside of Chicago. The daily deal was hardly dead.

"In International, business always comes first," Samwer said. "If necessary, we change a deal one minute before midnight. If a great deal comes in ten minutes before midnight, editorial has to do the write-up, just do it and get it up somehow online. Here, we were told and we're still told, it usually takes ten days, maybe we can fast-track it down to four days. And you get a budget, how much you can fast-track. They behave like AT&T." The international team scoffed at what it considered editorial's sway over the business and how they saw, as Hutzschenreuter put it, "the fun and the voice and the humor as being one of the key tools on how to sell."

"I think they were up to ten steps before a deal actually got live," Hutzschenreuter said.

"As a result, if you brought in a great deal that a lot of people will love, there was no way to launch that deal on a Saturday or on a Sunday or on a Monday," Stehle added. "You had this great deal lying in front of you and you were like, 'Hey, we can sell a lot of them, people will love it, it's the right day of the season, but we have to get it sold now.' But there was a delay of maybe one or two weeks before you could actually launch that deal. That was certainly one of the walls that the guys tried to tear down, and now there's a process for that."

Mason later said that the editorial lead-time question was simply part of the "operational stuff that we're working through." But in terms of putting new deals up at the stroke of midnight, the CEO noted, "The U.K. is a much smaller business than in the U.S. It was like that here when we were a couple hundred people." For his part, Aaron With had a dustup with Marc Samwer similar to the one Schwartz had, but the editor ultimately shortened the approval process in a way that still gave Groupon the time it needed to thoroughly vet and write up deals. Call it an uneasy truce. Given that the U.K. operation's run-and-gun style led to an embarrassing government investigation and settlement in the spring of 2012, it's reasonable to conclude that each side had important lessons to learn from each other.

The biggest thing the international crew did, overall, was redirect focus back toward the daily deal. "One of the things that I see as a constant danger to success is if you don't focus on the main two or three things you need to do right," Muhr said. Otherwise, it was like inviting a glutton to a buffet—too many choices could lead to unhealthy outcomes. "There are so many things you can do once you have a running business and it's so successful, you get distracted very easily," Muhr said. "And you need to concentrate on what's your core business. Where's your strength? Where are you stronger than the Google and the Yahoo! and the eBay, and where can nobody compete with you?

That is something that got lost a little bit in this multitude of options that came out. Too many choices, too many seductions. That is something we readjusted a little bit by saying, 'This is the core business.' That's where we need to be number one."

Getting there also required firing low-performing salespeople who'd been allowed to stick around during the ramp-up. In the early days, with an unknown brand, Groupon had attracted a young sales force, right out of college in most cases. And as the company grew, those folks recruited their friends, who came aboard because it had a reputation as a cool and exciting place to be.

"On the one hand it was great because it created the foundation for what they are," Muhr said. "It's a necessary first step. Even if you look at the U.K. today, you have a different set of people who joined initially compared to who's there now. But what changed is the way we look at recruiting and what we want. We believe we are a big company now, we have some standards, we give people incredible potential to earn money at a very, very early age, and we are not picky about where you're from, how your English is, if you have a Harvard degree. But you have to be excellent in what you're doing. So the filter of what's coming into the company has become a lot tighter, a lot more selective. There's also always been huge talent in the company, so some of the people helping us do this are also from the existing setup. Some of the city managers are from the existing force. It's more mixing it up with the right sort of injection from outside that makes it a very strong team."

The changes left a lot of Groupon salespeople complaining about their new management team. Glassdoor, a site where online employees rate their workplaces, saw a spike in negative Groupon notices from the sales team in the late summer and fall of 2011. A sampling of dire remarks from the anonymous kvetchers:

"Used to be a fun culture. Now it's all about the bottom line and feels like your typical call center." —August 19

"Goals are set in place that no one can reach. They are firing people left and right for no good reason. Cut commissions and eliminated bonuses. Sales staff make about 80% less than they did 5 months ago." —August 29

"They micromanage you, expect you to work 10+ hours a day and on Saturdays!!! . . . This used to be a fun, work hard–play hard place and the culture supported creativity and relationships. Now it's about how many calls can you make, close deals—and nothing is ever good enough." —September 4

"You're working in a call-center and cold-calling's your job. You're fighting with vendors, lying through your teeth, telling them that Groupon won't hurt their business, then begging them to sign up." —September 8

"Fire the new senior management team. Bring back the old culture, the old attitudes and bring back the hard work + fun = $$ and happiness. It's all gone. I don't know anyone who is happy anymore. Sad, sad, sad. Starting to see a mass exodus . . ." —September 9

"Some people will do better with fear tactics but most don't. So have fun hiring more people—they soon will realize how awful it is and then you can start all over again." —September 12

"The fun company culture is now dead and has been replaced by fear." —October 17

"Andrew—you should see how miserable your sales team
is now. Step up and be the CEO you used to be."
—September 4

In October, Mason described the situation as "a short-term period of a lot of noise and disgruntlement as we weed out the
bottom 20 percent, but what we'll end up with is a place where
people are surrounded by colleagues that inspire them and mo-
tivate them to work even harder, and it will be just a better
place to work and a more high-performance environment."

He called the German infusion—which included cutting the
commission sales reps earned on their $32,500 base salary from
2.5 percent of gross deal revenue to 1.5 percent—a net positive.
"International is a huge part of our business, and historically we
have almost run it as two separate businesses. Bringing Marc over
here is helping us turn it into one business where we communicate better, and culturally we're starting to converge where we
take some of the operational discipline that they have developed,
and they take some of the cultural things that we have developed.

"It's a process to work through," Mason said. "The stuff on
Glassdoor is a result of that. If you talk to the salespeople that
come from a sales environment like CareerBuilder, which has
something like 50 percent annual turnover, right now we still
have something like 20 to 25 percent. We were at like 10. So
we're firing more people now, but we're still not having anything near the attrition that you have with CareerBuilder, yet
if you go to the Glassdoor pages of CareerBuilder they are generally great. You have a lot of people here who have gotten used
to a country club kind of sales job, which was never the culture
we were trying to create."

Even on Glassdoor's Groupon review pages, there were some
signs of hope. "Overall it's not a bad place to work," one rep

wrote on September 10. "We still get paid good, have benefits, and a lot of freedom on the sales floor. Some days do suck, but some days are great. . . . At the end of the day it's a job, jobs are usually not supposed to be fun, carefree and easy and at the beginning of Groupon it was. Things have changed but I still have fun, close deals etc."

Another salesperson added on September 16: "You guys are great! Hardworking and there for us when we need guidance. Management is always thinking of ways to improve our work experience."

Every Monday, Muhr meets with city CEOs to review every deal they have in the works and how they're rolling them out. "It's donkey work, but it has to be done," he said. "I look at what's the deal, how could we improve it."

It didn't go well at the outset. "For the first two months, I ripped them a second asshole every time," Muhr said. " 'Would you buy this deal? Why would you buy this deal? It's crap.' They would just put up shit deals that they wouldn't even buy. Why would you buy 50 percent off an introductory gym membership when most of them you get for free? Why would you buy a car wash for twice the price that you normally would because the guy says he has a special method?"

By late September, Muhr said his direction was taking hold. "Two weeks ago and this week again, I went into this meeting and they got it. I had maybe two comments. One guy said, 'I know this deal's crap, I really want to improve it,' and I didn't even have to say anything."

Overall, Muhr was so bullish on Groupon's prospects that he could see the company hitting a $100 billion valuation someday. "It should be the Google of the local space," he said. "Local commerce is so big."

THIRTY-ONE

There was a hidden bonus to keeping the Germans close as well. A source close to the situation indicated that if the Samwers had known how vulnerable Groupon was operationally, they likely would have passed up their potential billion-dollar payday and competed directly with the company not only in Europe but in North America and the rest of the world as well. If Mason and Lefkofsky saw LivingSocial as a tough competitor, they were lucky that they didn't have to square off against the Samwers.

Georgiadis was not so fortunate. Though the COO character-ized herself as a woman of action, she actually created "analysis paralysis," Rob Solomon alleged. "It was ready, aim, fire, recali-brate, that's her approach. And the Germans and Groupon, the way we operated was ready, fire, aim, we'll fix it as we go, no time to over-analyze, make quick decisions."

In response to such criticisms, Georgiadis said, "I think it was hard for Rob to let go. He and I tried to have a really con-structive changeover. I think he probably sees me as this opera-tor. He was the cheerleader and I'm the operator. I look at it differently: I think everyone has to be a cheerleader and a vi-sionary no matter what stage you're at."

But Marc Samwer quickly grew frustrated with Georgiadis' deliberative approach as well. "Everyone realized this had to be done," he said of the restructuring. "The disagreement—not with Andrew and Eric, but with the rest of the organization—is how fast. But these things you can only do fast. You cannot drag them along."

As business development VP Sean Smyth put it, "Marc Samwer's point of view is, 'What are we doing this minute to make more money?' Margo is trying to set up systems and processes where we can scale and be a long-standing business. Margo is all about the brand and what do we represent and how are we doing what we do, and then you have others that are just about, 'How do I make as much money as possible today?' There is a huge clash going on internally right now about that."

A veteran consultant, Georgiadis was good at identifying problems, but internal critics said she couldn't pull the trigger on solutions. After a few months, people in the organization started working around her. At that point, the writing was on the wall. But as late as September 13, Georgiadis said her relationship with Mason was peachy: "Andrew and I literally sit three inches from each other every day. We spend a lot of time together as the senior team. We probably are in meetings almost every single day, multiple times a day, talking about critical business issues. We still run this very much like a start-up and we're a very kind of scrappy interactive group. When you're in lockstep as the leadership team it just makes it a lot easier.

"We definitely have a shorthand," she continued. "Andrew and I spend a lot of time talking about, 'Well, okay, do you want to take first on that or do you want me to deal with that? Do you want to go after that one?' 'No, you deal with that, I'll deal with that one.' So it's nice because we can kind of divide and conquer on things."

The next week, Georgiadis was gone.

THIRTY-TWO

Her departure was abrupt. During a tense conversation late in the evening of September 22, Georgiadis informed Mason that she was returning to Google as president of its North American operations; the announcement would go out the next morning.

Although she had reason to believe she might soon be pushed out if she didn't make the leap, the timing was dramatic. And since the poised and polished COO was not known as a high-drama person, the deal to return to Google must have been finalized rather suddenly.

Nine days before, she had sat for a lengthy interview for this book, an appointment she almost certainly would have rescheduled out of existence if she was certain her departure was imminent. In addition, just one day before she resigned, Georgiadis was interviewed by CBS News for a *60 Minutes* story on Groupon during which she acted as if her tenure at the company would be continuing. Her interview was not included in the finished segment.

"Margo and Andrew did work elbow to elbow, but they didn't get along, ultimately," a person close to the situation explained. "She was too corporate."

If she had waited just six more weeks to tender her resignation, Groupon could have gone public without a last-minute, top-level departure that had analysts wondering if Mason would ever get the company's operations running smoothly. That timing must have put a smile on the face of Google's Nikesh Arora, the man who brought her back into the fold.

The message from Arora, who'd been spurned by Groupon the past December and then watched the company announce Georgiadis' hiring on the exact day Google Deals launched, seemed clear enough: Just because you're in Chicago, don't think you can thumb your nose at Silicon Valley and get away with it.

Mason was heard to say that Georgiadis' departure just before the IPO was the kind of thing you'd have a good laugh about when it happened to some other company. And now the joke was on him.

The next morning, Mason called Mossler just after she had boarded a plane for Las Vegas, bound for a rare weekend off. When he told her the news, she got off the jet just before the door closed and started dealing with the fallout.

At 3:18 P.M., Mason sent an e-mail to Groupon's North American employees and to the corporate directors in Germany. The attempt to spin the departure was admirable, but it rang hollow to most observers: "As a fast-growing company, we've done a lot of hiring this year, including on our senior executive team. Since the beginning of 2011, we've made a total of 8 additions—that's 57% of the total executive team. It would have been great if I could say that we batted 1,000%, but in one instance, it looks like we didn't find a fit; after five months at Groupon, Margo Georgiadis, our COO, has decided to return to Google (her former employer) in a new role as President, Americas. We're disappointed that we were unable to make it work with Margo, but hiring isn't easy, and we support moving quickly when there isn't a match. It's the best way to do business."

Mason then broke some news of his own, indicating that Groupon's flirtation with the COO structure was at an end. "On the bright side, we've built a fantastic team that has proven itself highly capable, so this change won't have an impact on operations," he promised. "Specifically, here are the changes we'll be making:

- Marketing, under Rich Williams, will report into me.
- Business Channels, under Aaron Cooper, will report into me.
- NOW, under Dan Roarty, as a business channel, will report into Aaron Cooper.
- National Sales, under Lee Brown, will report into U.S. Sales under Chris Muhr.
- US Operations, under Hoyoung Pak, will report into me."

He then shared a note from Georgiadis: "Groupon is a great company and I feel privileged to have worked there even for a short time. It was a hard decision to leave as the company is on a terrific path. I have complete confidence in the team's ability to realize its mission."

Effective immediately, Mason had taken back direct control of Groupon's sales, channels, international, and marketing departments.

It was as good a time as any to yank off that particular Band-Aid. The damage from Georgiadis' departure was done: Losing a second COO in less than six months, especially while the company was pushing hard to go public, stoked the flames of the backlash narrative to new heights.

A couple of weeks later, Mason commandeered a conference

room to outline the new organization chart in a whiteboard tour de force. After first wielding his marker to sketch the old structure, he quickly erased it and filled in the new order of things, keeping up a running play-by-play as he did.

"You have Finance, Product, Engineering, COO, Corp Dev, Legal, and HR" reporting to the CEO under the old structure, he said, but "under the COO is where most of the company is, basically." Gesturing to departments under the CEO list, he said, "I've got a couple hundred people in here and maybe forty people here, five people here, six people here, and thirty people here." But under the COO, "you have Sales, International, Marketing and Operations, PR Communications, and Channels—Groupon Now! and product, and the Live Nation and Expedia partnerships.

"Where the COO model works is somewhere like Facebook, where you can say, 'Go do that so I don't have to worry about it,' and that's what I wanted," Mason continued. "I wanted a model where I could say this is the keep-the-trains-running-on-time stuff that you need just to keep growth going, and I'm going to find essentially a partner that is going to run that for me and that will allow me to focus on the future stuff, the product and engineering, corporate development, the strategy of the business.

"That seemed like a good model. The problem is, we are not like Facebook. Facebook is a technology company. We are fifty-fifty technology and sales, so we're this kind of cyborg where our product is our content. It's our deals, and in order to have continuously high-quality deals, you need to have this operational machine working really well. And some of the biggest mistakes that I feel that I've made are allowing myself to get too far away from these things."

He weighed the marker in his hand. "Shortly before bringing over Marc and then Chris, I remember sitting in and watching the flow of a deal—how a deal got created and some of the negotiating processes we were doing and thinking, 'Man, this needs to be weeded; this has just ballooned out of control.' The right hand isn't talking to the left and there are so many opportunities to fix this, and that's part of growing really fast, but I feel like if I hadn't allowed myself to think, 'Okay, somebody's got that,' it wouldn't have gotten as out of control."

As Rob Solomon had predicted, Mason ultimately did not need a high-performing COO; he needed to do away with the position altogether and operate Groupon in much the same way that Jeff Bezos runs Amazon.

"Getting rid of the COO is something that I can do only because we have got, at this point, really strong people in all these other roles," Mason said, pointing to high-performing divisions. Now, international, marketing, sales, and, for the time being, operations would report directly to him instead of through a COO intermediary. PR and communications would move under marketing, "and channels will eventually go into sales," he said. "I can only do it because I have an awesome head of product. I have an awesome head of sales. I have an awesome head of marketing. I have all these things that I didn't have when we first conceived of the COO role."

It was a commanding performance, and the new structure made sense. It was odd, though, how the new organization chart he'd drawn with red marker looked just like a circus tent, with all the lines leading directly to the ringmaster at the top.

Google's Nikesh Arora didn't take the opportunity to gloat when I reached out to him for comment on Georgiadis' departure. But Georgiadis was gracious enough to accept me as a LinkedIn connection. "As I am sure you know from our discussion, I was very passionate about Groupon and wish them every success ahead," she said via the service on October 16. "It was an extremely difficult decision to leave as you can imagine. Both

Groupon and Google are extraordinary places for different reasons and I feel privileged to have had the opportunity to be part of both."

After I mentioned her late-night departure, she remained on message, saying: "It's a fairly straightforward situation. Your comments sound more 'high drama' than is likely warranted." For good measure, she added: "I want only the best for Groupon and have a lot of confidence in the management team, etc. that we put in place. And, I feel very fortunate to have been offered an extraordinary opportunity to help shape the next wave at Google by Larry [Page] and Nikesh." Those guarded, highly politic statements made it even clearer that Georgiadis would have been unlikely to open up to me, or to *60 Minutes*, if she was certain she was headed out the door.

Two days later, I was having a drink with a colleague in Rebar, the mezzanine lounge at Chicago's Trump Hotel & Tower. A few minutes after we sat down, I noticed a familiar face across the room; Georgiadis was chatting with several people at a corner table. Was it a going-away party thrown by friends? Perhaps.

Georgiadis soon excused herself and left the lounge. When she returned, I said hello as she neared the table. She broke into a grin as she tried to make out in the dimly lit room which friend was hailing her. When she recognized me, the smile remained on her face, but her eyes told a different story.

"What a small world," she said gamely as I stood to shake her hand. I told her I was happy to be able to congratulate her on the new job in person and asked if this was a gathering in her honor. It turned out she was enjoying a drink with colleagues as well— the Chicago Google office was nearby and Georgiadis was working from there "for the time being." It made sense, given that her children were still in school on the North Shore.

We said our good-byes and she started to walk away, but something stopped Georgiadis after a few steps. She turned back to me and said, "You know, I wish the Groupon team nothing but the best. I talk to them all the time." With that, she went back to her $17 cocktail. She could afford it; she was about to make upward of $5.6 million on IPO day from her two hundred thousand vested Groupon stock options.

Not bad for 156 days' work.

THIRTY-THREE

One wonders just how much critical operational input Groupon's chief operating officer had toward the end when Andrew Mason was able to take off for an entire week immediately after Georgiadis left.

Mason and Marc Samwer had already effectively shut her out of the day-to-day decision making—their bias toward action having won out over what was seen as her tendency to foster "analysis paralysis"—so the CEO was able to take a refreshing break to marry his fiancée, Jenny Gillespie.

The couple boarded a private thirteen-passenger Gulfstream IV jet whose Rolls-Royce engines carried them to Telluride, Colorado, accompanied by close friends and family members—as well as Mason's iPad with its Groupon-green cover. But this was truly a time to unplug as much as possible after a grueling three years spent building the company.

Gillespie had quit her job at a children's magazine in the fall of 2010 to pursue her passion for music, just as Groupon was blowing up. In the intervening period, she had recorded an album of original material in a folk-pop vein while Mason worked insane hours feeding the Groupon beast. They had picked the site of the wedding a year in advance: Dunton Hot Springs, a Colorado ghost town that had been rehabbed into a luxury resort just one mountain over from Telluride.

One day a few months before the wedding, I was walking down a hallway with Mason at Groupon headquarters and asked him how the preparations were going. He said that, like a lot of guys, he was letting his fiancée mostly sort it out. He had the added advantage of being able to say things like, "Building the fastest-growing company in history here, dear; whatever you decide on the invitations is fine."

Mason did have an incredible idea for his bachelor party—he and his pals would rent out a Soviet-era military base in Poland where they could drive tanks and jump out of helicopters firing live rounds from rifles. "I want to kick a monkey out of a tree," he joked at one point. That plan fell through, though, which probably saved someone's life. But Mason and his pals were able to get away to Ibiza, the Spanish resort island, where they held a less insane party on a yacht.

And now here the couple was, taking in the Telluride Photo Festival and securing their wedding license in the San Miguel County Courthouse, a redbrick gem built in 1887 and restored to brilliant condition right up to the gold stars affixed to the façade. The resort itself fostered deep relaxation with its natural hot spring directed into an outdoor pool ringed with red rock and overlooking a lush alpine valley nearly as pristine as it was when the Ute Indians took the waters there long before gold miners arrived. It's also perhaps the only ghost town with a full spa. As if that weren't relaxing enough, the bed in the honeymoon suite greeted visitors with eight plush pillows and a comforter you could get lost in.

"Gonna go get married on a mountain," Gillespie posted on

her Facebook page September 27. "Why not. Yeah. Marriage. Let's DO THIS." They barbecued; they hiked; they kicked back with good beer. Mason and Aaron With caught up with a Chicago alley tradition—a beanbag-toss game known as bags or corn hole—on a recreation field complete with an open-air Ping-Pong table.

And then, on October 1, Mason capped off one of the best weekends of his life by donning a sharp blue suit and blue shirt offset by a yellow tie and boutonniere and meeting Gillespie at the outdoor altar. She looked fresh and radiant in a white off-the-shoulder gown with a spray of yellow flowers in her right hand and a simple strand of pearls around her neck, for a mountainside exchanging of vows in front of about fifty guests. Later that evening, Mason's mother beat Eric Lefkofsky in a drinking contest.

The city of Chicago was invited to celebrate along with the happy couple, after a fashion, that night. Groupon had booked Wrigley Field for its first-ever movie screening. The company packed the house, drawing better than the Chicago Cubs usually did, for the iconic Windy City comedy *Ferris Bueller's Day Off*. Beer flowed at the pinch-me price of three bucks a pop and the crowd set a Guinness World Record for number of people singing in the round by belting out a tipsy rendition of "Danke Schoen" in homage to Matthew Broderick's lip-synching parade performance in the movie.

As *Crain's Chicago Business* reporter Shia Kapos put it that night on Twitter, "I'm at Andrew Mason's wedding party—I mean Groupon's *Ferris Bueller* movie night at Wrigley Field." Just as the first Groupon was sold during Mason's birthday month in 2008, this was yet another milestone in the young CEO's life that dovetailed with a big day for the company.

Three weeks later, Gillespie performed live at a record store on

Chicago's North Side. She played a sampling of songs from her upcoming second album. Her mother and several friends were in attendance, but her husband couldn't be.

The idea was to record the live session for posting on the store's Web site, but the set faced several technical challenges. Two pre-amps were blown at the outset, necessitating a lot of microphone repositioning between songs as Gillespie switched between her Wurlitzer organ and two acoustic guitars. The space was too cramped for her to change setups easily, but she handled every challenge with calm grace.

Gillespie closes her eyes when she sings, and in the fleeting moments when she opens them you notice how large and liquid they are. Her thick brown hair falls just past her shoulders, casually curling at the ends, and her bangs hang low over her forehead. She cut a lithe figure in a light crepe blouse and black pants. Her full lips cracked a wry smile as she sang of a "beautiful, difficult man"—and there the eyes opened and she looked toward the front of the store for one beat as if Mason might just appear. But he'd already gone to New York City to present at Groupon's pre-IPO road show to investors.

As she continued sharing a suite of highly personal, often-melancholy songs ("When it's time to leave this body / Don't bury me / Carry my ashes to the sea") sung with lovely Joni Mitchell–style trills, a thought occurred: Beyond all his material wealth, Andrew Mason is a lucky man.

THIRTY-FOUR

Amid all the noise around the SEC and the Samwers' push to focus anew on G1 daily deals, Groupon kept expanding and refining its offerings. By mid-October, Groupon Now! continued to grow by double digits week after week. The mobile product still represented only a single-digit slice of the revenue pie, but it showed promise.

"The exciting thing about what we find ourselves doing is we're going deeper into mobile and doing things that we couldn't do when we first started the business, and at the same time we're going into new categories," Andrew Mason said. "We're laying new pipes for commerce to happen. We're balancing supply and demand through price and discovery. We're doing that in local, and now we have started doing it in travel and with product to some degree. In both cases, we have built this trust with consumers where we are able to fairly seamlessly transfer to a new category, similar to how Amazon did it early on."

One of Groupon's main men from Amazon, SVP of product Jeff Holden, outlined the company's expansion plans that fall. Mason brought him into the fold by acquiring Pelago, the company Holden founded in 2006 as "a real-world discovery product for consumers . . . which was all about helping people get out of their houses and into the real world and do interesting, cool, social things." Before that, Holden had spent nearly a decade at Amazon, where he had run the consumer division that delivered the Amazon Prime loyalty program and "all the magic that happens behind the scenes once you place an order."

So Holden's vision dovetailed nicely with Groupon's, and the company was glad to get his product expertise in the bargain as well as the perspective he had from living through the media and analyst backlash against Amazon. "None of the press negativity bothers me in the slightest," he said. "I'm less bothered by it probably than anybody here. This is exactly what Amazon went through and the key thing is focus . . . knowing what you want to focus on, what you're going to build, what's valuable."

Holden, forty-three, is a Detroit native, but he brought an outdoorsy Pacific Northwest vibe with him from Seattle, and his passion for creating great customer experiences is infectious. The more excited he gets, the faster he talks and the bigger he smiles, traits that are almost tailor-made to win Mason over.

When Groupon's CEO first met Holden in early 2011, he half-jokingly told the Amazon veteran, "I'm not necessarily psyched that my legacy is going to be that I brought the daily deal to humankind."

Holden was stunned. He had to get something straight. "I don't know if you're honestly being overly humble," he told Mason. "But just in case you're not, here's the way to think about that: You've afforded yourself the opportunity to invent. You've got this massive, thriving engine of people who care tremendously about your service, who engage with your service every day, and you get to invent for them. That's huge."

From Holden's perspective, the scale and scope of Groupon's daily-deals business makes all manner of other product innovations possible. "We built a two-sided marketplace: Each side is there because the other side is there," like at eBay, he said. Being the first mover in the space and ramping up so quickly helped Groupon overcome the chicken-egg problem of trying to attract customers without a critical mass of merchants or vice versa.

For instance, Holden said, "You can't do Groupon Now! without a critical mass of merchants and consumers at the same time. For someone who doesn't have nearly the reach we have, doing something like Groupon Now! is very, very hard. It's basically impossible. So there's a huge advantage there." He added that Groupon Now! could end up being ten times the business that G1 was. Eventually, instead of thinking of Now! as a place just to find deals, Holden believed consumers might end up seeing it as more of an overarching tool for serendipitously discovering cool things to do in their city—or wherever they're traveling—all at a great price.

Internally, Groupon developed a philosophy it called Triforce. As Holden joked during Groupon's IPO road-show presentation, the term was lifted from the video game *The Legend of Zelda*. In the classic fantasy game, the Triforce, aka Power of the Gods, is a golden triangle composed of three smaller triangles representing power, wisdom, and courage. Worthy souls who assemble the full Triforce are granted a wish. (If half the ethos of Groupon seems like one big inside geek joke, that's only because it is.)

At any rate, Triforce is geared toward serving three core merchant needs. With the sampling and awareness-building daily-deal tool, merchants could drive consumers to try their products and services. Groupon Now! helped them with yield management—getting rid of excess inventory or drawing in customers during slow times. "We're creating an ecosystem in which the merchant can turn a knob on price, and people behave instantly," Holden said.

The third leg of Groupon's Triforce model tackles the company's biggest challenge with merchants: showing them that deals can generate repeat business. If Groupon can crack the code on generating consumer loyalty, many of the criticisms leveled at it will fade away. That's a big if, of course, but Holden is eager to tackle it.

"As part of our operating system, we will provide merchants the ability to run a supersimple but supercompelling loyalty program," Holden said. With the Rewards leg of Triforce, merchants can set a spending threshold for customers. Once patrons hit that magic number, they can then earn Groupon deals for the business, which could give them a compelling reason to come back frequently.

"We think it's the coolest and most magical rewards experience out there," Mason said. "You walk into any random restaurant or spa, you swipe your credit card, and then you get an e-mail saying, 'How was your experience? You've earned $50 toward a free massage at Jack's Massage.'"

Once customers sign up for the loyalty program, they don't even have to know the merchant is enrolled in Rewards to receive offers, as long as they use the credit card on their Groupon account to make purchases. So earning rewards with local merchants "could be a complete surprise" for Groupon customers, Mason said. The Rewards program begins collecting customer analytics for all registered merchants passively, so online check-ins aren't required to track their visits.

To secure the visit-tracking technology, Groupon bought a company called Zappedy in July of 2011 for $10.2 million. "It allows us to interface with the merchant's credit-card terminal," Mason said. "We'll be able to compare the purchase patterns of Groupon customers to non–Groupon customers. We have always done this anecdotally, and we have some merchants that keep the data and it always ends up being good."

If all goes well, "you get to the point where businesses that have the Triforce tools are so much more successful on every measure than the ones that don't have the tools," Holden said. "That's where we want to be. We see our destiny as tied directly to the merchant's destiny."

Innovating new products and securing patents on them could help Groupon build a deeper moat around its business, again following the intellectual-property path that was so successful for Amazon with one-click purchasing and the like.

"We have to have a lot of IP being generated here," Holden said. "We can't not do that. We're going down that road now and we have a number of things in play." Banking patents can serve as a good defense if competitors start sniffing around the business for a payday. "If another company comes after you, and you have a huge patent portfolio, there's always some sort of exchange you can do or something where you can say, 'Well, look what we've got on you,'" Holden said.

In the end, he added, "Every innovation company has to have the same MO. Andrew and his team invented the daily-deal concept. It's really easy to say that's trivial in the way that people said one-click is trivial. But if it were trivial, someone would have done it before. It was a very successful, very creative strategy, and also very profitable. With innovation companies, the only defense is to continually innovate so people are skating to where the puck is, not where the puck will be. So you tend to see companies like Groupon get very secretive because the big weapon they've got is their innovation coming down the road."

On the consumer side, Groupon is deeply focused on personalization. "We invented this concept of Deal Tags, which is really cool," said Holden, who ran personalization for Amazon. "They will let you tell us, 'I love this deal,' via a specific tag. On one deal you might say, 'I like "bring the kids" deals.' Others might be 'adrenaline deals' or 'fountain of youth deals.'" Once Groupon knows the deal themes people are interested in, the company can make offers that may be more relevant to each customer.

It's quite a leap forward from Groupon's original "relevance engine," which relied primarily on a user's location and basic demographic data. "We still make mistakes of sending guys manipedis," Holden said in the fall of 2011. "We just started factoring in gender very recently. It's helping for sure. But we can get so much more precise and make it so much more visible: 'Here's the deal and here's why we're showing this deal. It's .2 miles from your home, it's an "adrenaline deal," and you say you love adrenaline deals.' You'll see a little heart lit up on it because you clicked it on a previous deal. It makes people go, 'This is so cool. It's targeted to me.'"

Groupon might even beat Amazon at the personalization game. "We're getting to comparable levels," Holden said. "Amazon's engine is not sophisticated; it's just operating on massive amounts of data."

The key to the tags is grouping deals into experiential themes instead of specific product and service categories. "If they're categories it would be things like 'spa,' and so I keep sending you spas and that's stupid," Holden said. "That's not what we want. But then 'pampered lifestyle' is something different. It might be about luxury things, it might be about [getting] off your feet and [letting] someone take care of it for you."

In theory, the harder Groupon pushes that button of how customers see themselves, the more engaged they'll become with the tagged offerings. "So a foodie isn't just about going into a different restaurant," he said. "It's also about things like wine tastings and gourmet-cooking shops." Ultimately, Groupon can infer from one purchasing behavior a nexus of related behaviors. That's the secret sauce of personalization. The goal is to avoid showing consumers deals that their purchasing patterns and tag selections suggest they're unlikely to want, Holden said. "But we do want to put things in front of you that you wouldn't have thought to look for."

In other words, Groupon wants to sell customers the thing they didn't know they wanted but are desperate to buy when they see it—the serendipitous perfect deal.

The engine works with Groupon's ancillary products as well. "With Groupon Live, we should be able to ask you about what genres of music you like, what specific artists you love, what kind of experiences at concerts do you want—do you want to be sitting outdoors in the grass or do you like going to a big venue?" Holden said. With Getaways, the questions might be along the lines of: Does a customer like urban centers? Or adventure travel? Or do they want high-adrenaline travel? Exotic places? Or a staycation?

Social networks can play a role as well. Holden described a Buy With Friends feature that would work particularly well with live events. Customers could buy a deal provisionally by essentially telling Groupon, "I want to go, but I only want to go if two or more of my friends will go with me," Holden said. "You set that number, go to Facebook, invite a bunch of people to be those two people or more, and have the thing tip when they say they're in. It's like microtipping for an individual social group."

Meanwhile, Holden's employee Mihir Shah, whose mobile-app company Mob.ly was purchased by Groupon in May 2010—the company's first acquisition, even before CityDeal—was busy cooking up mobile solutions at the Palo Alto, California, office. Since the acquisition, Mason has said several times that one of his few regrets was not opening a Silicon Valley branch sooner to tap into the deep pool of tech talent. Shah ramped up the action there quickly, along with Groupon chief data officer Mark Johnson, who had come over from Netflix. In March 2012, Groupon added another big gun to its Palo Alto office by hiring Curtis Lee from social-gaming firm Zynga as the new VP of consumer products.

Shah had been introduced to Mason by Accel's Andrew Braccia, the same guy who hooked Solomon up with the company. Holden called Shah "a total rock-star entrepreneur. He's freaking awesome to work with. And quickly created his own business unit within Groupon to run Mobile and Merchant. When I got here, his big concern was that I would take it all apart, dismantle it. I'm not going to touch that with a ten-foot pole. I love that. I want you to be that way. Andrew loves it, too."

The Mob.ly courtship was quick. With mobile heating up, Mob.ly, which had developed apps for major Web players such as restaurant-reservation booking engine OpenTable, had several suitors, most of them people Shah had known in Silicon Valley for years.

"Groupon came out of left field," he said. Shah had his first conversation with Mason via Skype. *Who are these guys way out in Chicago?* he thought. *How does this make sense when I can go with a Valley operation I already know?* Shah had run the product management team at Yahoo! and his Valley roots ran deep.

But the Skype conversation was intriguing enough to persuade Shah and Mob.ly co-founder Yishai Lerner to fly to Chicago for a meeting with Lefkofsky, Keywell, and Mason. Not twenty minutes into the chat, Lefkofsky said, "Okay, why don't you guys wait here? We're going to go talk for ten minutes and come back."

When they returned as promised, Lefkofsky started writing figures on a whiteboard in the conference room. "Look," he said. "Here's your valuation; here's some of the other terms; here's the deal we're willing to offer you. Here's basic information on the company financials. Why don't you go to lunch and come back and tell us what you think?"

Shah and his partner were stunned. It was such a refreshing change from the Valley culture they were used to, where corporate development departments often moved at a plodding pace. *Man*, Shah thought, *these guys can really focus and make decisions quickly. They realize mobile is going to be big, they want to be in the Valley, and they put an offer on the table immediately.*

Just like that, Groupon went from outside contender to winning bidder. Shah also was happy to see how entrepreneurial the culture was. He ran the product side of the Palo Alto office while Lerner headed up the engineering. Soon, Shah got the opportunity to sponsor potential deals for Groupon acquisitions, including the purchase of Zappedy, which brought even more entrepreneurs into the Palo Alto operation and reinforced the culture. They started the office with about six staffers. By the fall of 2011, it was up over 120, all concentrating on Groupon's mobile and merchant products.

Until the end of the year, when it moved into a larger space, the team worked out of three floors in a building with a big shaft running down its center. Shah's mobile and merchant products group took up the top floor, which had the vibe of a busy trading floor, with people claiming work space anywhere they could find it.

It was a bit of a mini–United Nations as well, with the team from Zappedy in one room represented by a large contingent of top-notch computer scientists from Chile. "Everybody speaks Spanish," Shah said. "And then we have the mobile team, which has people from Russia, India, China, every possible nationality you can think of. You can hear different languages all the time, and I think it's probably reflective of Groupon as a whole when you think about our global operation—which is perfect given that we're trying to build a global product in Palo Alto." Even though

CityDeal was on a different software platform than Groupon U.S., Shah insisted that they build their mobile products in concert.

"We went out to Berlin and we met with the people there and we formed the relationships," Shah said. "Now, except for a couple of countries, we essentially build all the mobile products for the world for Groupon out of Palo Alto. It's a close collaboration between the Palo Alto and the Berlin team. And it works."

Working with the rest of Groupon's far-flung operations has become second nature for the team. By the time Europe's winding down, Palo Alto is coming online. "You actually end up with a perfect cycle because they can do what they need to do and then you can come back the next day" and continue it, Shah said. A typical day might also start with a 6:00 A.M. videoconference call with Chicago.

"People always ask me: How do you work between Chicago and Palo Alto and the international product they built in Berlin? How is it possible to really coordinate as you're growing so quickly?" Shah said. "It's actually not that bad at all because that's how it's been from day one, really. For us, at least. It's just normal life for Groupon. Most companies that start in the U.S. take several years to build their U.S. business and they slowly buy and grow in other countries. For us, it happened within a year and a half of our existence."

In essence, Groupon was the first pop-up multinational company.

Mason is a frequent visitor to the Palo Alto office, grabbing the nearest free desk between meetings. Coming in from the outside, Shah couldn't believe the disconnect between the popular perception of the CEO and how he actually runs the business.

"We may not take ourselves too seriously as individuals, but we take our business ridiculously seriously," Shah said. "People are going to understand that more and more about us over time. I spent a year working directly with Andrew when I first started, and he is extremely focused, extremely competitive, and extremely serious about what we need to do and how we need to do it. If you were in as many meetings as I am with him on a daily basis, and you just look at the precision with which we're asking the questions of: Why did this happen? Why did this not happen? Why are we not looking at this? And, we need to look at this better. It's happening every day."

Shah described a non-political, rigorous, results-based culture in which those with a driven, entrepreneurial personality can thrive. "All the departments have their objectives and key results for each quarter and that's how everybody's measured," he said. "There's really nowhere to hide. This company is run in a very quantitative way. It's a great balance of very numbers-focused operational excellence combined with [the idea that] we're not going to be afraid to take chances and launch innovative new products."

Shah's goals with the mobile product were as ambitious as Holden's: "A few years from now, we can have several million small businesses around the world wake up every day and say, 'Wow, how did I run my business without the products and tools that Groupon offers?'" He envisioned a day when that suite of customer-acquisition and -retention tools would help small merchants level the playing field with retail giants like Walmart.

"The other thing that really excites me is that, given that we're all about local business and given how fast smart phones and mobile are growing, we're going to probably be one of the biggest mobile companies in terms of revenue," he said.

On the consumer side, Shah pointed out a surprising fact: Groupon has far more mobile users than Foursquare does. "So we can use our mobile apps to drive people into Groupon Now! or a regular G1 deal, a Getaways deal, very effectively," he said. "We're going to partner with people at Foursquare just to help distribute things like Now! deals, but we have a massive installed base of mobile users as well."

Beyond the size of its mobile base, even Groupon was surprised to learn that customers trust the brand so much they're willing to make large purchases on the go. "I didn't think that people would necessarily buy big-ticket items on their phone," Shah said. "But it turns out that people who like to use Groupon from their phone will buy anything on their phone, whether it's a Getaways deal or a Now! deal or a regular daily deal."

Even though many people planning a trip spend hours researching their destination and comparing prices on their laptop and desktop computers, Groupon quickly saw a spike in Getaways deals through its mobile app. "That's really indicative of what people are doing with their smart phones today, where it's just becoming sort of substitutional to their PC," Shah said. (In fact, 25 percent of Groupon vouchers sold in December 2011 were purchased via mobile devices.)

And since Groupon has a presence in nearly fifty countries, local commerce quickly becomes a way for it to give travelers merchant deals and recommendations in nearly every major city. "When you're traveling and you're about to go somewhere, it's a perfect time to pull out your Groupon mobile app and see what's available in that city and start buying some things as you get there," Shah said.

As he neared his year-and-a-half mark with Groupon, Shah remained bullish about its growth prospects. "I feel like we've just begun. It's easy for people to say, 'Oh, the company's big and it's got twelve thousand employees in fifty countries,' but I feel from the opportunity we have to transform fundamentally how local business works, it's just begun."

But could the promise of future revenues from these products justify the sky-high valuation Groupon was seeking in the IPO?

On September 22, I ran into Eric Lefkofsky at the Modern Wing of the Art Institute. We were there for a Goodman Theatre fund-raiser and we chatted briefly just a few feet from where Michael Bloomberg had his picture taken with Richard M. Daley and Rahm Emanuel after his pony-free tour of Groupon headquarters. Despite the latest round of shock headlines, Lefkofsky appeared sanguine. The third-quarter financials were going to surprise people—in a good way, he suggested. "I'd rather have a good business and bad press than a bad business and good press," he added. No wonder he was in a good mood: The quarterly report would end up showing Groupon near the break-even point and profitable in the United States.

THIRTY-FIVE

The going-public process had dragged on long enough for Groupon. It seemed as if the company was finally on a glide path to IPO when deal-aggregator site YipIt.com released a report in mid-September suggesting that 170 out of 530 Groupon competitors in the United States had shut down or been consolidated into another operation so far in 2011. Make that 171, as BuyWithMe, Groupon's very first clone, was about to be scooped up by deal site Gilt City after laying off more than half its staff. "The capital market's willingness to invest in daily-deal businesses has dried up," BuyWithMe's COO lamented just before the sale.

Mason started his road-show presentations in New York City on October 24, looking sharp in a blue suit and silver tie. He had some impressive numbers to share and a compelling story of future growth potential. But inevitably, bad headlines were just around the corner.

The problems started with a Louisville, Kentucky, area restaurant called Seviche. Mason used its successful Groupon experience to illustrate the benefits a typical business could reap from running a deal. Even after subtracting its cost of goods and services and Groupon's cut, the restaurant actually made a profit on each deal redeemed, Mason explained as he displayed a Power-Point slide headlined: "Why Seviche Loves Groupon." In fact, he added, the promotion had been so successful in generating repeat business that the fine-dining restaurant had expanded its seating as a result.

The only problem was, Seviche had changed owners after the deal ran and no one at Groupon had checked with the new guy to see if he would endorse the rosy picture the company planned to paint of the restaurant's experience. As it turned out, the new owners soon seemed to be saying they didn't see Groupon as a viable marketing opportunity. Rubbing salt, though no doubt salt of a very fine grade, in the PR wound, the owner told Reuters on October 25, in a story headlined "Seviche Doesn't Love Groupon Anymore," that the expansion "really had nothing to do with the Groupons." The new owner later told the company he'd been misquoted, but the cream had already curdled.

Meanwhile, a senior Morningstar analyst pegged the company's value at $5 billion, less than Google's 2010 offer and well below the $10 billion to $11.4 billion valuation the company was hoping to hit on IPO day. He also projected that Groupon would not become profitable until 2013. More negative headlines resulted when a comment Mason made to potential investors in Boston about culling the company's weakest sales reps was reported as a set plan to lay off 10 percent of the staff. The stories prompted Groupon to release a statement stressing that "Andrew Mason is talking about a performance-review process for managing out and replacing low performers that is common among the most efficient sales organizations."

And just to make the opening of road-show week complete, Groupon gave itself another black eye when its attorneys went after a parody site for trademark infringement. On one hand, the page, posted by an online retail site called runningshoes.com, used the Groupon logo and looked exactly like a deal page. On the other hand, it was labeled a "digital parody" and anyone who read the copy would immediately see that it was a gag.

The deal was for "Groupon IPO" and it peddled one share for sixteen dollars, or 60 percent off the forty-dollar price that had been bandied about earlier in the year. The deal description said it all: "Buy stock in one of the fastest start-ups in Internet history. Once valued at $25 billion, Groupon is now going for the estimated bargain basement price of $10.1 billion." The irony that the predicted valuation of a half-price deal company had dropped by more than half was a big comedic softball just waiting for someone to hit it out of the park. Customers were limited to only a million shares each, but those with extra money to burn were invited to sample other deals such as a Pets.com sock puppet for ten dollars, the official MySpace logo for one cent, or the Napster .com domain name for a buck.

The irony of a company that makes a fetish out of how funny it is sending attorneys after someone for parodying it was a tasty treat for the media. Stories of corporate hypocrisy are fun to read and write, after all. Even if Groupon technically had a case about misuse of its logo and other trademarks, why didn't management see that going after runningshoes.com would have critics racing for a chance to say Groupon could dish out the humor but couldn't take it?

"I guess we just didn't have our sense of humor that day," communications director Julie Mossler said.

In a more serious twist, Groupon also filed suit against three former sales managers it accused of taking trade secrets to Google Deals even though their employment agreements barred them from working for a direct competitor for two years. (The trio later countersued for punitive damages, calling Groupon's filing "a sham" that was designed to let the company "rifle through its newest competitor's pockets.") It was really starting to seem as if Groupon and Google had issues. Another stumble came when Groupon mistakenly told employees with stock options they could sell their shares on opening day when they actually had to wait through a customary 180-day lock-up period.

And with all that, one last trick still remained: Late on Halloween night, just four days before the IPO, Henry Blodget's *Business Insider* dropped a bombshell headlined: "Inside Groupon: The Truth About The World's Most Controversial Company." The story, based entirely on anonymous sources, contended that Lefkofsky had been the one to push group buying only to be ignored by an arrogant and stubborn Mason. Groupon editor-in-chief Aaron With, who was in the room for those meetings, forcefully disputed the story's assertion that Lefkofsky was "the real operator behind the entire enterprise during its early days."

It was a stunning turn of events: One of Mason's earliest colleagues from The Point was so disgruntled that he'd blindsided the CEO during IPO week. The article predicted that Groupon was "headed toward being quite profitable," but it was highly critical of Mason as a human being. Who had thrown him under the bus? Mason had planned to take the original Point team to New York City so they could celebrate the company going public together. But shortly after the article appeared, the Point posse's flights were canceled. Now, Lefkofsky, Keywell, and the road-show team would be the only executives to mark the day at NASDAQ. One day With was told he was going to the IPO event, and the next day he was told he wasn't. Though he didn't know why he and the other original staffers were disinvited, the snub didn't seem to bother him. There was always plenty of work to do in Chicago.

That moment felt like someone throwing the brakes on a runaway roller coaster: It was jarring as hell, but at least the ride had finally stopped. And not a moment too soon. As an investment banker who'd advised Google on its IPO told the *Chicago Tribune*, "Very few companies have this many missteps" on their way to going public.

As the week wore on, the question remained: Would all of these dark clouds clear in time for a successful IPO?

In truth, most of them already had. The Super Bowl "debacle" had led to Groupon's best sales week at that time. The SEC had approved the company to go public over the strenuous objections of the "Ponzi scheme" critics. Mason had remade the organization chart to eliminate his pesky COO problem. And the German-led overhaul of the sales process, though painful, was starting to show big results, with Groupon selling more than a million deals in one day for the first time on October 6—nearly three times the company's average second-quarter sales volume.

Propelled by an annual marketing budget on par with companies as large as Visa, Groupon now topped 142 million subscribers worldwide, 30 million of whom had purchased at least one deal. The company had worked with nearly eighty thousand merchants in the third quarter alone, selling 33 million Groupons around the globe during those months. And an astounding 54 percent of U.S. households with incomes over $150,000 now subscribed to a daily-deals site, according to an Accenture survey. As a result of all this positive momentum, Groupon's loss dipped to just $239,000 in the third quarter, more than $100 million less than it had burned through in the previous three months.

There were still caution flags, though—several of them. Revenue growth had slowed as the company dialed back its marketing spend; Groupon's overall take on the deals it sold had dipped to 37 percent in the third quarter, down from 42 percent a year earlier; and sales per employee during those months were $41,290 compared to $322,730 per staffer at Amazon. Meanwhile—no small thing—the long-term viability of the model remained unproven. But at least for now, the gamble of turning down overtures from Yahoo! and Google appeared likely to pay off. The offering was so oversubscribed that Groupon raised the number of shares available from 30 million to 35 million at the last minute and set a strike price of $20, above its filing target of $16 to $18 per share. The float was still a tiny 5.5 percent of the company's 632 million outstanding shares—the smallest percentage ever for an IPO—but most of the trend lines were looking up.

NOVEMBER 3–4, 2011

The night before the big day—call it IPO eve—Mason, Lefkofsky, and Keywell hung out with their spouses, a few key investors, and several high-level employees in the top-floor bar of the tony Hotel Gansevoort in Manhattan's Meatpacking District. It was a laid-back affair with bottle-service vodka drinks, and a DJ spinning dance hits in the corner.

Mason seemed a bit nervous, perhaps because he hadn't yet written his big speech for the NASDAQ cameras, but Lefkofsky was positively serene. Untucked shirts were still the popular sartorial choice for the men, but everyone looked like they'd picked out their sleekest ones for the big evening.

The next morning, Lefkofsky's assistant, Pat Garrison, was the first of the Groupon crew to arrive at the NASDAQ MarketSite studio in Times Square. She passed through security shortly after 8:00 A.M., followed by a guy delivering a sheet cake topped with the Groupon logo in fondant frosting thick enough to stop a bullet.

Upon arrival, the guests were invited to have a souvenir photo taken against a white screen. Through some computer wizardry, they all ended up looking like they'd appeared on NASDAQ's giant cylindrical screen overlooking Times Square.

Because NASDAQ is a virtual stock exchange, the MarketSite facility is all about creating pretty pictures for the investment world and for tourists passing by the windows that look directly into the ground-floor studio. A wall of monitors serves as the backdrop for the action, and on Groupon's IPO morning the company's stock was listed at the $20 strike price with the designation UNCHANGED, until trading began. After that, its every fluctuation was displayed on the screens in real time along with changes in the major market indices.

Outside the studio pit, a few dozen invited guests drank coffee and soda while bass-heavy inspirational music, like the kind played before NBA games, filled the air. Just above everyone's heads, several mini-television studios ringed the space so that business anchors could have the ticker screens as a backdrop from their second-floor perches.

Emily Chang had come all the way from *Bloomberg West's* California studio to cover the event, and she was pissed about being frozen out. Her pique didn't stop her from snapping a cellphone pic of the studio floor from Bloomberg's second-floor cubicle, however.

Mason at that point was sitting in a corner outside the pit with Jeff Holden giving him words of encouragement as the CEO worked on his brief remarks up until the last minute. As everyone grabbed coffees and sodas, Kevin Efrusy of Accel, one of the investors most instrumental in supporting Groupon's independent rise, echoed Mason and Lefkofsky's mantra that the IPO was merely one step, and an early one at that, on what they believed would be the company's long journey to market supremacy. Harry

Weller of New Enterprise Associates was on hand as well, but he didn't sing any Billy Joel numbers like he had during SXSW.

In keeping with the company's whimsical style, Mossler had suggested that the owners of Motel Bar—the guys who'd run the very first Groupon and fed thousands of its employees ever since—should ring the opening bell. The duo was so delighted by the honor that they ended up naming a sandwich after Mossler, which is available on Mondays.

When it came time for the introductions, NASDAQ CEO Bob Greifeld noted that Groupon was the third company Lefkofsky had taken public through the exchange. Only one other entrepreneur had pulled off that trifecta: Steve Jobs with Apple, Pixar, and NeXT.

Not bad company to be in, which made it even more curious that the exchange misspelled Lefkofsky's name on the giant screen outside. Maybe NASDAQ would get it right the fourth time.

Mason bobbled and nearly dropped the crystal replica of the MarketSite cylinder when Greifeld presented it to him, but the CEO managed to hang on to it as onlookers whispered that it looked like a bong.

After Mason thanked his investors and employees, the music grew increasingly loud. The Motel Bar owners sounded the market's opening bell and green confetti exploded into the air, one errant piece getting stuck to Lefkofsky's forehead for a minute until he finally swiped it off. The founders and other top executives basked in the moment, and applause erupted in the gallery as Mason embraced Lefkofsky at the lectern.

And then . . . everyone waited. It would be more than an hour, until 10:45 A.M., before Groupon shares began trading, and so the morning took on all the trappings of a wedding. There was champagne and cake. There was idle small talk. And there were photos outside in Times Square.

As the crew exited the building, Emily Chang raced up to Mason with her Bloomberg cameraman in tow.

"How do you feel?" she asked. "You must feel good."

The CEO just smiled at her and kept walking.

"Say something," she said, keeping pace. "Anything? What about Groupon's long-term future?"

"Try again, try again," Mason said, gently mocking her.

"Okay," Chang said. "How do you feel, Andrew?"

He flashed another grin and walked away. Make no mistake: These guys had paid close attention to a year's worth of bad press, and Bloomberg was near the top of their shit list. Chang did not disappoint, filing a remarkably bitter report later that day. "Unlike many public company CEOs, Mason and Groupon PR shut most media out of the event on the one day they should be claiming victory," she intoned, before citing "many analysts and investors who think Groupon's playing an investment game that may have dubious results."

Once the Groupon team was assembled on Times Square, passersby started taking pictures in front of Mason. One walked up to the group and said, "Does anyone know who these people are?" They were practically a tourist attraction, though not quite on par with the Naked Cowboy, the New York street performer famous for walking the square wearing tighty-whities and a cowboy hat while strumming an acoustic guitar.

Back inside, there was some brief drama. Lead underwriter Morgan Stanley thought the Groupon crew would be watching the first trade from the investment bank's offices, but since the company had already promised NASDAQ the honor, they ended up staying.

Groupon's first recorded public trade was for $27.93, a 40 percent pop over the strike price. A huge cheer went up in the gallery as the newly minted millionaires and billionaires toasted their good fortunes.

CFO Jason Child soon was set up on an uncomfortable chair in the arena for a live-remote interview with Jim Cramer on CNBC's *Squawk Box*. While Child waited for the segment to begin, his colleagues razzed him. "Imagine you're in front of a firing squad, but you don't know when they're pulling the trigger," Child responded.

When the CFO went live on the air, everyone immediately turned away from him so they could catch the full exchange on the monitors that hung in the area outside the pit. Much laughing and cheering ensued. The mood was further buoyed when word got out that the good sports at LivingSocial had forty pizzas from Motel Bar delivered to Groupon's Chicago headquarters by way of congratulations.

A few hours later, the leadership team was winging back to Chicago on Lefkofsky's jet—along with the Motel Bar owners, whom the chairman had invited to ride back in style at the last minute. With the stock closing its first day at $26.11 a share—a more-than-respectable 31 percent pop from the opening bell—the paper worth of the founders, early investors, and board members skyrocketed as the company earned a valuation of $16.7 billion.

All told, Groupon raised $700 million from the IPO, but analysts criticized the minuscule float as a gimmick to keep the share price artificially high by limiting supply. They also raised a red flag over a stock structure that would give the founders' preferred shares 150 votes each, thus guaranteeing them majority control.

But investors were willing to look past such concerns, at least for the day, to make Groupon the biggest tech IPO since, yes, Google raked in $1.7 billion in 2004.

Almost exactly one month earlier, Solomon had predicted a "good, not great" IPO. "I think it'll be high enough to vindicate not selling to Google, but it will be nowhere near the crazy numbers that people were talking about earlier this year," he said—especially the rumored $20 to $25 billion valuations that likely were coming from investment bankers looking for the business.

"I don't know where those crazy numbers were coming from," Solomon said. "They definitely were not coming from anyone at Groupon. We always said it would be really cool to be worth $15, $18 billion; $20 billion, that would be amazing." So after all the turmoil, the Groupon gang more or less got everything they had wished for.

Eric Lefkofsky alone ended the day up nearly $3.4 billion, his remaining 28 percent stake worth what Yahoo! had been willing to pay for the entire company a year earlier. That cemented his ranking on the *Forbes* 400 list of the richest Americans. His partner, Brad Keywell, was good for around $1.1 billion. He was actually edged out by Mason's $1.2 billion—but who was counting, aside from everyone?

The Samwer brothers saw a tidy $1 billion windfall for their opportunistic ways and operational excellence. Investors New Enterprise Associates and Accel Growth Fund made do with $2.3 billion and $863 million, respectively.

Former president and COO Rob Solomon banked a cool $105 million for his year of service, while his successor, Margo Georgiadis, knocked down $8.4 million for five months in the saddle. Ex-CTO Ken Pelletier, who'd been there for the Point days and a bit beyond, was now worth $70 million. Board members Howard Schultz and Ted Leonsis scored $49 million and $48 million, respectively. Director-level Groupon employees also ended the day as paper millionaires.

Of the three lead underwriters, Morgan Stanley took the lion's share of the banking fees at $17.3 million, with Goldman Sachs in the second slot at $8.7 million and Credit Suisse at $3.1 million. Eleven other banks helped underwrite the IPO, taking home a total of $42 million in fees.

Not bad for a three-year-old company started with a million-dollar investment.

Mason and company had survived the backlash, but the bruises remained. "It's so over-the-top that you're forced to develop a thick skin, which isn't necessarily a good thing I don't think, because it's great to be really sensitive to how your customers feel and how the public feels," the CEO said before the IPO. "But because you're prevented from actually saying or doing anything about it during the quiet period, the only way to deal and not blow your brains out is to learn to ignore it."

As 2011 sped toward its close, Mason held out hope that the Groupon bashing might begin to die down soon. "I think it will happen over the course of 2012," he said. "Silly season will be over hopefully a quarter or two after the IPO, but then I think the skepticism will slowly die out—there will just be more proof in the numbers.

"The numbers will say everything and then we'll just be in a lot of ways treated like a normal technology company," he predicted. "In terms of what I think we're doing five years from now, we want to be a part of local commerce in a really fundamental way. We want everybody to be thinking about Groupon on a daily basis whenever they're leaving the house to shop locally. And with the stuff that we're doing, I just get more and more excited every day about the potential for that to occur."

Solomon suspects Mason will be at Groupon's helm if and when that happens. "I think Andrew's the long-term CEO," he said. "It's going to be a very competitive, crazy period. But I do think he emerges as the guy who's running this company five years from now, ten years from now. I mean, it's him. It's his life, as Amazon is Bezos and Bezos is Amazon. Same thing here."

The actual NASDAQ trading operation is headquartered well south of Times Square, in lower Manhattan's One Liberty Plaza. The building looms over the former Liberty Plaza Park, now known as Zuccotti Park, where the Occupy Wall Street protesters famously had set up camp.

On the day of Groupon's IPO, musician David Crosby toured the park, scouting out the best place for him and Graham Nash to perform. Unlike Neil Young, they must not have been fans of Groupon the Cat.

The following Tuesday, Crosby and Nash slung acoustic guitars across their chests and led the Occupy activists in rousing a capella sing-alongs of "Long Time Gone," "Teach Your Children," "Military Madness," "What Are Their Names," and the duo's more recent indictment of capitalism's excesses, "They Want It All."

"This is a song for all these guys in the buildings down here," Crosby said, nodding toward NASDAQ headquarters directly across the plaza from where he stood.

"Want that Mercedes, that Gulfstream too / They want to get, get it from you," he and Nash sang. "They bleed the companies they're supposed to run / Ain't no different than taking your money with a gun."

On the unfamiliar verses, the crowd listened quietly, but it didn't take them long to pick up the chorus and join in: "They want it all, they want it now / They wanna get it and they don't care how."

The protesters weren't directing their ire at Groupon, not when they had big banks to attack, many of which, admittedly, had underwritten the IPO. But to have an icon of the 1960s protest movement like David Crosby plotting his latest political statement even as GRPN stock began minting billionaires a glow stick's toss away, well, it certainly underscored how far Mason had traveled from founding a crunchy-granola group-action Web site to joining the rarefied ranks of the wealthiest 1 percent in three years flat.

Without a doubt, Andrew Mason was still poised to change the world.

At least for now, though, that change would be measured in terms of how the world shopped.

THIRTY-SIX

After ending the year with seesawing share prices, thanks in part to short sellers and the record small IPO float, Groupon's first big splash in 2012 was a *60 Minutes* profile of the company that aired on January 15. Trotting out his polished aw-shucks act, Andrew Mason told Lesley Stahl, "Am I as experienced, or mature, or smart as other CEOs? No, probably not, but there's something, I think, very useful about having a founder as the CEO."

Watching him, one couldn't help but appreciate his increasingly assured demeanor and reflect on just how much public attention the goofball-executive shtick had generated for the company. Sure, some coverage of Mason's antics had been negative, but would Groupon's IPO have enjoyed nearly the buzz it did without him mugging for the cameras? Groupon had in fact gobbled up 69 percent of all media coverage of the daily-deals space in 2011, according to HighBeam Research, with LivingSocial a distant second at 15 percent. Consider: Zynga's shares fell 5 percent from their strike price on the company's first day of trading about a month after Groupon went public, even though the social-gaming firm was turning a profit, growing revenues, and earning high marks from analysts. Maybe Zynga needed a CEO with a knack for grabbing headlines. And maybe Mason and Lefkofsky owed the cyber-muckrakers a beer or two.

Groupon's big news, which wouldn't be revealed until February 8, was that the company had blown the doors off sales in the fourth quarter of 2011, raking in revenue of $506.5 million—an astounding 194 percent year-over-year increase. Unfortunately, Groupon had one more unwelcome surprise left to unveil from its wild IPO year, reporting a net loss of $42.7 million for the fourth quarter, or 8 cents a share, confounding analysts' expectations of a 3-cent-per-share profit. Its U.S. operation was profitable to the tune of $35 million, and the overall loss was due primarily to an abnormally high tax bill associated with Groupon establishing a new international headquarters in Switzerland. But the company's failure to inch into the black sent the stock price spiraling down more than 15 percent in after-hours trading until it came to rest less than a dollar above its $20 strike price. Leading his first-ever earnings conference call for investors and analysts that afternoon, Mason repeatedly stressed, in an accent that remained one *oot and aboot* away from sounding Canadian, that "It's still the early days" for the company, and "We believe we are on the cusp of a sea change in consumer behavior."

Mason pointed to several bright spots in the financials, including the fact that Groupon's subscriber-acquisition costs were dropping; the number of active customers (those who'd purchased at least one deal in the past twelve months) had risen to 33 million, a 20 percent year-over-year increase; annual gross billings per active customer had jumped to $188 from $160 in 2010; and overall revenue for 2011 had more than quadrupled to $1.6 billion against a cool $4 billion in gross billings.

All impressive numbers, certainly, but anyone listening in for a dose of Andrew Mason the entertainer hung up disappointed by his sober, even-keeled performance. The only big laugh of the call came after the CEO explained of an improved personalization tool, "It allows us to say, 'Please stop sending me pole-dancing lessons,'" only to have a caller pipe up that he'd like to keep receiving e-mails for those racy deals. (Mason did at least deliver an inside joke when he called the ability to nix those stripper lessons "a much-requested feature," a nod to previous teasing statements on the subject by *The Wall Street Journal*'s Kara Swisher.)

As if a Goldman Sachs analyst stealing the comedy spotlight from Mason wasn't evidence enough that February 8 was Opposite Day, none other than Henry Blodget of *Business Insider* bucked the mostly negative headlines that followed the earnings call by pointing out Groupon's $15 million in operating profit for the quarter (against losses of $336 million in the year-earlier period) and insisting that "the company has already proven the haters wrong."

With his eyes fixed firmly on future growth—and an expectation that all of Groupon's regional markets would be profitable within two years—Mason outlined how the company was quadrupling the company's technology-development workforce, now housed in a new Silicon Valley office, as it looked to keep honing merchant tools (such as the "remarkable, magical" Rewards program) and personalization options while still creating new products.

"The Groupon of five years from now will require investments in technology and innovations," the CEO said. "Despite rapid growth, we estimate that we participate in less than 1 percent of all local transactions." That left the company with a lot of running room. If Groupon could steadily enlarge its slice of the local commerce pie, the resulting revenue lift would be significant indeed.

Even without such an expansion, after more than six months of direct competition, Groupon was twenty to twenty-five times the size of Google Offers and Amazon Deals, and its deal margin (or "take rate") had popped back above 40 percent. Meanwhile, chief rival LivingSocial lost $558 million in 2011 on revenue of just $245 million, or less than one-sixth of Groupon's revenue for the year. With 150 million subscribers and some 250,000 merchant clients in forty-seven countries, Groupon's network effects were starting to look pretty formidable, especially as the company continued to refine its processes into a full-service "Local Merchant Operating System" that catered to an increasingly sophisticated and unforgiving client base. That was the way Groupon planned to win what investor relations VP Kartik Ramachandran called "the daily knife fight."

The day after the earnings call, even as Groupon's stock price continued to take a hit, investment bank William Blair & Company released a research note stating, "While it may take a few quarters to convince the critics, we believe fourth quarter was a solid first start for Groupon on the fundamentals." Goldman Sachs, Morgan Stanley, and Wells Fargo were similarly optimistic, with a Wells analyst touting Groupon's network effects to the *Journal*: "We believe the barriers to online commerce success in the daily-deals market are underestimated."

But analysts at J. P. Morgan and Colin Stewart raised a warning flag about slowing growth in Groupon's sequential quarterly billings. And Morningstar analyst Rick Summer, whose pre-IPO research note delivered a skeptical assessment of Groupon's prospects ("Barring significant innovation, we expect its lack of durable competitive advantage to become more obvious over the course of the next two years"), told *Crain's Chicago Business* after the earnings release, "We still don't have answers to the bigger questions, which are: How profitable is this business over the long run, and how big is this business?"

The skeptics had a field day on March 30, when Groupon

restated its fourth-quarter earnings and reported "material weakness" in its financial controls. This troubling turn of events, which cut Groupon's 2011 Q4 revenue by $14.3 million to $492.2 million and raised its net loss to $65.4 million from $42.7 million, was due in part to the company's failure to set aside enough cash of refunds on the bigger-ticket deals it was now selling. The company beefed up its accounting oversight to avoid future unpleasant surprises, but the stock was hammered as a result of the restatement, tumbling 17 percent on April 2, the first trading day after the announcement, leaving the stock nearly five dollars below its strike price. "We remain confident in the fundamentals of our business," CFO Jason Child said, even as at least one analyst downgraded his rating on GRPN to "sell" and Groupon's old pals at the SEC reportedly contemplated launching an investigation.

Despite such worrisome pitfalls, Groupon now considered itself big enough to see Amazon as its main competitor and set out to relaunch as more of a full-spectrum e-commerce site. Ultimately, there were two sides to the e-commerce equation: demand fulfillment, such as customers traditionally going to Amazon to purchase an item they already had in mind, and demand generation—those same consumers looking to Groupon for cool deals to buy on the spur of the moment. Increasingly, Amazon and Groupon were invading each other's front yards with pop-up lemonade stands.

"We think we can become the next great e-commerce company alongside Amazon," Lefkofsky declared as 2012 got under way.

It'll take years to know whether Groupon can realize that vision—and the company will have to start regularly turning a profit and get its financial controls in order first to avoid an untimely demise. But given the strength of its IPO and the vast untapped reaches of the world's local commerce markets, Groupon's audacious act of walking away from Google's nearly $6 billion offer might just go down as one of the ballsiest gambles ever to pay off in the history of corporate America.

ACKNOWLEDGMENTS

Thanks first and foremost to Julie Mossler, without whom this project would not have happened.

I'm grateful to everyone at Groupon who gave me wide-open access to the organization for nearly sixteen months starting in October 2010. It's rare that a group of sources will be as forthright about their failures as their successes and will actually go out of their way to provide a warts-and-all account of what was a truly wild and wooly period.

Andrew Mason was not thrilled about the idea of having a book written about Groupon while it was still in its infancy, but knowing someone was going to publish one given the feverish interest in the company, he acquiesced to me as the devil he knew. Given that he was running the fastest-growing company in history, Andrew was generous with his time, and he shared a tremendous amount of useful information. Even if he has regrets, I'm thankful that he gave me the opportunity. Eric Lefkofsky was there when the chips were down. Rob Solomon went above and beyond the call long after he'd left Groupon.

Thanks also to Aaron With, Joe Harrow, and the other OGs of The Point—Matt Loseke, Steven Walker, Zac Goldberg—as well as Brad Keywell, Darren Schwartz, Sean Smyth, Margo Georgiadis, Jeff Holden, Mihir Shah, Pat Garrison, Sophie Hinkley, and everyone else who helped me out at Groupon. The international team of Marc Samwer, Chris Muhr, Emanuel Stehle, Jens Hutzschenreuter, and Raj Ruparell was forthright and on the case. And a tip of the cap to my sources outside of Groupon as well.

I am truly blessed when it comes to editors and agents: Dan Weiss, Matt Martz, the entire St. Martin's team, Robert Gottlieb, Alanna Ramirez, and Melissa Flashman, thank you for your insights, your advocacy, your time, and your patience.

Speaking of patience, thank you to my family—especially Heather, Nick, and Emma—for their support while I worked on this book, and to the wonderful friends who rooted me on, shared their insights, and listened to me yammer.

Thanks to Robert Feder and Keir Graff for their keen reading eyes and keener advice, and to Sam Weller for the research assistance. And many thanks to my incredibly supportive colleagues at *Time Out Chicago,* where this project got its start as a cover story edited by the one and only Laura Baginski, with an interview assist on Steve Albini from Jake Malooley. I'm fortunate to work with all of you.

Finally, thanks to you for reading this book. For ongoing Groupon updates and to share your thoughts, please visit franksennett .com.